Creating Person-Centred Organisations

Strategies AND Tools FOR Managing Change IN Health, Social Care AND THE Voluntary Sector

Stephen Stirk and Helen Sanderson

Jessica Kingsley *Publishers*
London and Philadelphia

Figure 12.1 from Smull, Bourne and Sanderson (2009) on p.270
is reproduced with kind permission from the authors.

First published in 2012
by Jessica Kingsley Publishers
116 Pentonville Road
London N1 9JB, UK
and
400 Market Street, Suite 400
Philadelphia, PA 19106, USA

www.jkp.com

Library of Congress Cataloging in Publication Data
A CIP catalog record for this book is available from the Library of Congress

British Library Cataloguing in Publication Data
A CIP catalogue record for this book is available from the British Library

ISBN 978 1 84905 260 3
eISBN 978 0 85700 549 6

Printed and bound in Great Britain

Contents

List of Figures

Acknowledgements

In this book we share the story of disability charity United Response. We are grateful to the following people for their help with this: Shonagh Methven, who provided Chapter 10 on enabling risk as well as other insights into the use of person-centred practice; Bob Tindall, who gave us many helpful directions to follow from the benefit of his broad knowledge and experience of the field; and Su Sayer OBE for her long experience of developing United Response and permitting us to use so many examples of what has been done there. Nick Rogers, Tim Jones and Diane Lightfoot provided additional information and examples from United Response. Diane also provided invaluable help on the accuracy of the material. John Hespe shared his knowledge and experience of organisation design and development, and helped with many technical aspects of the subject matter.

Mary Beth Lepkowsky is a consultant to non-profit organisations in the USA and Organisational Development Manager for Tri-Counties Regional Center in California. Helen Sanderson and Mary Beth have been further developing the concept and practice of person-centred teams, and Mary Beth co-authored Chapter 9, based on their book *Person-Centred Teams*.

This book builds on Helen's earlier work in 2003 with Richard Williams called *What are we Learning about Person-Centred Organisations?*; and Chapter 2 is based on an existing paper produced by Helen Sanderson Associates (HSA).

The appendices are 'Progress for Providers'. The first Progress for Providers is an overall self-assessment for progress in delivering personalisation, and was developed by Helen Sanderson, Kim Haworth (Commissioner for Lancashire County Council), Tracey Bush (Alternative Futures Group) and Ben Harrison (United Response). The second Progress for Providers is for managers to self-assess how they are using person-centred practices, and was developed by Ben Harrison (United Response), Ruth Gorman (IAS Services and HSA), Jackie Fletcher (Dimensions), Michelle Livesley and Helen Sanderson (HSA), Kim Haworth (Commissioner for Lancashire County Council), Lisa Keenan (Joint Commissioning Support Manager for Leeds City Council) and Andy Rawnsley (Head of Service, Leeds City Council).

In this book we share stories and examples from a range of other social care and health organisations. Some organisations were happy for us to name them, and others preferred to stay anonymous. Thank you to everyone who shared their stories with us, in particular to Jackie Fletcher and Steve Scown from Dimensions; Paul Roberts and Agnes Lunny from Positive Futures; Ruth Gorman and Owen Cooper from IAS, Marianne Selby-Boothroyde and Aisling Duffy from Certitude; Michelle Livesley, Jo Harvey, Jonathan Ralphs, Alison Short, Gill Bailey, Lorraine Erwin, Vicky Jones and Charlotte Sweeney from HSA; Richard Williams from Options; Tracy Myerhoff from Hull City Council; Ruth Sutherland and Kathryn Smith at Scope; Fran Winney and Loraine George from Care UK; Suzie and Jennie Franklin and Independent Options; Bill Mumford and Brenda Mullen from MacIntyre; Brian Hutchinson and Lisa Watchorn from Real Life Options; Freya El Baz, Nicola Gitsham, Jon Ralphs, Julie Bray and Jaimee Lewis.

Thank you to Kerry Buckley from HSA for all her help with the references; Julie Barclay for designing the additional figures and illustrations; Henry Iles for Figure 2.26; and Max Neil for allowing us to use the 'Achievement exercise' in Chapter 6.

The learning shared in this book has been developed in partnership with an international community around person-centred practices. Michael Smull is the Chair of the Learning Community for Person-Centred Practices, and Helen Sanderson is the Vice-Chair. Michael Smull and members of the Learning Community developed the person-centred thinking tools shared in this book. You can learn more about the work of the Learning Community at www.learningcommunity.us.

You can learn more about United Response at www.unitedresponse.org.uk. For further information and support in implementing person-centred practices, see www.helensandersonassociates.co.uk. For materials and resources on person-centred practices, see www.hsapress.co.uk.

Chapter 1

Person-Centred Organisations

A person-centred organisation has people at its heart – both people it serves and people it employs. This has an impact on the whole organisation's processes and structures, and transforms the traditional organisational hierarchy putting decision-making as close to people supported as possible. The DNA of a person-centred organisation is using person-centred practices to deliver its vision and values.

Sanderson and Lepkowsky[1]

Introduction

Personalisation demands fundamental changes for organisations. It means people having better lives through more choice and control over the support they use. Services need to be designed and delivered according to what is important to the people who use them, and provided in ways that help people be active and contributing members of their communities.[2] For many, if not most, organisations this will require changes to systems, processes, practices and cultures. This transformation is more likely when person-centred practices are embedded throughout an organisation, changing the ways that teams meet; that staff are supported; and that leaders lead. This book explains how this means becoming a person-centred organisation – and how to do it.

A person-centred organisation has people at its heart – both people it serves and people it employs. You will see person-centred practices embedded and consistently used within a person-centred organisation.[3] Working towards being a person-centred organisation is not easy, and we share what gets in the way in health and social care. However, the benefits are tangible – in the outcomes for people supported, the culture, conversations and practices, as well as in hard organisational results. For example, using person-centred practices has been a substantial contributing factor in reducing staff turnover in the national disability charity – United Response – that serves as an extended case study throughout this book. Having previously been competitive – and in line with industry norms – the organisation's staff turnover reduced by 41 per cent in the three years after implementing person-centred practices: with consequent savings on resourcing and training costs.

It becomes a virtuous circle – by staff using person-centred practices, people have more choice and control in their lives; staff are clear about their role, are well supported and their talents and interests are used to support people; staff stress is reduced (because of role clarity and good support) and work feels good (staff can see the difference they are making, and enjoy using their interests to support people) so turnover is low. Consistent support from well-motivated and supported staff with a sure sense of purpose and values makes it more likely that people have choice and control in their lives.

As mentioned earlier, this book draws extensively on the experiences of United Response, and, together with examples from other health and social care organisations, we share how person-centred practices can be used with or instead of conventional organisation design and development techniques and approaches, and demonstrate the dramatic and culture-shifting results of person-centred practices. The book is for leaders in any organisation that wants to deliver personalised services, in health or social care. Throughout the book we have used the phrases 'people we support' or 'people supported' to represent people who use health and social care services. If you happen to be reading this book as a colleague in another type of sector or business, then we also invite you to read on, because we believe there is much that can be learned from these experiences for mainstream business practice.

The idea for this book arose from the learning that we acquired while working together at United Response; from Helen's work with providers, health and social care organisations; and from a wider learning community around person-centred practice. Helen's interest in person-centred organisations started with her PhD in organisational change and person-centred planning. Stephen experienced the difference in a person-centred organisation as he moved from the pharmaceutical industry to his role as Human Resources Director at United Response. Since 2005, United Response has been specifically introducing person-centred thinking tools and practices into the way the organisation works.

Person-centred practices refer to the range of practical person-centred thinking tools and skills that people can use with individuals, teams and organisations. The international Learning Community for Person-Centred Practices, which Helen leads in the UK, originally developed these tools. They emerged from a style of planning for individuals called person-centred planning. You can find a full description of the history and development of person-centred thinking and planning in the companion book to this volume, *A Practical Guide to Delivering Personalisation: Person-Centred Practice in Health and Social Care*, also published by Jessica Kingsley Publishers, which serves as a guide for individuals on how to deliver personalisation through simple, effective and evidence-based person-centred practice.[4]

Key elements of a person-centred organisation

The key elements of a person-centred organisation will echo what you already know about excellent organisational practices. The differences lie in a relentless focus on what matters to the people whom the organisation supports, and on community contribution.[5] A person-centred organisation extends being person-centred to staff, who are supported to bring their 'whole self' to work, and use their talents and interests to offer the best possible support to people. The culture in a person-centred organisation could be summed up as one of trust, empowerment and accountability.

The early work describing a person-centred organisation suggested eight key elements that are the foundation of a person-centred organisation.[6] These are:

1. Visionary leadership
Person-centred organisations have a clear vision and mission, with leaders who motivate, inspire and ensure that everything is aligned to deliver this.

2. Shared values and beliefs
Everyone shares, can articulate and most importantly demonstrate the person-centred values of the organisation.

3. Outcomes for individuals
Everything is orientated to achieving the outcomes people who are supported want in their lives – from day-to-day routines to how they want their lives to be in future. Person-centred organisations know whom they serve and what people expect from their service, and they deliver this.

4. Community focus
Community is important. Both the people supported and the organisation contribute to and feel part of their local community.

5. Empowered and valued staff
Managers work with staff in a person-centred way – ensuring that teams have a clear purpose, know what is important to each other and how to support each other, and match roles to strengths and talents as much as possible. Staff are appreciated, valued and listened to in a person-centred organisation. People are respected, trusted and accountable in their work, and hierarchical structures are flattened.

6. Individual and organisational learning
A person-centred organisation is also a learning organisation, continuously developing and improving. Learning takes place at all levels, and learning from people supported directly influences staff, team and organisational development. You would expect to see creativity, action learning, innovation and enterprise in a person-centred organisation.

7. Working together
Working together starts with the people supported, in co-designing what they want their service to look like. Decision making is as close to them as possible, thereby empowering teams to make decisions with the people supported with as little bureaucracy as possible. Person-centred organisations are built through partnerships with their stakeholders.

8. Person-centred practices embedded throughout the organisation

The whole organisation shares a common language and practices to deliver the other seven key elements. This is part of the DNA of the organisation – person-centred practices are simply the way things get done, to achieve the best outcomes and lifestyle for the people supported.

In person-centred organisations, these key elements are delivered by using person-centred practices throughout all organisational processes and structures. These person-centred practices are used to build on, and occasionally replace, conventional business practices.

In the following chapter, we catalogue the person-centred thinking tools and practices that this book refers to in each chapter. Chapter by chapter we will now share what we are learning about achieving the key elements of a person-centred organisation within the structures and processes of organisations. We discuss creating a powerful vision and clarifying values in Chapter 3, together with suggestions for building your organisation's mission, business strategy and plans. Chapter 4 looks at the overall organisation and business process that may be the starting point for implementing changes to your organisation design to achieve high performance in these key elements. In Chapter 5 on working together, we look at co-production and partnership, with a particular focus on communities. Translating all this into a person-centred culture, Chapter 6 summarises and explores a set of practices that you would expect to find in the culture of a person-centred organisation. You will see the focus on outcomes for individuals through all chapters, but especially in Chapter 5 on working together and Chapter 11 on quality. The chapters on human resources (Chapter 8) and change management (Chapter 12) offer ways to demonstrate empowering and valuing staff. Chapter 8 looks at the range of people processes that align the procedures and processes of an organisation with the values of person-centredness.

We review the internal organisational aspects of partnership and collaboration in Chapter 9 on person-centred teamworking, which looks at a detailed process for creating and maintaining high-performing and focused teams. How leaders might behave in such a person-centred organisation to support the vision and values and develop the ways of working is discussed in Chapter 7 on leadership. This chapter also suggests a wide range of appropriate behaviours and styles of working that can be applied across the whole organisation. Chapter 10 focuses on what we consider to be a critical aspect of the focus on outcomes for individuals, enabling risk taking, and offers a complete approach to supporting and allowing risk taking to happen in a thoughtful, controlled way. Finally, in Chapter 12, our chapter on change management, we propose a process and set of tools and techniques that bring people on board and encourage them to maintain these new ways of working. You will find a self-assessment in each chapter based on 'Progress for Providers'. Progress for Providers is a self-assessment developed by providers and commissioners to help providers think about their progress in personalisation. The two original versions are in the appendices: one aimed at senior managers, and one for first-line managers.

We have seen that there can be different ways of running an organisation, and we believe these ways of working can be used elsewhere in business, potentially to make a lot of people's lives more fulfilling.

Given that the experiences derived from the work of United Response lie at the heart of this book, we provide the following brief description of the organisation for your reference. The story of the charity outlined here begins to illustrate some of the challenges that were faced in becoming person-centred, and how United Response addressed them. These challenges will be explored in greater detail in the chapters that follow.

United Response

> In over 35 years in this work, I have not come across anything that builds a positive culture, and creates change in the way that person-centred practices have done in United Response. Person-centred thinking tools make sense to people in their daily work, and they have been keen to help the organisation in moving forwards. This does not always happen in traditional organisational development.
> (Bob Tindall, Managing Director, United Response)

United Response today is an organisation supporting around 2000 people, with over 3000 staff working across England and Wales. In 2011, the organisation had an annual budget of around £70 million.

Over the course of the last 40 years, a tiny charity operating out of one house in West Sussex grew to become one of the country's largest social care providers – without losing its focus on people. This book shares how United Response got there – charting the journey to becoming a person-centred organisation and sharing the person-centred practices used along the way.

The beginning of United Response

Su Sayer OBE co-founded United Response in 1972. For its first home in Tillington, West Sussex, she found in the middle of a small country village an old rectory that had been donated by a family who were keen to see a different kind of support for local people with learning disabilities. The organisation was founded at a time when people with learning disabilities did not generally live in the community, so this was something of a radical and pioneering move. The name 'United Response' was coined to reflect a desire for everyone – from all parts of the community – to come together with people with learning disabilities and to work together to support them to live independently. So a meeting for everyone in the village was held during which they were told about plans to convert the house so that people with learning disabilities could live nearer their families rather than being sent away to long-stay hospitals, as was the norm at that time. People were very concerned because in those days they didn't know much about learning disabilities – so much so that they were concerned about the safety of their children and asked whether they could have street lamps installed in the village. They were reassured that it would be OK, and they never did have street lamps!

United Response discovered a dual role: not only did the organisation need to take the lead in providing what would later be described as 'care in the community', it also needed to educate the general public so that they could understand what people needed and how best to be supportive. For example, the local Post Office (where people supported went to pick up their benefits) asked if they could learn what to do if someone had a seizure in the shop. It very rarely happened but once or twice it did. Everyone knew exactly what to do and there was no drama.

Growing as an organisation

From these small beginnings, United Response began to grow, initially from its original base in Sussex, establishing a second residential home in Bognor in 1977 and a further two services in Petworth and Crawley. By 1979, it was the largest charity working with people in West Sussex. In 1981, the charity began investigating the potential of offering its first services in the North, growing steadily in the North throughout the 1980s. This was followed by significant growth as a result of a major transfer of support from Barnardo's as a group of young people made the transition into adulthood and needed a different approach to their support. The charity continued to grow steadily, supporting an increasing number of people as they moved from hospital or other settings.

Other types of support were also added to the range of services being provided. In 1990, United Response began working with people with mental health needs, predominantly in the South East, but also in other parts of England. And, as the reputation of the organisation grew, other local authorities and commissioners began to have confidence in its ability to take on large pieces of work, leading to growth in the numbers of people supported particularly in the South West and North East of England, and within some London boroughs. More lately, having concentrated entirely on operating in England, United Response has begun to offer services and support in South Wales, with growing success. In the last five years in particular, growth in numbers of people supported has exceeded expectations, and the organisation has had to learn how to bring on board new staff and people and to support them quickly and effectively.

United Response today

Today United Response provides support to people in most areas of England and in South Wales. It is highly dispersed, working in well over 250 communities. The organisation aims to achieve a balance that ensures that people are supported consistently well, with clear evidence of positive changes in their lives, without a level of prescription to managers and support staff that could undermine local initiative and innovation – in other words, taking a person-centred approach to staff as well as to the people supported.

Support is provided to many people with complex disabilities – for example, 40 per cent of people supported do not speak. To prevent people's life chances being compromised, people must be supported by staff who are determined to assist them in making positive changes in their lives. The risk of misunderstanding and making the wrong assumptions about people is substantial, and many people have had damaging life experiences in the years before coming to United Response.

Challenges and solutions in developing as a person-centred organisation

As the organisation grew and began to support more and more people with significant disabilities, the team faced the challenge of how to support managers to ensure that people who used services had great lives, even if they did not use words to communicate. The solution was the widespread implementation of active support.[7] Active support is a proven model of providing care to people with intellectual disabilities, using a range of engagement and communication techniques and styles to foster successful enabling relationships between support workers and people supported. This formed the foundation of encouraging people to be engaged in some meaningful activity, and the challenge then became to link this with people having a fuller life outside their front door, as well as inside it.

This led to the creation of United Response in Business (set up as a trading arm of United Response to provide work opportunities for people with learning disabilities) and The Inclusion Team (a small group of people focused entirely on improving the range of engagement tools, techniques and mechanisms used by support staff), which helped more people in getting work and being part of the community.

The context in the UK was changing, with a new focus on person-centred approaches. It also became clear that people were more engaged, but how can you ensure that everyone is working in a person-centred way? How could staff understand how everything fitted together?

The solution to this was to design and introduce 'The Way We Work', an innovative person-centred planning framework for bringing about culture and organisation change (see Chapter 6 for a detailed explanation of this). This was introduced in 2001 and became the summary of how the organisation would go about its work and support people. This was within the framework of the newly developed Department of Health guidance on person-centred planning and person-centred approaches.[8] It signified a diminishing corporate emphasis on process and a greater emphasis on outcomes. Active support subsequently became known as 'person-centred active support' in United Response.

This culture change led to people having a stronger common sense of mission and purpose, but the challenge now became how to make sure this was making a difference in people's lives everywhere. When an organisation is growing and has high staff turnover leading to increased costs, how can you focus on culture as well as business results?

The solution for this challenge was for managers and staff to use person-centred thinking tools and practices through the implementation of a culture change programme. This programme was originally called 'Good2Great', and was then retitled as 'Developing the Way We Work' (explained further in Chapters 6 and 12). Introduced by Michael Smull and Helen, Good2Great originally started in the North West division of United Response. The changes were highly successful for people supported, staff and managers, and led to a National Training Award for the difference the programme had made in people's lives. The next challenge was how to scale this up from a pilot to become national practice. To do this, the solution was to build local capacity by training trainers and developing divisional leadership teams.

One successful outcome of the use of person-centred tools was that people were involved in planning their own lives. The next question was, 'But how can you get everyone involved in setting the direction for the organisation and linking the learning of all stakeholders together?' To do this the organisation set about implementing a process to draw input from the people supported into the business planning and strategy of the organisation. This person-centred practice was called 'Working Together for Change', and is explained in Chapters 2 and 5.

The next challenge, as well as everyone consistently working in a person-centred way, was how to ensure that all the formal policies and procedures were aligned to support person-centred working. There is an obvious dichotomy between an overt focus on the importance of individual needs and desires, and a rules-driven policy environment. The two cannot work together very comfortably. Changes were necessary, therefore, to recruitment processes, how teams operated and quality management standards, as well as to introduce person-centred reviews, change the culture of risk management and adopt person-centred thinking tools in the performance management process. Essentially this meant a complete review of human resources and risk processes.

As these issues were addressed, it became clear that a solution was needed to keep moving forward and improving, which led to the introduction of new ways of measuring progress and achievements, using a mixture of conventional indicators and widespread storytelling and knowledge sharing.

Latterly, as a result of widespread economic changes, the challenge was that everywhere there were severe financial pressures. In a time of cuts, how do you keep moving forward? The way that United Response chose to address this was to engage the energy of staff across the organisation to innovate and generate creative ideas for cost saving, while maintaining the quality of support and moving into new areas of business.

United Response is not 'there' yet, because being a person-centred organisation means ongoing learning and change. However, in the following chapters you will learn more of the practical solutions drawn from United Response's experience in facing challenges and finding solutions, and also from other providers and organisations in health and social care.

What gets in the way of organisations being person-centred?

In 2000, the government introduced person-centred planning into its policy for people with learning disabilities[9] and then for everyone using adult social care in 2007 with 'Putting People First'.[10] From the emergence of person-centred planning in government policy to today with the focus on personalisation, it was evident that expecting staff to behave in person-centred ways would require a change in the way that they were supported and managed. However, over a decade later, person-centred organisations are still very far from the norm. Here are some reasons why that might be the case.

'It is only about listening to people and we do that already.'

We have heard being person-centred described as simply listening to people. Our experience is that most staff require practical ways or tools to enable them to listen well, and support and coaching from their managers to act on what they hear. Staff using person-centred practices, and listening well, will only be able to make limited change if person-centred practices are not embedded throughout the policies, procedure and culture of the organisation.

'There are too many competing pressures on us.'

There are many competing pressures that can detract from vision and mission, and for some leaders these become so pressing that they lose their sense of mission and people become secondary to regulation or reputation. Organisations that support vulnerable people can face challenges in helping people assert their rights, because it may bring them into conflict with people who do not recognise those rights. This can lead to political, financial, stakeholder or media pressures.

'We can get away with not being person-centred – no one asks about this.'

Regulators may not be able to see what is happening, and, if families and allies are not aware of negative practices, then unscrupulous providers can 'get away' with not being person-centred.

'Funding is scarce – we need to focus on money and savings instead.'

Some organisations simply value money over outcomes for individuals. Other organisations believe it will cost too much to be person-centred. Research suggests that it does not cost more to implement person-centred planning and the United Response experience suggests that investment in training and building internal capacity was required and paid dividends in the long run – for example, savings based on staff retention cutting agency spend.[11]

'Some staff are trying their best – but it does not matter as much to managers. We talk the talk but don't walk the walk.'

This is an issue of leadership will and focus. If nobody corrects or modifies poor practice, and it is tolerated, then the message is clear – person-centred practice is not really important, irrespective of what organisational standards, policies and communications say. We think that competence in person-centred practices requires the same expectation and attention as health and safety training and compliance. Being person-centred is not the icing on the cake – it *is* the cake.

Why work towards being a person-centred organisation?

Becoming a person-centred organisation means ensuring that your structures, processes and culture all align to enable people to have choice and control over their lives and their service. This will mean the organisation can do the following.

- Make maximum use of every opportunity offered for learning and growth. Every day in the life of someone who receives support we are given new evidence of what is important to them and how they want to live and be supported; what is likely to work in the future and what is not likely to; real-time opportunities to engage people in what matters to them, build on what works and discard what does not.

- Address dilemmas that can occur in everyday life by training and supporting staff to think about how to approach them in ways that do not rely on the use of power over people, but instead offer the maximum opportunity for personal choice and learning through experience.

- Collate what is learnt so that everybody involved in the support of someone can share the learning. This learning is often achieved by families and friends over many years of living alongside someone.

- Embed a common language and set of practices that can be used in everyone's role within a culture of trust, empowerment and accountability. The majority of social care staff do what they do because they want to make a positive difference in the lives of people they support – the person-centred tools and practices reinforce this sense of mission, provide practical ways to deliver this, encourage positive risk taking and maximise creativity. Innovation and creativity are crucial to people having more fulfilling lives – the higher the level of creativity brought into play by staff, the more opportunities and scope for people supported to expand the boundaries in their lives and contribute to communities.

Person-centred practices are powerful in introducing change for staff as well as for people the organisation supports. The strongly creative approach referred to earlier, if applied by organisations, can unearth undiscovered potential in colleagues too.

The main benefit, however, is the development of a person-centred culture and positive habits across support staff and other organisational staff. Successfully applied, person-centred practices become the norm and will result (and have often resulted, in the case of United Response) in people doing their jobs very well indeed with the minimum amount of prompts from their line managers. This is important in a time where personalisation and personal budgets are delivering greater control to people. Support staff (and their managers), who are used to using their judgement and not having to rely on the instruction of those senior to them, will thrive in such context.

We come back to United Response to explain this. The benefits of the organisation's investment in embedding person-centred practices can be seen primarily in the lives of the people supported, and then in staff retention and morale – team working is different, meetings are different, and staff are helped to think about enabling risk in a different way. Finally, the benefits can also be felt in terms of the reputation, partnerships and impact of the organisation.

Impact on people

Here is a story of someone we will call Graham that illustrates the impact on people, and what that means for staff.

> Graham has been supported by United Response in London for a few years, before which he spent the best part of 20 years in other care establishments. He was born with serious physical disabilities, including profound deafness, facial disfigurement and fused fingers, as well as a learning disability and some difficult medical conditions. Graham is profoundly deaf and doesn't really speak.
>
> Staff realised that to support Graham properly they'd need to learn how to communicate with him in a way that made sense to him. They used person-centred thinking tools around communication, took up training in accessible communication and began talking to him using a type of sign language, Makaton. The better they became at signing, the less Graham was prone to outbursts of frustration. He gradually started using the signs to tell staff what he wanted, and, for the first time, started having a say in his own life.
>
> Then over the past couple of years, local United Response managers worked in partnership with the local authority to give Graham – and other people whom the organisation supports in the area – control of his daytime budget allocation – effectively a personal budget for his daytime support. Alongside this, the support team used community mapping to create an interactive multimedia map of the community to support Graham to make real choices about his day-to-day life.
>
> Graham navigates around the map with great dexterity and is able to choose his daytime activity. Staff know what is important to him and the best ways to support him, including how he makes decisions. He now goes horse riding, to the cinema, on day trips and out for lunch. He has even showcased the multimedia tool at external events. As one local commissioner commented, 'I've known

Graham for nearly 20 years before he came to United Response, but this is the first time that he's been able to tell me – himself – that what he REALLY likes is a curry and a pint!'

Most importantly, Graham's support worker, Adam, says: 'It is incredible how much happier Graham is since we started working this way. He is a classic example of someone with learning disabilities whose appearance is deceiving. Because he looks different and can't speak, people never understood him and assumed he wasn't capable of being independent. But, after a lot of work and patience, the future finally looks bright for Graham. Who knows what he's capable of achieving next?'

Impact on staff

'We trained staff in using simple person-centred thinking tools to help them resolve the kind of dilemmas which cropped up regularly, and to work more effectively in teams,' said Bob Tindall, the Managing Director of United Response. 'Staff became even more enthusiastic about what they were doing, and this had a huge positive impact on the people we support. Obstacles which had seemed major before became manageable by applying these tools.'

The impact on staff coming to the organisation from providers with traditional approaches, or perhaps with fixed views about what 'care' should mean, can be seen in terms of the culture, which the organisation has instilled, moving as shown in the following table.

From	To
Doing things *for* people	Doing things *with* people
Risk assessment as *prevention*	Risk assessment as an *enabler*
Focus on people we support *or* staff	Focus on people we support *and* staff
Focus on what's important *for* people	Focus on what's important *for* people AND what's important *to* them
People have *disabilities*	People have *abilities*
See the *problem*	See the *person*

Impact on the organisation, its business and other stakeholders

Here are some of the tangible business outcomes achieved since person-centred practices were introduced:

- Lower staff turnover and improved staff stability. Costs of recruitment and training are lowered.

- As a consequence of lower staff turnover, levels of temporary and agency staff usage are lower, bringing lower staff costs through reduced agency charges but also through the greater effectiveness of regular staff.

- Improved motivation and a positive culture leading to reduced absence rates and the consequential costs of sick pay, replacement staff and additional training.

- Business growth, through creating a reputation for quality and consistency of service that people trust, with a creative and innovative edge.

- Recognition through awards – for example, National Training Awards, Investors in People, Investors in Diversity and Excellence awards for skill training.

An important message in this book is that embedding person-centred practices into your organisation is not the outcome: it is developing your organisation to deliver choice and control for the people you support, and using all the skills and talents of your staff to achieve this.

In each chapter we help you to find out how you are doing by introducing a checklist based on Progress for Providers. These checklists both describe the detail of what you would expect to see in a person-centred organisation, and also give you an opportunity to celebrate the areas that you are doing well in, and to think about areas that you want to develop.

Conclusion

We think that working to become a person-centred organisation can make a big difference – to people you support, your staff and how your organisation works. This is the only way to deliver personalised services in organisations. The story of United Response, and other social care and health providers, illustrates what can be achieved. We hope that this book is useful along your journey of development – as a leader and in your organisation.

Chapter 2

Person-Centred Practices and Conventional Organisation Development

Using a small set of value-based person-centred thinking skills at all levels of the system will drive change throughout the system.

Smull, Bourne and Sanderson[12]

Introduction

Person-centred organisations employ person-centred practices to deliver the best possible service to the people they support, using the commitment and talents of their staff to achieve this. Traditionally, person-centred practices have been seen as only relevant for use with people who use services. We think that delivering great outcomes for people can only be delivered through using the same person-centred practices with staff, and within the structures and processes of the organisation.

At their heart, person-centred thinking tools are simply a different way to have a conversation. The thinking, learning, decisions or actions from this conversation are then recorded and acted on. Person-centred thinking tools and practices can sit alongside, enhance and sometimes replace conventional organisation development practices. Instead of repeating summaries of what each tool is throughout the book, we have produced a catalogue of them in this chapter for you to refer to. Starting with where person-centred thinking tools have come from, we then introduce the person-centred thinking tools and conclude with four person-centred practices used in teams and organisations. We then provide a summary of the main organisational development tools that we refer to throughout the rest of the book.

The origins of person-centred thinking tools

Person-centred thinking tools have their foundation in person-centred planning – an approach to social justice and inclusion originally developed in supporting people with learning disabilities.[13] The Learning Community for Person-Centered Practices mainly developed these tools, and the foundation skill underpinning them is being able to separate what is important *to* someone from what is important *for* them, and finding a balance between the two.[14] Other tools have been adapted from management practice – for example, the 'Doughnut' is taken directly from Charles Handy's work on organisational behaviour and management.[15] Person-centred thinking tools have also been developed from the contributions of leaders in the disability inclusion movement and personalisation – for example, Beth Mount's relationship circle,[16] John O'Brien's work[17] and Simon Duffy's decision-making agreement.[18]

Person-centred thinking tools enable staff to deliver person-centred support to individuals by helping to answer the following questions:

- How does the person want to live and be supported?

- How can the person have more choice and control in their life?

- What is our role in delivering what is important to the person and how they want to be supported? How are we doing in supporting the person in the way they want to live? How can we work together to keep what is working and change what is not working?

- How can we keep learning about the person and what we need to do to provide the best support?

Each person-centred thinking tool does two things. It is the basis for actions and it provides further information about what is important to the person and how they want to be supported. This information is recorded as a person-centred description and may start with information on just one page (a one-page profile).

Similarly, using person-centred thinking tools with staff and teams enables managers to answer these questions:

- What are the gifts and strengths of each team member and how can we use these to provide the best support to people?

- What is important to each team member about their work? What does this mean for the way that I work with them?

- Specifically, what support does each team member need to do their best work? What does this mean for me and how I support them? What does it mean for how I communicate with them?

- What do I expect from each team member – their core responsibilities? Where is the space for them to use their own judgement and be creative?

- How can we as a team keep learning and recording and acting on what we are learning? About what to build on? About what to change?

- How can I get the best fit between team members, and their role or the people they support?

In the next section we introduce each tool and provide an example or story to illustrate how they are used with individual staff, with teams, and within organisational processes. The examples are taken from health and social care, and we have included a couple from business – from an events organiser and a consultant – to demonstrate the breadth of contexts in which person-centred practices can be used.

'Important to and for'

The first and fundamental person-centred thinking skill is to be able to learn what is important to someone, what is important for them and the balance between the two. Learning what is 'important to' and what is 'important for' has to be done before you can help find the balance. 'Important to' includes the people, interests, pace of life and possessions that really matter to you, and that define the quality of your life. What is 'important for' you are the things that need to happen to keep you safe and well. Everyone finds that what is 'important to' them and what is 'important for' them are in conflict from time to time.

One-page profiles

There are person-centred thinking tools and conversations we can use to draw this information out, such as asking about morning routines, good days and bad days. This provides information about what is important to you, and how you need to be supported. This information is recorded in a one-page profile. A one-page profile typically has three sections – an appreciation about the person; what is important to them from their perspective; and how to support them well.

Many innovative organisations committed to developing as person-centred organisations are requiring all their staff and managers to have one-page profiles, as well as enabling everyone they support to have one. It is not uncommon to read directors' one-page profiles on their organisation's website as a way of introducing themselves. Some people use one-page profiles to share information about what matters to them and how to support them at work. For direct support staff, it is important that their profiles include information about their passions and interests so that these can be matched with those of people supported. Figure 2.1 shows Helen's one-page profile, which includes how to support her at work, and personal information.

The following quote demonstrates how one-page profiles are used within the organisation Dimensions.

> When Dimensions was first introduced to the one-page profile, it was clear to see how useful they could be in sharing important information about people in a succinct and meaningful way. A one-page profile tells us about the person. It tells us what others like and admire about the person; what is important to them and how to support them well. This simple inclusive approach to completing a one-page profile appealed to us and it was agreed that we would use them initially when working with families and people with learning disabilities and with individual budgets, paying particular attention to how we might match people with the right support staff.[19]

> We started to think about how we might introduce one-page profiles to people who we supported across the organisation. This came at a time when the organisation was undertaking a review of many of its systems and processes, and a time of changing regulation within social care. In response to the changing demands and requirements of the internal and external environment, we developed Dimensions standards. These standards would ensure not only regulatory compliance but make

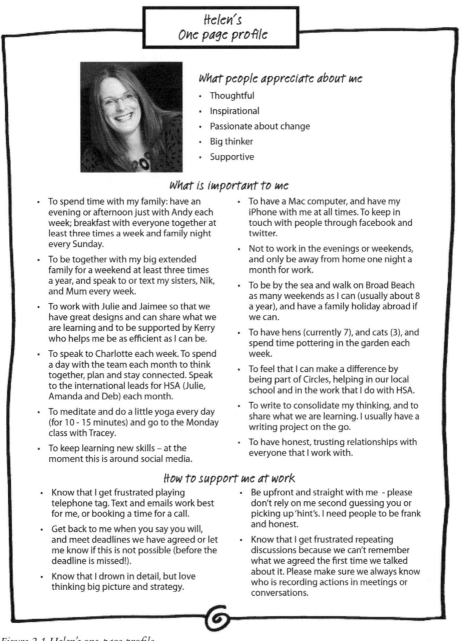

Helen's One page profile

What people appreciate about me

- Thoughtful
- Inspirational
- Passionate about change
- Big thinker
- Supportive

What is important to me

- To spend time with my family: have an evening or afternoon just with Andy each week; breakfast with everyone together at least three times a week and family night every Sunday.

- To be together with my big extended family for a weekend at least three times a year, and speak to or text my sisters, Nik, and Mum every week.

- To work with Julie and Jaimee so that we have great designs and can share what we are learning and to be supported by Kerry who helps me be as efficient as I can be.

- To speak to Charlotte each week. To spend a day with the team each month to think together, plan and stay connected. Speak to the international leads for HSA (Julie, Amanda and Deb) each month.

- To meditate and do a little yoga every day (for 10 - 15 minutes) and go to the Monday class with Tracey.

- To keep learning new skills – at the moment this is around social media.

- To have a Mac computer, and have my iPhone with me at all times. To keep in touch with people through facebook and twitter.

- Not to work in the evenings or weekends, and only be away from home one night a month for work.

- To be by the sea and walk on Broad Beach as many weekends as I can (usually about 8 a year), and have a family holiday abroad if we can.

- To have hens (currently 7), and cats (3), and spend time pottering in the garden each week.

- To feel that I can make a difference by being part of Circles, helping in our local school and in the work that I do with HSA.

- To write to consolidate my thinking, and to share what we are learning. I usually have a writing project on the go.

- To have honest, trusting relationships with everyone that I work with.

How to support me at work

- Know that I get frustrated playing telephone tag. Text and emails work best for me, or booking a time for a call.

- Get back to me when you say you will, and meet deadlines we have agreed or let me know if this is not possible (before the deadline is missed!).

- Know that I drown in detail, but love thinking big picture and strategy.

- Be upfront and straight with me - please don't rely on me second guessing you or picking up 'hint's. I need people to be frank and honest.

- Know that I get frustrated repeating discussions because we can't remember what we agreed the first time we talked about it. Please make sure we always know who is recording actions in meetings or conversations.

Figure 2.1 Helen's one-page profile

it clear that best practice approaches would also be a fundamental requirement of the organisation. The one-page profile was seen as one of these requirements.

As we progressed on our journey towards personalising services and we became more familiar with the benefits of having a one-page profile, we extended its use to include all staff across the organisation and the Board of Management.[20] We kept the implementation under review and learnt along the way how best to introduce the profile and the need to be clear with instructions and expectations. We developed a standardised template, 'top tips' for staff to follow and a brochure for guidance.

The senior management team set the benchmark by completing their one-page profiles and making them publicly available to all via the Dimensions website and internal intranet.

Dimensions have continued to find additional benefits from the one-page profile and how to maximise its use, from recruitment and selection, induction, team building, performance management, project work, and introductions and getting to know people.

The table below provides an overview of some of the business processes Dimensions uses profiles in and the expected outcomes. It is not an exhaustive list and we are discovering more and more ways to use the one-page profile all the time. As can be seen, the one-page profile approach is routinely built into our policies and procedures from a person's first day with us, whether you work for us, receive support from us or you are meeting with us. (www.helensandersonassociates. co.uk/blogs/dimensions/2012/1/18/101-ways-to-use-one-page-profiles.aspx)

Business process	Outcomes
Recruitment and selection	
Shortlisted candidates are sent our one-page profile template and 'top tips', asked to follow the guidance and to bring the completed one-page profile along to the interview. Additionally we use one-page profiles to best match people and teams.	The completion of this task: • demonstrates whether the candidate can follow instructions • provides information that is not easily evidenced from an application form and often not drawn out at interview • can be used to test candidate's openness • can be used to help people to recall visually who they have seen.
Performance management	
Used in both supervisions and appraisals to ensure staff are being supported properly and to make sure we know what is important to people. We discuss whether anything needs to change.	The one-page profile ensures that good support with the appropriate resource is in place for staff. It promotes discussion and can enable issues of capability to be addressed to the benefit of both employee and employer.

Learning and development, project work and teams

The one-page profile can be used in a number of ways in this area – for example, team building and induction.	In both team building and induction the one-page profile is used to ensure that team/individuals are all familiar with each other, know what is important to each other and how best to support each other. This reduces the chances of potential conflict because colleagues understand each other better. Additionally they can be used to inform team plans and project plans so everyone is clear about each person's role.

Introductions

Dimensions uses the one-page profiles to introduce people to each other within the organisation and outside the organisation.	People are encouraged to send one-page profiles prior to meeting individuals, teams, families or external bodies. We have found that they are a good way of sharing information about each other before meeting and putting a face to a name. We also request others to complete one-page profiles before meeting with us. For example, when a number of people we support met with the Department of Health we requested that one-page profiles were completed by the ministers.

A person-centred team plan is a description of the team – its purpose, the one-page profiles of team members, how decisions are made, what is working and not working for team members, and the actions agreed to change what is not working and ensure that the core responsibilities of the team are being met.

It can start with people's one-page profiles and a statement or purpose, and then grow from there. Many teams get started with a 'one-page team profile'. This is a description of each team member, what is important to each person, how best to support each person, and what the team's purpose is.

Figure 2.2 is a graphic template that many teams have used to begin a one-page team profile.

'Good days and bad days'

'Good days and bad days' is a person-centred thinking tool that simply asks a person to describe what a typical day is like, then a really good day, and a really bad day. This tells you what needs to be present for them in their day-to-day work life to have good days, and what needs to be absent. In team working, we can ask people to describe in detail 'a good day at work and bad day at work'. Once we know this we can ask, 'What will it take for you to have more good days at work and fewer bad days? What do you need to do?' Figure 2.3 shows Helen's example of a good day and a bad day at work, and her action plan to have more good days at work.

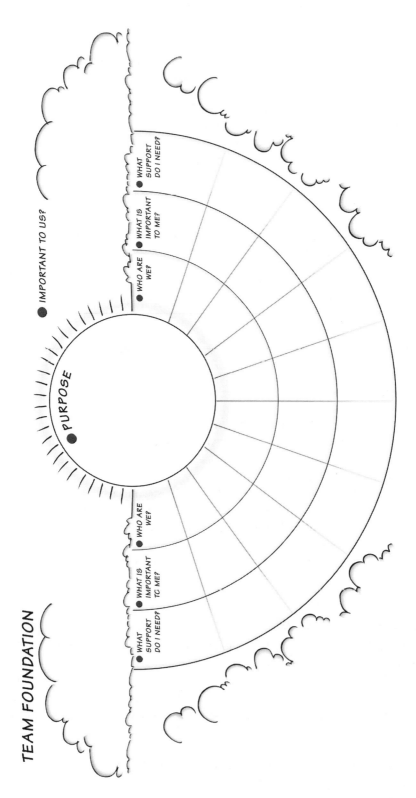

TEAM FOUNDATION

PURPOSE

IMPORTANT TO US?

WHO ARE WE?

WHAT IS IMPORTANT TO ME?

WHAT SUPPORT DO I NEED?

WHO ARE WE?

WHAT IS IMPORTANT TO ME?

WHAT SUPPORT DO I NEED?

Figure 2.2 Person-centred team foundation template

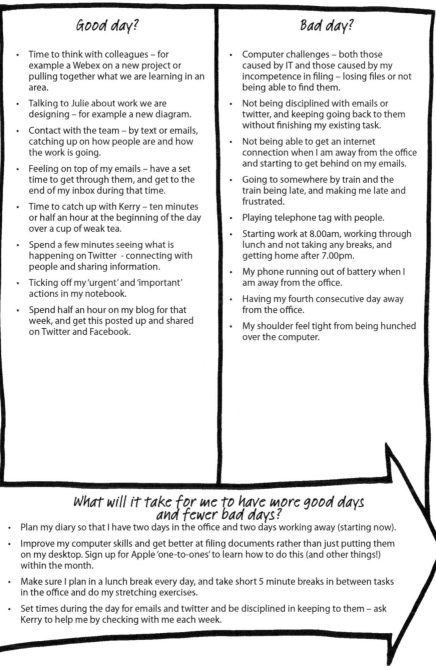

Good day?

- Time to think with colleagues – for example a Webex on a new project or pulling together what we are learning in an area.
- Talking to Julie about work we are designing – for example a new diagram.
- Contact with the team – by text or emails, catching up on how people are and how the work is going.
- Feeling on top of my emails – have a set time to get through them, and get to the end of my inbox during that time.
- Time to catch up with Kerry – ten minutes or half an hour at the beginning of the day over a cup of weak tea.
- Spend a few minutes seeing what is happening on Twitter - connecting with people and sharing information.
- Ticking off my 'urgent' and 'important' actions in my notebook.
- Spend half an hour on my blog for that week, and get this posted up and shared on Twitter and Facebook.

Bad day?

- Computer challenges – both those caused by IT and those caused by my incompetence in filing – losing files or not being able to find them.
- Not being disciplined with emails or twitter, and keeping going back to them without finishing my existing task.
- Not being able to get an internet connection when I am away from the office and starting to get behind on my emails.
- Going to somewhere by train and the train being late, and making me late and frustrated.
- Playing telephone tag with people.
- Starting work at 8.00am, working through lunch and not taking any breaks, and getting home after 7.00pm.
- My phone running out of battery when I am away from the office.
- Having my fourth consecutive day away from the office.
- My shoulder feel tight from being hunched over the computer.

What will it take for me to have more good days and fewer bad days?

- Plan my diary so that I have two days in the office and two days working away (starting now).
- Improve my computer skills and get better at filing documents rather than just putting them on my desktop. Sign up for Apple 'one-to-ones' to learn how to do this (and other things!) within the month.
- Make sure I plan in a lunch break every day, and take short 5 minute breaks in between tasks in the office and do my stretching exercises.
- Set times during the day for emails and twitter and be disciplined in keeping to them – ask Kerry to help me by checking with me each week.

Figure 2.3 Good days and bad days with actions

'Working and not working from different perspectives'

This is a way of looking at a situation and analysing what is working and not working from different people's perspectives.

The tool is useful in three ways:[21]

1. It is a simple way to analyse what is happening, and it surfaces where there are areas of disagreement so that it is clear where there is agreement and where there is difference.

2. It is powerful to look at areas of disagreement in the context of what people see as the same. It enables people to see things 'all the way round', to stand in different people's shoes and to hear it from their perspective.

3. It prevents us from inadvertently changing things that are working.

Dan is the manager of a small printing firm in the North West. He uses 'Working and not working from different perspectives' in his monthly one-to-ones with the staff. He asks each member of staff to bring a list of what is working and not working from their perspective, and he prepares a list of what is working and not working from his perspective. At the meeting they look together at what is working, which Dan says is such a different way to start these meetings. Then he listens to what is not working from the staff member's perspective, and shares his list of what is not working. Together they action plan what they can do to make sure that what is working keeps happening, and change what is not working.

Dan says, 'By using what is working and not working, I have found out about problems that I would never usually have got to know about. For example, I would not have guessed that something that was not working for Carol was how stressful she found the journey to work, and how she worried about being late. It was simple enough to suggest that she had a flexible half an hour at the beginning of the day. This means that, if she comes in 15 minutes later at the beginning of the day, she works 15 minutes later at the end of the day. Carol says this has made a big difference to how stressed she feels coming into work, and makes her days better.'

Figure 2.4 is an example of using 'Working and not working' to review an event, from the perspective of the participants, the event organisers and the venue staff.

In the same way that we can look at what is working and not working from different viewpoints, we can also look at what success means from different perspectives. This is a key element of 'Working Together for Change', introduced later in this chapter.

Communication charts

Up to 97 per cent of communication is non-verbal, and using a communication chart with a team helps you understand their nuances of communication. There are different variations of communication charts used with teams. The first is the same communication chart that is used with people supported. It has four columns, written in either the first or the third person – 'at this time...', 'I do this...', 'it means...' and 'I would like you to...'

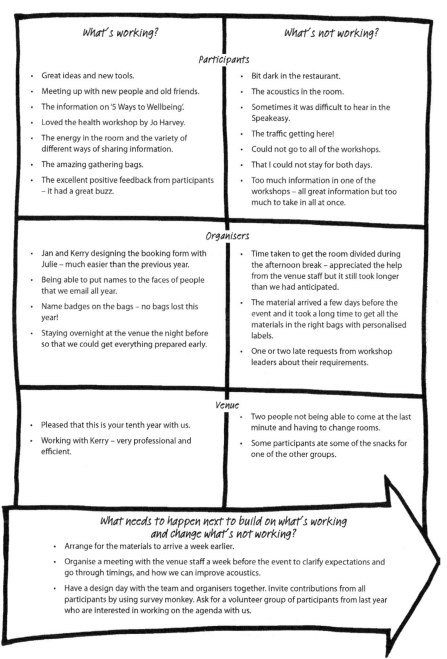

Figure 2.4 Working and not working from different perspectives

Lucy and Ken were part of a health team, and their manager introduced communication charts as part of team building, to improve communication within the team. Figure 2.5 gives two examples, from team members Lucy and Ken, from the team's communication chart.

When Ken is...	he does this...	he would like you to...
Bored	• Daydreams, switches off, doesn't talk.	• Nudge me, change subject and let me say something.
Embarrassed	• Goes quiet, looks down at feet – dwells on it for hours – gets preoccupied.	• Leave me, let me talk through when I am ready. Help me put it to bed.
Inspired	• Jiggles about, talks fast, nods lots, arms go like windmills.	• Help me turn ideas into action.
Worried	• Frowns, goes quiet and thoughtful.	• Give me a chance to come back later when I've thought things through. Don't pressure me, but let me talk when I am ready.
Angry	• Goes very quiet, sulks even, opts out, looks annoyed.	• Leave me alone until I calm down.
When Lucy is...	**she does this...**	**she would like you to...**
Bored	• Looks switched off, maybe yawns and doesn't contribute.	• Bring me into the discussion.
Embarrassed	• Goes red and quiet.	• Leave me until my acute embarrassment has gone then let me speak.
Inspired	• Talks a lot or tries to butt in with her idea, jiggles about in her seat and waves her arms.	• Listen calmly to my idea and talk it through with me.
Worried	• Holds her arms across, is defensive and goes quiet.	• Listen carefully; don't dismiss it as nothing.
Angry	• Either goes very quiet or looks very unhappy or bursts out with it, in a very aggressive manner.	• Listen to what I have to say but in a calming way. Don't aggravate me by arguing aggressively with me.
Pleased	• Grins a lot, looks animated.	• Ask me what I am so pleased about, because I always like to talk about things.

Figure 2.5 Team communication chart

Another form of communication chart focuses around what stresses people, how people react to being stressed and communicate this, and what helps (what the person can do themselves and what they would like another person to know or do).

A consultant was using a personality profiling called the Myers-Briggs Type Indicator with a team to help them think about their personality types and what those meant for how they worked together as a team.[22] She helped them to think about what made each person most stressed, how this would appear to others in the team, and how they could support each other with stress. She used the 'stress and support communication chart' to record what the team learnt (see Figure 2.6).

Name	What makes me most stressed	How I react to being stressed	What I can do	What helps What I would like you to know or do
Sally	• Feeling forced to make decisions too quickly or close tasks too soon. • Being disrespected or my competence being doubted. Feeling as though I've done something badly. • Having my work closely supervised which makes me feel as though my skills aren't being recognised. • Too much time working alone, getting no input or feedback from others. • Restrictive rules that make it difficult to be creative. • Being overloaded by small details – either imposed by others or myself. Being surrounded by clutter (ugliness) that I can't make sense of – either visually or as part of a big task.	• Withdraw, avoid people, avoid the specific task/issue that I am struggling with – procrastinate. • I work harder and longer – try not to think about it. • I display extremes of emotion and activity. • When disrespected, I can become passive and withdraw rather than defend myself, or make a joke that makes others think I'm okay with it, then feel angry with myself later on. • Punish myself, particularly by eating really bad food.	• Pay attention to my body - massage, horse riding, hard physical work. Especially outside, walking, exercise, yoga. Remember to breathe and eat! • Map my work tasks to see how they relate to the big picture/future goals. • Buy time before making commitments - ask to hear more about it, say I need to consult with the team before committing. • Set priorities and check which tasks will fit with the strengths of other team members and then delegate. • Remember to do some things slowly. Take time to read nurturing things like Leunig, pick flowers and arrange them. • Plan and structure my office time, make lists at least weekly and make them visible so I can't hide from them.	• When I'm having a complete freak out, listen without interrupting first, suggest a brisk walk outside, then start asking questions/making suggestions. • Ask if I have a list at the moment. Nag or remind me to make lists and check if I've thought about how to link the boring things to the big picture. • Help me break big things down into small tasks or just prompt me to do this. • Help me plan time to do something physical/outside/nurturing. Send/email me short, inspiring reads (poetry/prose almost always works better than non- fiction). Suggest we do something together. • Ask me to talk you through the main things I have to do at present, offer to do things, reassure me that you will only offer if it's genuinely okay with you – although tedious for you, I will need this reassurance every time. • If I've gone underground, check whether I'm okay, know that if I'm not ok, I'm likely to cry and that will help. • If you know/suspect I'm stressed, ask questions to prompt me to think ahead about healthy food. Actions: • Record team expectations and distribute to team. • Write out some scenarios and an appropriate script for saying no. • Develop a code to write next to things on my to do list so I know how they fit with the big picture. • Copy each week's list and stick up. • Ask Kate if she can give me a weekly list reminder.

Figure 2.6 Stress and support communication chart

Finally, a third version of a communication chart is simply about when and how people prefer to be contacted. This is particularly important for dispersed teams and people who work from home. A national consultancy team used the communication chart shown in Figure 2.7 to make it easier for team members to know the best ways and the best times to get hold of each other.

Decision-making agreements

Personalisation requires that people who receive services have the most choice and control possible over their lives and services. One way to ensure this is to use a decision-making agreement that describes how people are involved in important decisions about their lives, and clarifies the role of staff in this.

Mary uses mental health services. Her team worked with her to develop the decision-making agreement shown in Figure 2.8.

At a team level it is crucial that teams understand how decisions are made and what their role is in this. Another version of a decision-making agreement describes the important areas in which decisions are made within teams, and how the decisions are made. Figure 2.9 is an example from a training team, describing the decisions that individual trainers can make, and the decisions that the managers and the senior manager make.

Matching

Typically when organisations look at the skills required to support someone, they limit themselves to the general skills needed to support the person – for example, if the person has epilepsy, they will often look for candidates who have previous experience or can demonstrate skills in supporting people who have epilepsy. People who have personal budgets looking to employ personal assistants often use a similar approach.

This process is unlikely to produce good matches (that is, where there are common interests and compatible personalities between people who want support and staff who can give it).

The Matching person-centred thinking tool is a simple way to record what is needed to get the best match between those who use services and those who provide them (see Figure 2.10). Finding a good match is one of the most important decisions to make in providing person-centred support. It is a win-win situation when we take into account a staff member's characteristics and interests, as well as their skills and experience. We are then more likely to get a match that is enjoyable for everyone. When staff enjoy their work, they are more likely to stay longer in the role, increase the stability for the person supported and decrease the turnover for the organisation. It could be argued that we are less likely to see issues of abuse and neglect when we pay good attention to matching people well. The same tool can be used within teams to recruit a new team member.

Who	The best ways we can communicate together
Terry	I like email as I am more likely to remember what was agreed. I check most days. I do not take offence at being reminded of things I have forgotten. Try my home number as well as my mobile as mobile reception isn't great where I live. Texting is fine also. Phone me anytime before 10.00pm but not between 6.00 and 7.30pm unless it's very quick and you don't mind being drowned out by children. I am appalling at sending out letters and cards, sorry.
Linda	I always have an admin day on a Monday and tend to check my emails throughout the week. My preference is that we communicate by text, emails or face-to-face conversation. I am really not a lover of the phone (land-line or mobile) and much prefer face-to-face conversations or emails. Feel free to contact me on my mobile at any time and if I am unable to take your call, I will get back to you at my earliest convenience. I am happy to hear from you up until 9.00pm in the evening; but will let you know if it is not convenient.
Claire	If you need to get information to/from me it's better to text or phone. Leave a message. I like to be specific in writing emails; don't put too much information in. If it's really detailed, put bullet points, be clear and detailed about what you want me to do. Worst time to call me is between 5.00 and 8.00pm. I hate text conversations but I see the use of text as information.
Gareth	Email works best for me. I work at my desk 4 days a week so I am able to pick up urgent requests/comments/information via email. If you like to talk rather than email this is ok as long as I have a pen (This is really important!) and paper and will follow this up with a written email. Text is great for me if bits and bobs of information but nothing difficult to get my head around that I need an email copy of. I work 8.30 – 4.30pm five days a week.
Helen	I work best by email. I check my email Monday to Friday. Text is a good way to get me during the day and definitely if you need something urgently. I work hard to keep my evenings and weekends work free so only phone me at home in emergencies please.
Ralph	I prefer most of our communication to be via telephone calls. The best number to phone me on is my mobile and I will tell you if it is convenient to talk as this may be dependent on travelling and children. Anything you need me to do or we have agreed together needs to be confirmed by email by either of us to provide a record or a gentle reminder. I do not take offence at being reminded of things I have forgotten.

Figure 2.7 Team contact chart

What decisions are made?	Who makes the decision?	Who makes the decision? If it's not me why does someone else need to make the decision?	What support do I need to make this decision?
• Spending money under £5	• Mary	• I make this decision. I am able to choose between two choices when presented to me.	• When I go to the shop I want staff to present me with two choices of an item that I like and is recorded in my person-centred plan. Sometimes I would like staff to support me to explore choosing items I have not tried before.
• Spending money under £50	• Mary and SW	• Team members will need to support me with making larger purchases as I do not have the capacity to understand money and its value. Accept that I may make my choice on what I want to buy based on what it looks like.	• If the item is an item to look at (like a painting) then staff can present choices to me and I will choose. If it is any other sort of item staff will have to choose for me based on information that is in my person-centred plan.
• Money up to and under £500	• Mary and HM	• As I do not have capacity to understand money or the function of the items I am purchasing I will need someone that knows me to do this. As this is a large sum of money to protect me from abuse, the manager of the team that support me should sanction all items of expenditure in this range.	• Staff should show me pictures and explain to me what is happening at every stage.
• Money over £500	• Mary, family, HM and my appointee	• I do not have capacity to understand money or the function of the items I am purchasing, I will need someone that knows me to do this. As these items are expensive I want my family informed of the purchase but the people that support me on a day to day basis are the people best placed to choose the item that I would choose. My family and appointee should be involved to protect me from abuse.	• The manager of the team that supports me should consult my person-centred plan and staff members that support me and know me well to make the decision of which item to purchase. Staff should ensure that they get appropriate value for money.
• Money over £2000	• Mary, my appointee, family and HM	• I do not have capacity to understand money or the function of the items I am purchasing I will need someone that knows me to do this. As these items are very expensive I want every one in my circle of support to be involved in this decision to make sure they choose the item I would want and protect me from abuse.	• Staff should show me pictures and explain to me what is happening at every stage. Staff members will then need to agree the cost with my appointee.
• When to get up, if I want to go out, if I want to leave an activity, if I want to start an activity	• Mary	• I can make my wants known well to others. I like to wake up when I am ready and go to bed when I feel tired. I can show that I want to go out by leading someone to where I want to go; this is also how I show that I want to start an activity. When I want to leave an activity I will get up and walk a way from the activity.	• The manager will research the purchase with my staff team and using my person-centred plan. The team will inform my family and appointee of the choice before the item is purchased.
• Clothes	• Mary and SW	• I can choose between choices of clothes presented to me.	• Staff should show me pictures and explain to me what is happening at every stage.
• Planning day to day activities	• Mary and SW	• I do not have the capacity to understand what different activities are unless I am doing them or how to plan events. I will need support from the people that work with me day to day.	• The manager will research the purchase with my staff team and utilising information in my person-centred plan. They will discuss ideas with my family. Once a decision is made this should then be shared with my family and appointee to agree the expenditure.

Figure 2.8 Decision-making agreement

Decisions we make as individual trainers	Decisions we make together as a team	Decisions the managers make	Decisions the senior manager makes
• How we deliver the content of training to our customers according to their outcomes. • How the training will be structured – time scale and the specific dates that it will happen. We do this together with the customer. • Which additional materials to use on courses to complement core materials. • How we involve other people, locally and nationally, in training and development. • How best to build a supportive and professional relationship with our customers. • How to deal with problems that arise. We make the initial decision about whether we can deal with this individually or need support from other team members or the managers.	• How we are working together collectively to meet our purpose and vision. • The core responsibilities for trainers regarding content of courses and where judgement and creativity can be used. • How we contribute to, and develop our publications to share with the rest of the company (in all divisions). • How we used the talents of the team in relation to the work we do, in ways that reflect our gifts and passions.	• The overall look and feel of the intranet. • The service budget and what we need to do to keep to it. • What opportunities to pursue and to look at creating in order to further our work within the company.	• Who is leading on what development areas. Matching interests, strengths and opportunities and talents. • Which relationships and partnerships to develop. • How to share the work of the team within the company.

Figure 2.9 Team decision-making agreements

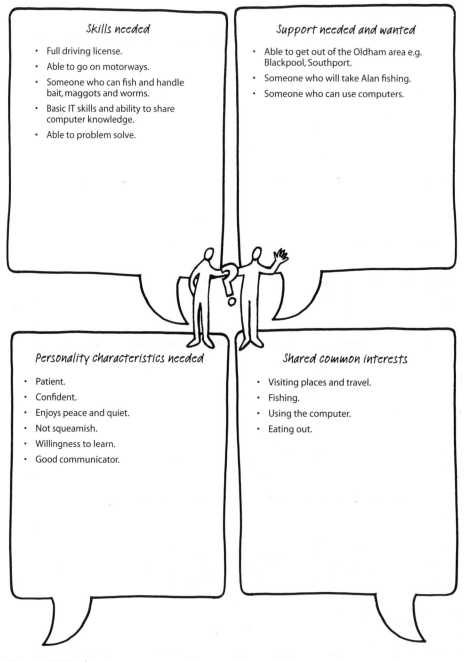

Figure 2.10 Matching

Skills needed

- Full driving license.
- Able to go on motorways.
- Someone who can fish and handle bait, maggots and worms.
- Basic IT skills and ability to share computer knowledge.
- Able to problem solve.

Support needed and wanted

- Able to get out of the Oldham area e.g. Blackpool, Southport.
- Someone who will take Alan fishing.
- Someone who can use computers.

Personality characteristics needed

- Patient.
- Confident.
- Enjoys peace and quiet.
- Not squeamish.
- Willingness to learn.
- Good communicator.

Shared common interests

- Visiting places and travel.
- Fishing.
- Using the computer.
- Eating out.

The Doughnut

Charles Handy originally developed the concept of the 'doughnut', and this is how he describes it:[23]

> The heart of the doughnut – the core – contains all the things which must be done in that job or role if you are to succeed. In a formal job, these are listed as your duties. The next ring is our opportunity to make a difference, to go beyond the bounds of duty, to live up to our full potential. That remains our ultimate responsibility in life, a responsibility always larger than duty, just as the doughnut is larger than its core.

Doughnuts that are 'all cores and no space around them' are all predictable, planned and controlled. Roles that are mainly space, with little 'core', have almost no limit to what can be done. This can make life very stressful for managers, because it suggests that there is no end to their work and there is always more that they are responsible for.

Michael Smull further developed the concept of the doughnut to include a third circle, to identify areas that are not the responsibilities of staff.[24] Therefore, the person-centred thinking tool, the Doughnut, has three rings:

- The inner core reflects the core responsibilities of staff or people providing support.

- The next ring shows areas where staff need to exercise their own judgement and be creative. These are areas where people must make decisions, problem solve and think creatively about possibilities and potential.

- The final ring is areas beyond the scope of the staff member's role and responsibilities. All roles have limits and boundaries, some of which are formally in place and some of which are informal – for example, family preferences or respect for cultural differences.

Figure 2.11 shows the doughnut developed by an admin team in United Response.

One way that Doughnuts are used in organisations is to clarify expectations and firm up job descriptions. Job descriptions can be written using the headings from the Doughnut. One organisation used the Doughnut to make a job description clear and personalised to Jennie (see Figure 2.12). Jennie is a young woman with autism, who, together with her family and Circle of Support, commissioned Independent Options to provide support to Jennie. The job description used the Doughnut to clarify the expectations of staff in relation to:

- Jennie herself

- the family (and Circle of Support)

- the organisation.

The headings of the Doughnut were used within the job description.

You can also use a 'shared' Doughnut to identify and communicate the different responsibilities and areas for creativity for people or organisations working together. Figure 2.13 is an example of a Doughnut used by a project manager from one organisation and the person who was co-ordinating the work from another organisation.

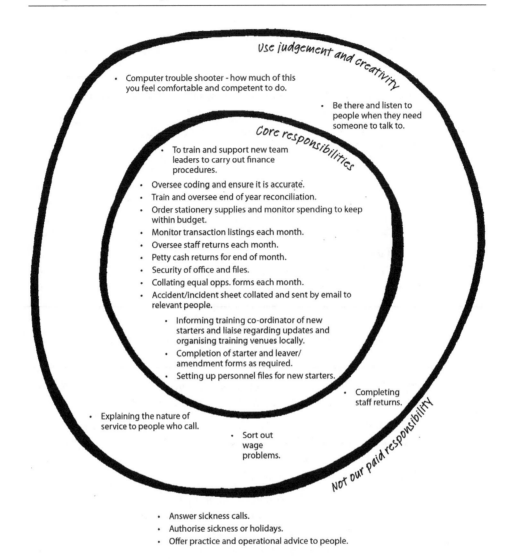

Figure 2.11 The admin team Doughnut

4 Plus 1 questions

This is another tool for reflection and learning about what works and doesn't work. It asks the following questions:

- What have we tried?
- What have we learned?
- What are we pleased about?
- What are we concerned about?

The answers to these questions lead to the 'Plus 1' question, which is:

- Based on what we know, what should we do next?

	Core responsibilities	Use judgement and creativity
Responsibilities to Jennie	1. To communicate well with Jennie. This means knowing how to communicate with Jennie and how Jennie communicates, and to use her communication system and visual cues daily (described in detail in her Person Centred Plan). To support Jennie in her decision-making, so that Jennie increases the amount of choice and control that she has in her life.	
	2. Support Jennie in her relationships (for example, arranging for Jennie to meet up with her friends, supporting Jennie to send birthday cards) and enable her to be part of her local community.	1. Helping Jennie to meet new people, establish new relationships, and be part of her local community.
	3. Support Jennie in all the activities on her weekly timetable and discuss any suggested changes with Suzie (Jennie's Mum).	2. Supporting Jennie to try new activities that she may enjoy (based on what we know is important to Jennie and how to support her).
	4. Work in a person centred way with Jennie, going at her pace, supporting her to develop her interests. This may include practical assistance, support, teaching, advice, role modelling, encouragement and positive feedback.	
	5. To support Jennie to eat healthily and stay safe (there is detailed information about this in her person centred plan).	
	6. Support Jennie a respectful, dignified way. Her personal care routines are described in her person centred plan.	
	7. To support Jennie in managing her own home, including domestic duties, paying bills, shopping, cooking, and budgeting.	
	8. To have a positive, enabling and thoughtful agreed approach to enabling Jennie to take reasonable risk.	

Figure 2.12 Extracts from the job description for Jennie's team leader

Purpose	Core responsibilities	Use judgement and creativity
Freya • Freya's role: to project manage the overall programme from the customer's perspective and coordinate all other input. To communicate progress both internally and externally.	• To collect relevant material and information for communications/meetings. • To collate any reports that may be required. • To deal with any problems/complaints/issues. • To liaise with Michelle and schedule regular meetings/updates. • To clarify who to liaise with in relation to invoicing. • To coordinate programme dates.	• How to involve Michelle. • When to involve others in these meetings/updates.
Michelle • Michelle's role: to coordinate and manage the delivery team's involvement.	• To coordinate all of the delivery team's input into the programme, including; providing dates for training, meetings etc., ordering of materials and invoicing. • To liaise with Freya and schedule regular meetings/updates. • To capture any ongoing learning from the teams involved and to coordinate the documentation for this. • To be responsible for liaising with individuals, families and teams in relation to the planning and/or training.	• How these are delegated within the team. • When to involve others in these meetings/updates. • What documentation to use.

Figure 2.13 A shared Doughnut

These questions are powerful to use in meetings, one-to-ones (supervision) and reviews, or to reflect on a particular issue or project. This is an efficient way to gather collective learning and to make it visible to everyone. One approach used at meetings by a community team is to put up sheets of flip chart paper, each with a different question, and to ask people to write answers on them. This ensures that everyone's perspective is heard, and also that issues are addressed and not overlooked.

Figure 2.14 is an example from a project team that had been working to develop individual service funds. As part of one of their project meetings, they used the 4 Plus 1 questions to reflect on what they had achieved and what they wanted to focus on next.

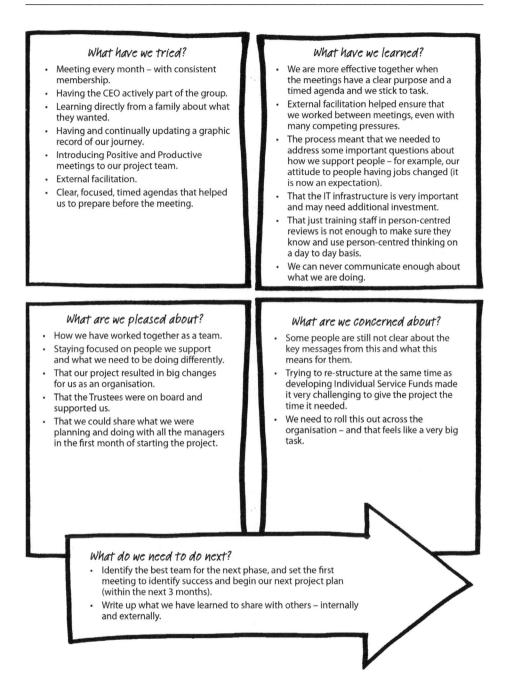

What have we tried?

- Meeting every month – with consistent membership.
- Having the CEO actively part of the group.
- Learning directly from a family about what they wanted.
- Having and continually updating a graphic record of our journey.
- Introducing Positive and Productive meetings to our project team.
- External facilitation.
- Clear, focused, timed agendas that helped us to prepare before the meeting.

What have we learned?

- We are more effective together when the meetings have a clear purpose and a timed agenda and we stick to task.
- External facilitation helped ensure that we worked between meetings, even with many competing pressures.
- The process meant that we needed to address some important questions about how we support people – for example, our attitude to people having jobs changed (it is now an expectation).
- That the IT infrastructure is very important and may need additional investment.
- That just training staff in person-centred reviews is not enough to make sure they know and use person-centred thinking on a day to day basis.
- We can never communicate enough about what we are doing.

What are we pleased about?

- How we have worked together as a team.
- Staying focused on people we support and what we need to be doing differently.
- That our project resulted in big changes for us as an organisation.
- That the Trustees were on board and supported us.
- That we could share what we were planning and doing with all the managers in the first month of starting the project.

What are we concerned about?

- Some people are still not clear about the key messages from this and what this means for them.
- Trying to re-structure at the same time as developing Individual Service Funds made it very challenging to give the project the time it needed.
- We need to roll this out across the organisation – and that feels like a very big task.

What do we need to do next?

- Identify the best team for the next phase, and set the first meeting to identify success and begin our next project plan (within the next 3 months).
- Write up what we have learned to share with others – internally and externally.

Figure 2.14 4 Plus 1

Learning logs

The learning log is a process of reflection and learning about what is happening. Recording what works makes it more likely that an activity or event will happen again.[25]

The information from the learning log has to be used in the same way as the 'Working and not working' information is used.

- Those things that are working need to be maintained.
- Those things that are not working need acting on to change them.

This is particularly important when someone is being supported by more than one person, to ensure that learning is shared and acted on.

Learning logs are also used by teams that are not directly supporting people. One leadership team uses them in their team meetings to reflect on significant events that happen. Certitude, a service provider in London, uses learning logs with the leadership team to record and learn from employee-related issues (see Figure 2.15).

'Presence to Contribution'

'Presence to Contribution' is a person-centred thinking tool that can help to look at connections and contributions. It enables people to think about what they do and where they go in their community, and how these activities could be developed further to provide opportunities for contribution.

Teams and organisations can adapt this person-centred thinking tool to look at their presence in their community and how they are making a contribution. A provider organisation was thinking about how it could get involved in timebanking, and Figure 2.16 is a Presence to Contribution around 'timebanking' as the area of potential connection and contribution.[26]

Histories

Reflecting on our past can reveal what is important to us, and what our qualities are. You can approach this in different ways: either by plotting a chronological timeline of your work life or whole life or by pulling out themes – for example, 'What are the seven experiences that have made you who you are today?'[27] You can record a history in words, graphics or use multimedia. Consider using them individually or to capture a team's or organisation's history. Nicola used a history map to think about a career change:

> Nicola worked with a colleague, Jaimee, to map her work history when she was thinking about her future career. She looked back to her first job as an occupational therapist, then becoming a manager (lecturer) and later a director of a Trust. She thought about the jobs that she had loved – for example, leading the 'Getting A Life' programme for the Department of Health. Jaimee helped her to reflect on each period of her work life and think about what had worked and not worked for her, and what this suggested about her qualities, gifts and talents. This information helped Nicola to think about what was important to and important for her in her work, and therefore what needed to be present (and absent) in whatever work she did in the future: 'This exercise helped me appreciate what I'd achieved, identify the type of change I still wanted to see, and reinforce the type of role and people that energise me.'

certitude

Learning Log: April 2011

Each Leadership Team member should complete a line (or more!) of the log in relation to an employee relations issue – ideally within the last 6 months. Giving as much detail as possible (albeit in bullet points for ease) would be good. To aid learning, it would be good for Mark, Jan, Janette and Mary to share this with their teams so we can get as wide a perspective as possible.

At May's Leadership Team meeting we will spend some time looking at our learning from this and what this means in terms of actions for change.

Date	What was the situation? What happened?	Who was involved?	What did you learn about what worked well?	What did you learn about what didn't work?
What does this mean we need to keep doing or do differently?				

Figure 2.15 Learning log

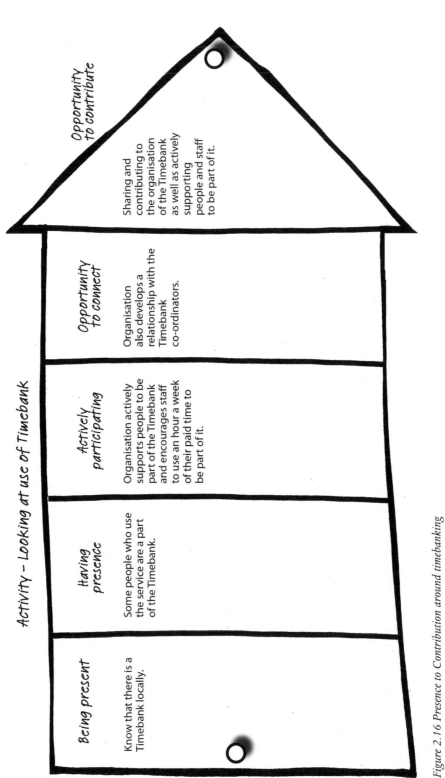

Activity – Looking at use of Timebank

Being present	Having presence	Actively participating	Opportunity to connect	Opportunity to contribute
Know that there is a Timebank locally.	Some people who use the service are a part of the Timebank.	Organisation actively supports people to be part of the Timebank and encourages staff to use an hour a week of their paid time to be part of it.	Organisation also develops a relationship with the Timebank co-ordinators.	Sharing and contributing to the organisation of the Timebank as well as actively supporting people and staff to be part of it.

Figure 2.16 Presence to Contribution around timebanking

Figure 2.17 shows the template used to record Nicola's work history.

IAS is a provider organisation in Greater Manchester. Owen Cooper, then the Chief Executive, gathered a group of people together to develop a graphic of the history of the organisation. This is how he explained the purpose of this to his managers in an email:

> One of the activities we've talked about doing for a while is a historical analysis of the company that draws out what the foundations really are, what the values and beliefs of the company are, what the characteristics of the company are and who's been central to that. This will look at how we've evolved, what our strengths are and what keeps us strong. This is less about specific people or events and more about the values and characteristics about the company... It's also about recognition and appreciation of what the foundations are.[28]

Owen gathered together people with a long history in the organisation, who shared stories of what they remembered. There was a timeline on the wall, and, once people had shared their story, they put the name of the story on a card and attached it on the timeline. A graphic facilitator created a colourful record of this history. The huge poster was shared at the event to create the organisation's statement of purpose, and it was later updated for the company's ten-year anniversary (see Figure 2.18). This inspired people to do histories of the local services – for example in Oldham, Michelle, the Head of Service, asked managers to work with their teams, individuals and families to capture the history of their services. People brought photos and mementoes to bring their storytelling to life, and created a graphic that captured their shared history.

Purpose and success from different perspectives

A person-centred organisation has a clear, shared purpose and one of the ways to achieve this is to think about purpose from different perspectives.

- What is your purpose in relation to people you support?
- What is your purpose in relation to staff?
- What is your purpose in relation to the organisation and how it works?
- What is your purpose in relation to the local community?

When IAS was developing its statement of purpose as a whole organisation, it asked every team, parents' forums, self-advocacy groups and commissioners to contribute. Everyone was asked to think about these questions in a variety of ways to enable people to contribute their perspective. The information was shared through posters at a 'Statement of purpose day', and from this the organisation co-produced its statement of purpose (see Figure 2.19).

Another way to approach this is to use the same perspectives and think together what success would mean – again, from different perspectives:

- What does success mean for people you support?
- What does success mean for staff?

My Work Timeline

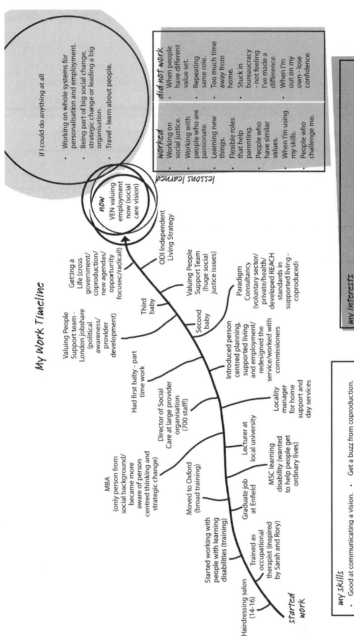

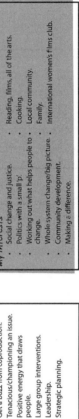

started work

- Hairdressing salon (14-16)
- Trained as occupational therapist (inspired by Sarah and Rory)
- Started working with people with learning disabilities (training)
- Moved to Oxford (broad training)
- Graduate job at Enfield
- MSC learning disability (wanted to help people get ordinary lives)
- MBA (only person from social background/ became more aware of person centred thinking and strategic change)
- Lecturer at local university
- Director of Social Care at large provider organisation (700 staff)
- Had first baby - part time work
- Locality manager for home support and day services
- Valuing People Support team - London jobshare (political awareness/ provider development)
- Introduced person centred planning, supported living and employment and redesigned the service/worked with commissioners
- Getting a Life (cross government/ coproduction/ new agendas/ opportunity focused/radical)
- Third baby
- Second baby
- ODI Independent Living Strategy
- Valuing People Support Team (huge social justice issues)
- Paradigm Consultancy (voluntary sector/ private/health/ developed REACH standards in supported living - coproduced)
- now VEN valuing employment now (social care vision)

if I could do anything at all
- Working on whole systems for personalisation and employment.
- Being part of big social change, strategic change or leading a big organisation.
- Travel - learn about people.

lessons learned

worked
- Working on social justice.
- Working with people who are passionate.
- Learning new things.
- Flexible roles that help parenting.
- People who have similar values.
- When I'm using my skills.
- People who challenge me.

did not work
- When people have different value set.
- Repeating same role.
- Too much time away from home.
- Stuck in bureaucracy - not feeling I've made a difference.
- When I'm out on my own - lose confidence.

my skills
- Good at communicating a vision.
- Passionate/listening to people.
- Get people to buy into ideas and change.
- Experience of health and social care practitioner/ manager, director, breadth of experience in sector, worked across Gov.
- Get a buzz from coproduction.
- Tenacious/championing an issue.
- Positive energy that draws people.
- Large group interventions.
- Leadership.
- Strategic planning.

my interests
- Social change and justice.
- Politics with a small 'p'.
- Working out what helps people to change.
- Whole system change/big picture.
- Community development.
- Making a difference.
- Reading, films, all of the arts.
- Cooking.
- Local community.
- Family.
- International women's films club.

Figure 2.17 Work history

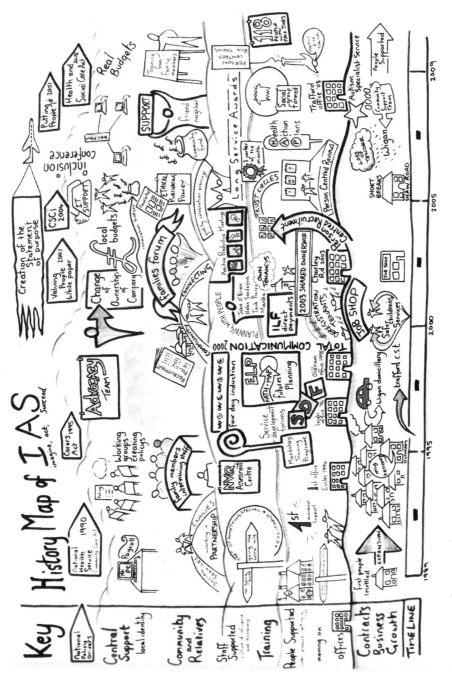

Figure 2.18 IAS history graphic

IAS
Imagine, Act, Succeed

People we support

- Are encouraged and supported to dream.
- Are given opportunities to demonstrate their capacity and resourcefulness.
- Have a choice over where they live, who they live with and how they are supported.
- Have the opportunity to direct how their service is delivered.
- Have contributions to make to their communities.
- Have opportunities to get to know and be known by as many people as possible.
- Live as valued members of their communities, surrounded by a wide network of family, friends and neighbours.

Company

- We continue to learn through encouraging and celebrating good attempts.
- We promote decision making to be as close to the person as possible.
- We create a person centred company where everyone matters.
- We support fair and ethical business practice.
- We develop a "can-do" culture
- We work in partnership with our allies as "together we're better".
- We make time to reflect on practice and re-visit our purpose.

Staff

- Have the opportunity to contribute and influence the development of the service.
- Feel their gifts, skills and contributions are acknowledged and appreciated.
- Have their passion and creativity released by adapting jobs to match a person's strengths and gifts.
- Listen to people and act on what has been heard.
- Act together from a shared sense of purpose.
- Have an opportunity to discover and do what matters.
- Challenge the low expectations that people we support generally experience.
- Are acknowledged as resources in their own communities.
- Know what is expected of them at work and are supported to achieve this.

Community

- We strive to increase the community's ability to include everyone.
- We create opportunities for people to get to know each other and develop friendships and relationships.
- We promote equal and respectful relationships.
- We highlight peoples gifts and qualities.
- We counter discrimination through positive participation.
- We invest in and promote local communities through using local facilities and resources.

Figure 2.19 IAS – our purpose in relation to people, staff, the organisation and community

- What does success mean for the organisation?
- What does success mean in relation to your contribution to the local (or wider) community?

This can be further developed into a one-page strategy summary.

This is where the links between the purpose of the organisation, what success looks like from different perspectives, how person-centred practices can help to deliver what success means, and how this is measured, come together. Figure 2.20 is an example:

What success means to:

Individuals
* I have friends and am valued as a citizen in my community.
* I am listened to and supported in the way I want to be.
* I live the life I choose and make my own decisions.

Staff
* I am listened to and valued.
* I am proud of the job I do.
* I make a difference.

Organisation
* We use person-centred practices in all we do, at all levels of the organisation.
* We can demonstrate that we achieving outcomes for people.
* We keep learning and developing and challenge any perception of "good enough".

We can deliver success by using:

* Communication charts.
* Decision making agreements.
* Relationship circles.
* Matching.
* One page profiles.
* Presence to contribution.
* Person-centred reviews.

* Positive and Productive meetings.
* Person-centred supervisions.
* Person-centred teams.

* Individual Service Funds.
* Working Together for Change.

We measure success by:

* The number of person-centred reviews.
* The number monthly reviews - using working and not working with actions.

* Staff satisfaction survey.
* Survey of sickness rates.
* The number of person-centred team plans.
* The number of person-centred supervisions and staff reviews.

* Increasing our scores using Progress for Providers.
* The number of people with Individual Service Funds.

Figure 2.20 One-page strategy

Relationship and community maps

Relationships are central to person-centred organisations. Mapping out relationships is important for teams and organisations, encouraging people to think about who is important and what needs to happen for these connections to develop and grow. In business terms the activity is similar to stakeholder mapping.

A relationship map is usually three concentric circles with a person in the middle. It can be sectioned across to indicate different groups of people.

Debbie is a consultant working with organisations in health and social care. She used a relationship map as part of her business planning to map out who her existing customers were, and to identify potential customers and important partners in her work. She therefore split her relationship circle into three.

Existing customers – Debbie put the names of the customers with whom she had a very close relationship, and who had invested in longer term programmes, in the first circle. In the second circle she put customers with whom she had worked to deliver multiple training and learning opportunities, and in the outer circle she listed those with whom she had only worked on one course.

Potential customers – in the inner circle Debbie wrote the names of people with whom she already had a relationship, and who had expressed an interest in her work. In the second circle were people she knew, and who could be interested in the learning opportunities or consultancy she offered. In the outer circle she listed people whom she knew of, but did not know personally, who had similar interests and could be seen as potential customers.

Partners – in this section Debbie focused on people with whom she worked, who shared the same mission, and who were already working with her (for example, as part of an action learning set, a co-author of a paper describing what they were learning). She put the names of these in the inner circle, and those more loosely connected (for example, people she knew on Linked-In) in the second and third circles.

Debbie used the relationship map to think about and develop actions around how she could invest in her relationships to move people from the outer circles to the inner circles.

Figure 2.21 shows the relationship circle divided into three, in the way that Debbie used it.

We have put relationship and community mapping together because communities are about relationships, and good community maps are always about people.

Person-centred organisations have a strong focus on communities. This is in relation to people they support, to enable them to be contributing and valued members of their community, and as an organisation, looking at what the contribution of the organisation could be.

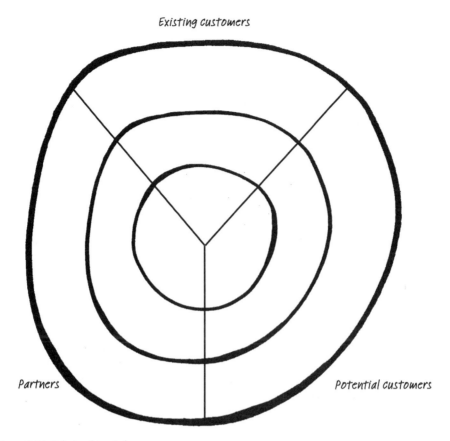

Figure 2.21 Relationship circle

United Response uses interactive multimedia community maps to enable people to map and think about their community, and to look for opportunities to connect and contribute.

When we think about an organisation's contribution to communities, we can think of community in several ways. One way is a community of people – for example, as an organisation, United Response makes contributions to the wider community of people with learning disabilities. This includes providing practical easy-to-read tools and information that helps people to know and exercise their rights as equal citizens, such as accessible information on politics and voting ('Every Vote Counts') and on money management and banking ('Making Money Easier'). United Response campaign at local and national level on issues that people supported say are important to them – for example, running a project to help prevent bullying and harassment of people with learning disabilities on public transport ('UR on Board') and raising awareness of the importance of social care ('Life Support'). There are also communities of interest – for example, an organisation could map out the communities of interest that relate to its purpose. For example, there is a community of interest about person-centred practices led by the Learning Community for Person-Centered Practice with an annual gathering, online forums, community websites such as www.thinkandplan.com, an email list-serve and a Facebook page. Provider organisations can make contributions to communities of interest – for example, by supporting people to contribute their learning and examples, and to generate and respond to messages on the list-serve.

As well as communities of people, and communities of interest, there are neighbourhood communities. United Response makes a contribution to a number of local communities that have actively supported the development of timebanking to benefit the community as a whole.

Mapping community, whether at an individual or organisational level, can be powerful when used alongside the Presence to Contribution person-centred thinking tool to go from 'Who and what is here?' to 'What connection and contribution can I/we make?'

These are the main person-centred thinking tools that we refer to in this book. There is a much longer list, and for more information go to www.helensandersonassociates.co.uk, www.learningcommunity.us and www.thinkandplan.com.

Person-centred practices

'Person-centred practices' is a term that covers both person-centred thinking tools and practices that share the same values and may utilise a number of the tools. In this book we introduce person-centred reviews, 'Positive and Productive Meetings', person-centred recruitment, person-centred one-to-ones (supervision) and 'Working Together for Change'. We introduce these approaches in the relevant chapters, and here is a brief summary.

Person-centred reviews

Person-centred reviews were originally developed in schools to support young people in transition from school to adult life.[29] The approach then spread to be used in adult services, in health and social care.[30] Now, the person-centred review process is also used with teams, to review how the team is doing both in delivering on its purpose and working together. The process uses the person-centred thinking tools 'Important to and for' and 'Working and not working from different perspectives'. Teams can look at what is working and not working in relation to people (relationships and supports), performance (core responsibilities, policies, procedures and resources), and process (how members work together, decision making, etc.) to identify action plans to sustain or enhance each aspect of the team.

In IAS, teams use person-centred reviews to review their teams each year. Chief Executive Ruth Gorman says:

> The introduction of the person-centred review process has changed the culture of the organisation. It is a fantastic way to use common language for all connected to IAS. Using person-centred reviews in teams, to review what is important to the team and what is working and not working from different perspectives, has resulted in better working relationships, a clearer understanding about the

direction of each team in the organisation and their commitment to our statement of purpose. We continue to develop our thinking in this area by introducing the person-centred review process for all staff rather than an appraisal. This 'work review' is based on the same headings, and it enables people to really focus on what they are contributing to the lives of the people we support, how they are engaging with their team and the organisation.

Here is how the questions used in a person-centred review can be adapted to be used within a team:

Headings used in a person-centred review	Headings used in a team review
What do we appreciate about the person?	What do we appreciate about our team?
What is important to (the person) now?	What is important to us as a team now?
What is important to (the person) for the future?	What is important to our team in the future?
What does (the person) need to stay healthy and safe, and supported well?	What support does our team need to do our best work • from each other? • from the manager? • from others?
What questions do we need to answer?	What questions do we need to answer? What do we still need to figure out?
What is working and not working from different perspectives?	What is working and not working from the perspective • of each team member? • of the manager?

'Positive and Productive Meetings'

This is a fresh approach to meetings that uses a person-centred approach and focuses on sharing roles and responsibilities in meetings and ensuring that roles reflect people's gifts and talents. Positive and Productive Meetings require clarity over decision making, and clear, outcome-focused, timed agendas that enable people to think together and make decisions, rather than just using meetings as a way to share information. The meeting process ensures that everyone is listened to and contributes to decision making (see Figure 2.22).

Many organisations have used Positive and Productive Meetings as a way to start to move towards a person-centred culture, and to deliver personalised services.[31] Michael Smull, the founder of the international Learning Community for Person-centred Practices, describes Positive and Productive Meetings as a key way to achieve person-centred cultural change.[32]

Summary of positive and productive meetings process

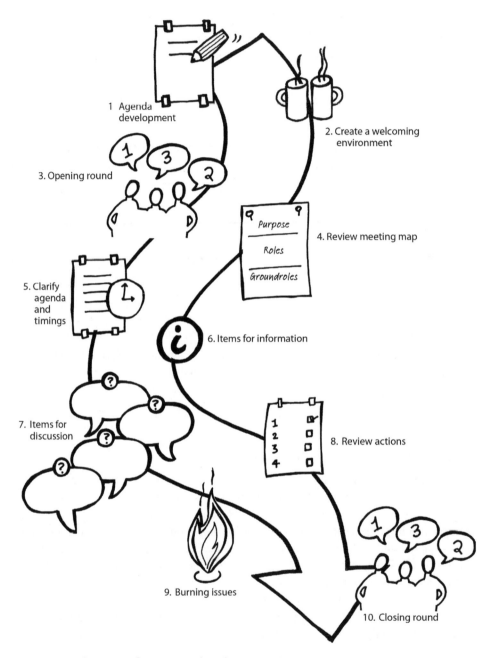

Figure 2.22 The process of a Positive and Productive Meeting

United Response provided coaches to assist managers and staff to embed person-centred thinking within all their management practices. They introduced Positive and Productive Meetings early on in the change programme. In this new way of running meetings, rounds are used to ensure that everyone in the meeting is heard. Agendas are written in a new way, clearly saying what the issue or question is, how long the discussion of it will last and how people need to prepare for the meeting. Sarah, a divisional director, describes the difference that using Positive and Productive Meetings has had:

> I changed the meetings across the organisation and the way colleagues talked to and supported each other. They had been monthly meetings from across the three areas and they were all very business focused with me in the chair. It was all quite dry really. Now we focus on practice and moving forwards. The meetings are more creative, and we use person-centred thinking tools to help people to prepare. We share roles in the meetings and the end result is better, more enjoyable meetings with sharply improved attendance.

Person-centred recruitment

The person-centred recruitment process uses person-centred thinking tools to try to get the best possible match between the person (or team) and the candidate (see Figure 2.23). The process starts with person-centred information, and this is used to develop the person specification and job description. It is very important that everyone involved is clear about how decisions will be made, and how the person, or their family if relevant, will be central in the decision making. Using a decision-making agreement can help here. To get the best match, you are matching to the values and culture of the organisation and then the person or the team. The Matching tool is central to the person-centred recruitment process. Joe's story illustrates the difference that getting the best match can make in someone's life:

> Joe was resettled in 1994 from a long-stay institution with three other men. The match wasn't perfect but the men lived together as best they could in a large purpose-built bungalow. Although this appeared to be OK for Joe, it was clear that his routines had a huge impact on the other men. Joe is a 'very lively, rough and tumble type of guy' with a great sense of fun. He loves boisterous, knock-about fun. Touch is also very important to him because he has a visual impairment.
>
> The staff were skilled at supporting Joe; however, he could inadvertently put the other men at risk if they were in the immediate vicinity when he was being boisterous. As he preferred to spend the majority of his time at home, the bungalow practically became a no-go area for anyone but him and his staff team. He couldn't seem to tell the difference between day and night, and because of this has never established a regular sleeping pattern. He also refused to be in a bed, and this meant that the lounge area was his 24 hours a day unless he was out and about. His erratic sleep pattern required staff to be awake and around for him at all times; this had an impact on the quality of sleep that the other men had and they were regularly disturbed by Joe's night-time activities. With three other men whose support needs could be as intense as Joe's, dividing staff time

became increasingly difficult. Joe also has pica and will put anything in his mouth and try to eat it. He wore specialised clothing to prevent him ripping his clothes and eating the material, and because of this required intense observation and support. Outside his home, Joe required 2:1 staffing levels for his own safety. Staff were finding it really hard to cope. Each of the four men had an individual person-centred review, and the 'what's not working' made very clear the impact that Joe's lifestyle was having on everyone.

The local authority had been aware of the situation throughout, and had been supportive of many initiatives and interventions that had been tried to reduce the impact on Joe's co-tenants. They had even provided some additional hours for Joe's support. None of this made the difference that was needed and it was eventually agreed that Joe would move into his own tenancy, with his own staff team.

Joe already had a one-page profile, and the staff worked on the 'matching' person-centred thinking tool to think back over the years of working with Joe what type of person he enjoys being with. They decided that the ideal person would be lively and relatively loud; confident; outgoing and fun. Essential skills and knowledge would include being a driver, and being connected in and knowledgeable about the local community. The shared interests they were looking for in the person were a love of walking, swimming and food – eating out and cooking.

So...a loud, fun-loving foodie – sounded like Jamie Oliver would be perfect! The manager used the information from Joe's one-page profile and the 'matching tool' to develop the job description and person specification. The existing staff who had a good relationship with Joe and fitted the specification were invited to move with him, while the recruiting of his own team began.

The advert introduced Joe by using the 'appreciation' section of his one-page profile and gave information about the kind of person being sought. It was put in local places like the Post Office and a local newspaper.

Using this process, to get the right staff for Joe and his own place made a huge difference to his life, and the life of the men he used to live with. Today he has a regular sleep pattern and sleeps in a bed. He only has 1:1 staff now, instead of 2:1, he no longer has waking nights and his pica has significantly decreased. His manager attributes this to having the right staff with the right qualities and the best match for Joe.

The one-page profile format can be used in recruitment as well. Figure 2.24 is an example.

Person-centred one-to-ones (supervision)

One-to-ones or supervision can be experienced by staff as a negative, almost punitive experience. This person-centred approach to one-to-ones focuses on their being opportunities for appreciation and feedback, reflection on progress and learning and an opportunity for shared problem solving (see Figure 2.25).

Innovative organisations are using staff members' one-page profiles within one-to-ones, asking what is working and not working from the individual staff member's perspective, sharing what is working and not working from the manager's perspective and then agreeing actions that build on what is working and address what is not working.

Summary of Person Centred Recruitment Process

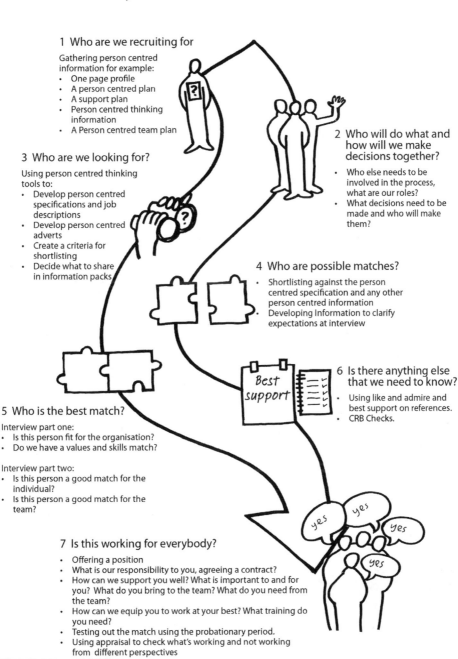

1 Who are we recruiting for

Gathering person centred information for example:
- One page profile
- A person centred plan
- A support plan
- Person centred thinking information
- A Person centred team plan

2 Who will do what and how will we make decisions together?
- Who else needs to be involved in the process, what are our roles?
- What decisions need to be made and who will make them?

3 Who are we looking for?

Using person centred thinking tools to:
- Develop person centred specifications and job descriptions
- Develop person centred adverts
- Create a criteria for shortlisting
- Decide what to share in information packs

4 Who are possible matches?
- Shortlisting against the person centred specification and any other person centred information
- Developing Information to clarify expectations at interview

5 Who is the best match?

Interview part one:
- Is this person fit for the organisation?
- Do we have a values and skills match?

Interview part two:
- Is this person a good match for the individual?
- Is this person a good match for the team?

Best support

6 Is there anything else that we need to know?
- Using like and admire and best support on references.
- CRB Checks.

7 Is this working for everybody?
- Offering a position
- What is our responsibility to you, agreeing a contract?
- How can we support you well? What is important to and for you? What do you bring to the team? What do you need from the team?
- How can we equip you to work at your best? What training do you need?
- Testing out the match using the probationary period.
- Using appraisal to check what's working and not working from different perspectives

Figure 2.23 The process of person-centred recruitment

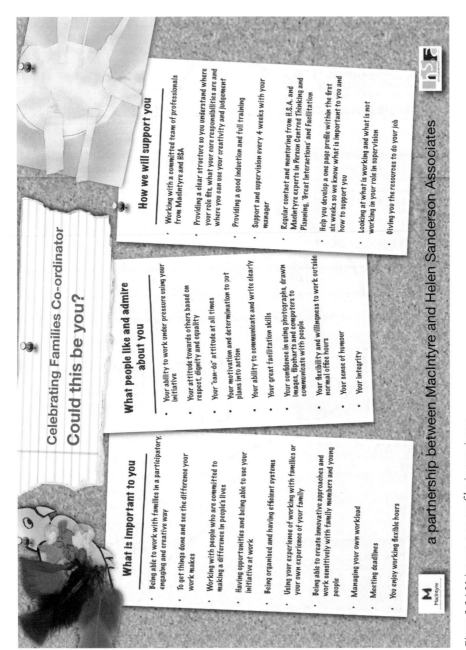

Celebrating Families Co-ordinator

Could this be you?

What is important to you

- Being able to work with families in a participatory, engaging and creative way
- To get things done and see the difference your work makes
- Working with people who are committed to making a difference in people's lives
- Having opportunities and being able to use your initiative at work
- Being organised and having efficient systems
- Using your experience of working with families or your own experience of your family
- Being able to create innovative approaches and work sensitively with family members and young people
- Managing your own workload
- Meeting deadlines
- You enjoy working flexible hours

What people like and admire about you

- Your ability to work under pressure using your initiative
- Your attitude towards others based on respect, dignity and equality
- Your 'can-do' attitude at all times
- Your motivation and determination to put plans into action
- Your ability to communicate and write clearly
- Your great facilitation skills
- Your confidence in using photographs, drawn images, flipcharts and computers to communicate with people
- Your flexibility and willingness to work outside normal office hours
- Your sense of humour
- Your integrity

How we will support you

- Working with a committed team of professionals from MacIntyre and HSA
- Providing a clear structure so you understand where your role fits, what your core responsibilities are and where you can use your creativity and judgement
- Providing a good induction and full training
- Support and supervision every 4 weeks with your manager
- Regular contact and mentoring from H.S.A. and MacIntyre experts in Person Centred Thinking and Planning, 'Great Interactions' and Facilitation
- Help you develop a one page profile within the first six weeks so we know what is important to you and how to support you
- Looking at what is working and what is not working in your role in supervision
- Giving you the resources to do your job

a partnership between MacIntyre and Helen Sanderson Associates

Figure 2.24 Using one-page profiles in recruitment

Summary of person-centred supervision (one-to-ones)

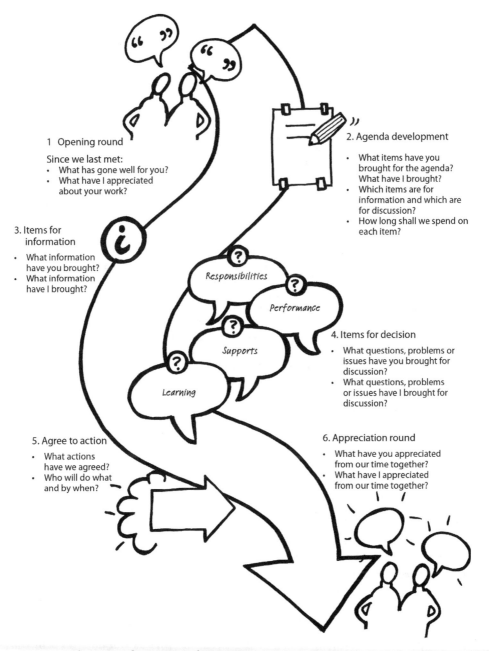

Figure 2.25 The process of person-centred supervision

Carolynn, a manager, was trained and coached to use person-centred supervision by Michelle, and this is how it changed her thinking and practice:

> Carolynn believed that staff had a historical perception of supervision being punitive and therefore a negative experience, regardless of how she had tried to approach it. Staff saw supervision as a time to be 'told off'; therefore, there was a reluctance to attend and contribute. Carolynn said that sessions were often one-sided, with her setting most of the agenda. She made up for this by ensuring that lots of informal, unplanned support was given with an open-door type of philosophy.
>
> Because of this, there was a tendency for structured supervisions to be infrequent although informal guidance was available at any time. The point of supervision of staff is to allow for time and space to focus on supporting them through the structural and ideological changes taking place, and to focus on the outcomes for the individuals being supported. Staff needed to understand their role within the changes and the one-to-one time afforded by supervision ensured that there were opportunities to reflect on this. Michelle had an individual session with Carolyn and this equipped her with a person-centred process that she could follow, and which would help her to better support her staff team. They explored how the content of supervision should have a focus on what they were learning about the people they supported and the team, and how they were progressing with the outcomes developed via the support planning and subsequent planning opportunities. Carolynn said that she felt more confident to support people by using the supervision process and the structure had really helped her to have more meaningful conversations with staff.
>
> She realises now that, before this process of change, her supervision of her staff and also those she supported was not always 100 per cent person-centred – despite aiming for it to be so. Originally staff meetings focused on policy and procedures because that was what staff were most concerned about.
>
> This support focused Carolynn's management style and made her feel as though she was focusing her efforts on her staff in a more productive and fruitful way. She said, 'It was the best training I have ever done! Being able to say to my staff, what do you want to get out of your supervision?; and moving away from the negative associations of staff supervision, was great!'

Working Together for Change

This is a collaborative, eight-stage process that takes person-centred information from person-centred reviews or what is working and not working for people, and uses this to inform strategic change (see Figure 2.26).

It has been used in schools, by the Department of Health, and in adult health and social care, and it is now being used instead of staff satisfaction questionnaires by some providers.[33] Using the process instead of staff satisfaction questionnaires involves taking anonymous information from staff one-to-ones or appraisals about what is working and not working for staff, and then a group of staff and managers clustering this to identify themes. Looking at all the 'what is working' for staff can provide information about what is working overall. Managers and staff can then agree strategic actions to ensure that what is working is available to all staff, as well as actions to ensure that what is working can continue. Theming what is not working reveals the main areas of discontent within the staff groups across an organisation. The process includes ways to understand why this is happening, and then the group agrees success indicators about each aspect that is not working. Once there are clear success indicators, the group decides on strategic actions to change what is not working and move towards these success indicators.

Figure 2.26 The 8-stage process of Working Together for Change

The purpose of this book is to show how person-centred thinking tools and practices can be used alongside conventional development tools for teams and organisations. Therefore we are ending this chapter with a summary of some of the conventional tools that we refer to within the book. It is not the purpose of this book, however, to go into these conventional tools in detail, and so only short descriptions are given in the table below.

The table gives only some examples of the kind of tools and techniques that can be used to address certain issues.

Typical tool and purpose	Short description
Resistance management	Methods used to find out how people feel about a change or event they are facing, and how strongly they are seeking to stop that happening to them. Also the ways in which the resistance is then dealt with in order to ensure that a change or event is successful, and the impact on the people affected is minimised as far as possible.
Role clarification	A way of being clear about who is doing what in relation to any particular activity, task or role. A common tool is RACI analysis – responsibility, accountability, consultation and information. A variation on this is RASI – responsibility, accountability, supporting, information.
Visioning	How a business decides the big picture view of its future aims and objectives. Sometimes done by brainstorming, or by drawing cartoons or graphics of the future desired position. It can also be done by creating a vivid word description of the desired state.
Objective setting/ SMART	How people lay out the more detailed definition of the things they will achieve in a given timeframe. Typically many organisations work on a one- to three-year timeframe and include detailed financial and other hard measures that confirm the level of success. Sometimes these are expressed as 'critical success factors'. At an individual level, objectives tend to be set annually or sometimes semi-annually or quarterly, and a common tool is to use the SMART acronym: S – Specific, M – Measurable, A – Achievable, R – Relevant, T – Time bound.
Performance management	The process of measuring how well people and organisations are doing, and identifying what actions to take to improve performance or develop competence. Here you will frequently see supervision and appraisal tools and techniques at an individual level, and the use of key performance indicators and critical success factors at an organisation level.
Employee relations management – discipline, grievance, capability, absence management	The policies, procedures and practices that determine how the working relationship between an employer and employee are managed. This will include formal policy and procedure documents and other protocols that may be written or unwritten. An identifying characteristic of the processes in this area is that they will be predominantly formal in their style and implementation. Techniques may also include mediation, consultation and negotiation, for example. This area is also typified by formal terms of reference for representative bodies.
Communications strategy and planning	Strategy documents that lay out the broad direction and things to be achieved through communication, and the key groups of stakeholders who need to receive attention. Plans that detail the people who need to be communicated with, the timescales and subject matter of communications, the method of delivery, and who will do it.

Employee engagement	How staff in the organisation are encouraged to do more than just turn up for work, and to take an active part in seeking to further their contribution to the success of the organisation (and of course, themselves). Techniques have previously mainly focused on involvement of colleagues in improvement projects, or in consultation and so on. The modern definition now includes a much broader thinking about reward and recognition, and the overall well-being of colleagues, so that they are motivated and equipped physically and mentally to give their engagement. This includes motivation techniques, the specific range of tools and techniques that encourage employees to perform at their best. This will be a vast range of approaches from monetary rewards, through recognition for achievement, and incorporating the interpersonal skills and techniques used by managers in their communication with colleagues and management of staff activity.
Strategic and business planning	The way in which an organisation goes about explaining what it is here for and how it will pursue its aims in order to justify and maintain its existence. There are a multitude of tools and techniques available here, some of which are mentioned elsewhere in this summary. Common analytical tools that encourage thinking about the aims and objectives for strategic and business planning include SWOT and PEST analysis. SWOT – identifying Strengths, Weaknesses, Opportunities and Threats. Strengths and Weaknesses are referenced to the internal aspects of the organisation, while Opportunities and Threats are related to the external environment. As such, SWOT quickly gives an all-round view of the business context. From here, leaders can decide the appropriate steps to take to respond to the nature of that context, and allocate priority for resources. PEST is a broadly similar tool. The PEST analysis looks at likely changes in the *political, economic, socio-cultural* and *technological* factors and seeks to predict the extent to which change is likely to occur and its possible consequences for the organisation. This enables the organisation to design strategies to manage these factors.
Team development planning and implementation	Team assessment tools are common here, generally based on some assumed or researched set of team performance criteria, of which there is a vast range. Another popular approach is to have a new team start-up approach, combining a range of 'getting to know you' activities with other exercises such as role clarity and visioning. These are often based around a specific team model.

cont.

Typical tool and purpose	Short description
Culture assessment	Common tools in this area include quasi-numeric assessment tools that seek subjective assessment of defined criteria using a numeric rating scale. This can range from quite simple versions, using a shortlist of preferred cultural characteristics to the relatively more complex as used in the approach favoured by Robert E. Quinn,[34] which builds a considerably more multi-faceted model of a culture.
	An alternative approach is to carry out a number of diagnostic interviews, generally based around some key 'issue' questions, and then to analyse the data into a summary set of key cultural indicators for an organisation. It is often the case that such diagnostics are designed and agreed for the specific organisation, but are also frequently based on prior experience of such exercises when carried out by experienced consultants.
Project planning and management tools	The wheel has been reinvented numerous times in the area of project planning and management, and there are volumes of tools and techniques. Generically these fall into some form of task scheduling tool, which may range from something as simple as a spreadsheet or an action plan on a piece of paper, through common systems such as Microsoft Project up to highly detailed and complex custom-designed software for large multi-faceted projects.
	Other typical project monitoring and management tools would include such as Go/No Go Criteria checklists, and project progress review meetings.
Continuous improvement tools	These are very common, particularly in the high-volume manufacturing industry. Tools include 'the Five Whys', Fishbone diagrams, Kanban, Pareto charts, histograms, flow charts, waste elimination tools, and so on.
	The modern approach to these is often referred to as Lean, or Six Sigma, or Lean Sigma, and, in summary, tends to focus on waste elimination and process reliability. Some of the tools have also been adapted successfully for office and administration environments, and other work situations.

Conclusion

Person-centred practices offer a way to develop services that can deliver personalisation. We are not assuming that they will replace the wealth of organisation development tools, but that they can add to a richer, fuller toolbox with which to bring about change with a person-centred ethos.

Chapter 3

Vision, Mission, Values and Strategy

A small body of determined spirits fired by an unquenchable faith in their mission can alter the course of history.

Gandhi[35]

Introduction

Stephen Covey says that being successful requires 'beginning with the end in mind'.[36] For organisations this means knowing what success looks like, and what your mission is. Almost every management text will tell you about the importance of vision, mission and values. We want to explore what this means in the context of a person-centred organisation. In this chapter you will find more detail of how person-centred practices can enhance conventional approaches to creating a vision, mission, strategies, a set of values, and a robust business planning process.

Vision, mission and values – what do they mean in a person-centred organisation?

Although these terms are all familiar, we start by clarifying what each of them means and how they link together.

Term	Definition
Vision	A vivid and compelling description of the big outcomes for the organisation and its stakeholders. The 'bright star'(s) we are aiming for.
Mission	A mission statement captures an organisation's reason for being. A clear mission statement will answer the questions: Who are we? What do we do? For whom do we do it? Why do we do it? (Collins 2001).[37] This statement should describe the journey that the organisation is taking to reach those bright stars, how it will travel and who it will work with on the way. Some organisations use the term 'purpose' rather than mission.
Core values	Core values are essential and enduring principles and beliefs that guide work behaviour, relationships and decision making. Core values are ones that we should strive for despite external environment changes.

cont.

Term	Definition
Strategies	Strategies answer the 'how' we will do it, and focus on longer term direction to set parameters for business planning.
Business planning	The process that translates the longer term vision, mission, values and strategies into shorter term achievable results.
Local action plans	The process that implements the business planning objectives and measures.

Without a clear vision and mission, an organisation will struggle to create a consistent long-term strategy. If you don't know where you are going, you could end up somewhere you really don't want to be (or anywhere will do!).

An organisation without shared values does not know what it stands for, will lack credibility with the people who use, or who could potentially use, its service, and risks losing the loyalty of its key resource – the people who work in it. A person-centred organisation will have a clear vision of what it wants to achieve. This vision and mission are underpinned by shared person-centred values or beliefs, and, most importantly, the values will be evident in everyone's behaviour, and throughout strategies, policies and procedures within the organisation. Let's look at each of these in turn, and then you can assess where your organisation is in relation to vision, mission and values.

Person-centred vision and mission

A vision statement captures where an organisation wants to be. It is usually timeless, and constant, unless the fundamental purpose of the organisation changes. Both the vision statement and the mission statement will reflect the core values of the organisation. The core values are the enduring principles that guide the organisation, and are consistent even as the wider context changes. This is how Scope describes its mission and vision:

> We see the person and we set no limit on potential.
>
> We believe in independence, inclusion and freedom to choose.
>
> Everyday life equality.
>
> No more. No less.
>
> Together we can create a better society.

Person-centred values

It is the values of an organisation that really tell you what the organisation is. In particular, they will give you a strong sense of how the organisation conceptualises being 'person-centred'.

United Response describes its values as follows:

We are committed to improving the lives of the people we support. We do this chiefly through our person-centred approach, which puts people at the centre of all our activity – whether that's day-to-day support or advocacy on matters that affect them.

We respect and promote the rights of every person we support. As such, we campaign around issues that are important to and for them – in our own right, as well as members of the Learning Disability Coalition and the Voluntary Organisations' Disability Group.

Here are the values and beliefs of a supported living organisation called Options.[38]

This is what we expect of all our staff:

- Integrity – We seek in our actions, in what we do, to reflect what we say and believe. We say what we mean and mean what we say.

- Commitment – We work hard to enable people we support to achieve their goals. When the going gets tough we stick in there. But we are also committed to balanced lives. As we seek full lives for the people we support, so we seek to ensure staff do not work excessive hours and have time for themselves and others outside of work.

- Enabling – We support each other to develop our skills and abilities and to use them effectively for the benefit of those we support. Therefore we don't jump in to do everything ourselves, but look to developing and using the skills of others.

- Confidentiality – We share specific, private information on a 'need to know' basis and within supervision systems. We do not gossip about others and we do not create negative reputations for people we support.

- Challenge – We rigorously debate our differences of opinion and see such debates as healthy and positive. Once a decision is made, we work wholeheartedly towards the agreed decision.

- Listening – We listen to each other and don't jump in with our own views before considering others. This reflects our respect for each other.

- Recognition and encouragement – Appreciation and encouragement are great motivators. We seek to identify opportunities to praise and encourage each other and we celebrate success.

- Rigour – We act and make decisions on what makes a real difference to the quality of life of those we support. When necessary we take hard and painful decisions about making sure Options works effectively.

- Teamwork – We recognise each other's different skills, experiences and abilities and seek to use each to work as a team and to support each other in good and in bad times.

- Learning – We are creative and try different ways of doing things. We make mistakes, but after they occur we learn from them to ensure they do not happen again.

- Vision – We have a clear sense of purpose and direction.

- Risk taking – We are willing and keen to take thought through risks and make sure we learn through every experience, the good and the bad.

Our beliefs

We believe that all people should have the opportunity to live a fulfilled and meaningful life which includes:

- The power, authority and resources to control our own lives.

- A sense of belonging and acceptance for who we are.

- Being treated with dignity and respect.

- Participating as valued members of our own communities.

- Having new life opportunities and enriching life experiences.

- Meaningful and loving personal relationships.

- The opportunity to express our own cultural and spiritual beliefs.

- Access to good health care.

- Taking responsibility for what we can or ought to do for ourselves.

- Caring about and helping those around us.

Having a written vision, mission and values does not of course mean that they are owned or acted upon by the organisation.

Living the values throughout the organisation

Success means more than just good paper with well-crafted, person-centred and shared statements. It means everyone in the organisation working in ways that reflect the vision and values. While most organisations will profess to have values, it is the sense that you get of the depth and breadth of them throughout an organisation that is the true measure of how real they are. Another benefit of this is that those who evidently don't share the values are easily spotted!

How well the values are evident throughout the organisation is dependent on five issues:

1. How they were developed in the first place and the level of involvement of staff and stakeholders in this.

2. How they are communicated and used throughout the organisation.

3. Whether staff are recruited to these values, and whether their training reflects them.

4. How the leaders of the organisation are seen to live the values.

5. The consequences of not working in ways that are consistent with the values.

The next time you are with a group of colleagues, or running a training session, see how many people can quote the mission of the organisation. Usually it is not many! That is not as important as their answer to the question, 'What have you done today that reflects the values of the organisation?' One health and social care leadership team has this as the first question at each quarterly meeting, and asks everyone to share one thing that they have done over the last month that reflects living the values of the organisation.

When you think about the values held in your organisation, how are they put into practice on a day-by-day basis? Does everyone recruited to the organisation have these values? Does the recruitment and selection process focus on these? Does the induction programme develop people's understanding of these values into deeper perspectives that will inform and direct the work each staff member does every day, even every hour? Does ongoing training, mentoring and support to staff develop the outworking of these values? Do one-to-one or supervision sessions enable people to work through issues in implementing values, and clarify what staff are responsible for in living and working to these values? Does the way that the organisation spends its money reflect the values of the organisation? Does decision making at every level of the organisation – from team meetings to the board – keep coming back to the values that are held by the organisation?[39] 'The acid test of values is the day-to-day actions and decisions of the leaders in an organisation. Leaders will reinforce or undermine the organisation's stated values by what they do everyday in work.'[40]

Mark Friedman suggests an alternative approach.[41] Rather than deliberating over vision, mission and values, he recommends you go straight to action. His '7 Performance Talk to Action Steps' skips past the headings of mission, vision, values and purpose, straight into strategy, and asks seven questions instead.[42] These are:

Step 1: Who are our customers?

Step 2: How can we measure if our customers are better off?

Step 3: How can we measure if we're delivering services well?

Step 4: How are we doing on the most important measures (baselines and causes)?

Step 5: Who are the partners that have a role to play in doing better?

Step 6: What works to do better, including no-cost and low-cost ideas?

Step 7: What do we propose to do?

The full seven questions take us into the realm of quality management and measurement (see Chapter 11). Friedman suggests that many organisations seem to think that the mission statement must be perfected before they do anything else. As most organisations have an established purpose, he proposes going straight to thinking about the difference an organisation is trying to make for its customers.

We think you need clear, shared values and purpose, and a strong focus on action and making a difference. How is your organisation doing with this?

What does success look like? How are you doing?

The following table is a way to rate how you are doing with your vision, mission and business strategy. You can use this table to rate your own performance using a scale of 1–5, where 1 is very poor, 2 is poor, 3 is fair, 4 is good and 5 is excellent, to give a first assessment of your progress as an organisation.

How are you doing with developing and communicating and acting on your vision, mission and values? How are you delivering this through your strategy?

Measure	Rating (1–5)
Our mission, vision and values were developed with people we support, families and staff.	
They reflect a person-centred ethos and personalisation.	
They are expressed in everyday language.	
We use them in our training and our meetings, and everyone knows them.	
Our policies and procedures support our mission, vision and values.	
We have a strategy for delivering person-centred support and personalisation in the organisation (for example, developing individual service funds).	
Our strategy has resources to implement it.	
We know how we are doing in delivering our strategy to deliver person-centred support and personalisation – what is working, what is not working and what we are doing next.	
We aggregate information from people we support, together with their families and other stakeholders (for example, through person-centred reviews). This information sets the direction of the organisation and provides important information for our overall business and strategic planning.	

Developing vision, mission and values using person-centred practices

> The process of visioning is starting with a blank sheet of paper. It is about visualising a future desired state, a picture of where and what we would like the organisation to be in the future, without being constrained by such factors as funding or resources, and then working backward to develop an action plan to get us there. It is about imagination and discovery versus analysis and forecast. (Jim Collins[43])

Developing and embedding vision, mission and values for the organisation is best done with as many people as possible across the breadth of the organisational roles, and ideally with other stakeholders as well. We can break this down into stages of the overall process called 'business strategy development' as follows.

The first stage is developing vision, mission and values statements. The second stage of business strategy development is strategic planning, which takes into account what we know today plus lessons learnt from the past, and develops a plan to place the organisation in a better competitive or business continuity position for the future. It deals with scenarios, broad direction and the positioning of the organisation as a provider of choice, either in terms of volume or specific niches, rather than specific shorter term activities. It is the business planning process, the third stage that deals with those shorter term activities. Here you would expect to find the specific objectives, targets and measures, and the action plans to achieve them. The final stage is implementing the business strategy through the local organising of action plans and team activities that deliver the results.

At the end of this chapter we summarise these stages, and the conventional business tools and person-centred practices that you can use for each.

Here are how some of the person-centred thinking tools and practices can be used to inform vision, mission and values.

Person-centred practices	How each practice can inform vision, mission and values
'Important to/for'	Knowing what is important to an organisation is another way to describe the organisation's *values* and *purpose*.
The Doughnut	Can be helpful in defining the *mission* or *purpose* statement – what is core to your mission and what is external to what you do?
History	Looking back at this history and telling stories about it can be used to describe the *values* in an organisation. Knowing where you have come from is also important in thinking about the future *vision* of an organisation.
Purpose or success from different perspectives	Identify what different people and stakeholders would see as the purpose of the organisation, or what success means to them. This can inform *vision* and *mission*.

There are different ways that organisations can use these person-centred practices. You can start with what matters to people, using 'Important to and for' as IAS did; or you can look back at your organisation's history and share stories about this before then looking forward, as United Response did. Here are these examples in more detail.

Using 'Important to and for' to develop a statement of purpose for the organisation

IAS provides support to people in Greater Manchester. Owen, the then Chief Executive, gathered a group together to think about the mission and purpose of the organisation. The group included direct support staff, managers and admin team members, and they became the design team for this 'statement of purpose' work. The group based this work on the person-centred thinking tool 'Important to and for'. They decided to start by exploring what is 'important to' and then address what is 'important for' during the strategic planning stage. The group came up with a list of questions to help people in various roles think about what was important to them in the organisation. They organised training for all the first-line managers to help them work with their teams, think about the questions, and record their answers.

Each team manager was asked to schedule time in a team meeting to think about the questions. Two development workers were available to coach and support the managers. The development workers also spent time with people who used the service (through self-advocacy groups) and parent forums.

Two months later a huge gathering was held, where two representatives from each team, the self-advocacy groups parents and commissioners were all invited. The room was decorated with balloons, each with powerful statements about inclusion and social justice, and people sat at round tables with a facilitator. Around the room were all the posters from the teams and advocacy groups with their understanding about what was important to IAS, based on the four headings. The day was an opportunity to look at all the posters, and the facilitators worked with the table groups to identify the key issues and phrases that resonated with everyone about what was important to IAS. At the end of the day the design team took these, and drafted them into the organisation's statement of purpose – what is important to IAS? Figure 3.1 shows the final result.

Using 'history' to inform the future vision

The directors' team at United Response wanted to start developing their vision and strategy around personalisation and self-directed support.

They started by developing a graphic history map. This depicted the development of the organisation as a journey. They told stories and shared examples of where the organisation had come from, the ideals of Su, the co-founder, and how they had grown and developed. They used this to think about the values and ideas that were embedded in the organisation, and what these could look like as they responded to the personalisation agenda. From the history, they then looked at the present, and then moved to their vision for the future, and what personalisation could mean for people and the organisation – as a natural progression and the logical next step in their person-centred approach.

Strategic and business planning

Once you have your vision, mission and values, the second phase starts to describe how these will be implemented over the medium to long term – the strategic plan. Once again the initial focus should be on people you support as the starting point. Who are you supporting and what do they want? Then you dig deeper into how you deliver your products and services to them. What are your product and service (support) options, and how will you go about continually improving them to maintain that matching with the people you support? Next, how do you display your unique offerings, perhaps through quality, efficiency and effectiveness?

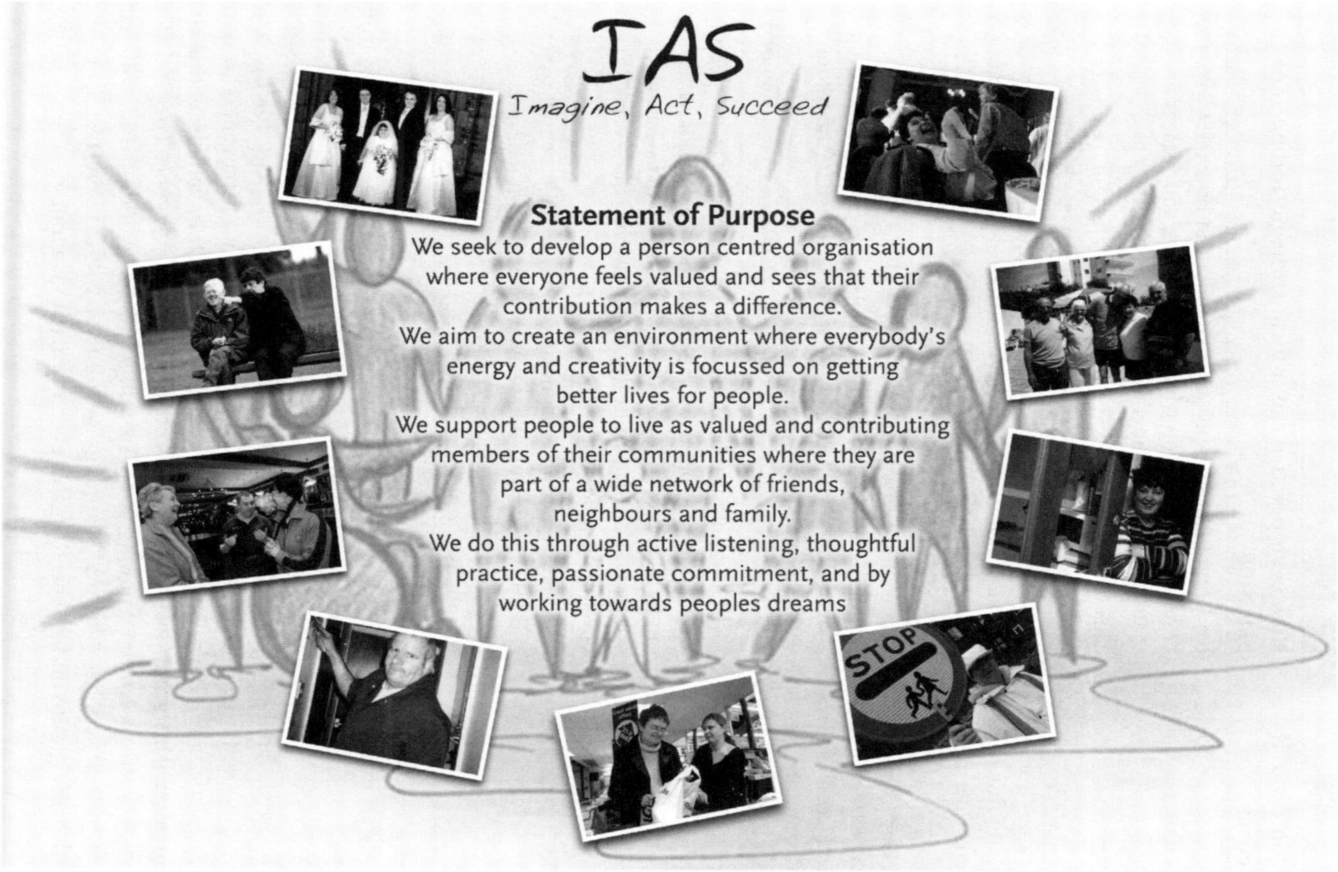

IAS
Imagine, Act, Succeed

Statement of Purpose

We seek to develop a person centred organisation where everyone feels valued and sees that their contribution makes a difference.

We aim to create an environment where everybody's energy and creativity is focussed on getting better lives for people.

We support people to live as valued and contributing members of their communities where they are part of a wide network of friends, neighbours and family.

We do this through active listening, thoughtfull practice, passionate commitment, and by working towards peoples dreams

Figure 3.1 IAS statement of purpose

What differentiates you from any other provider? How do you assess your critical success factors?

Here is how some of the person-centred thinking tools and practices can help.

Person-centred practices	How each practice can inform strategic and business planning
'Important to/for' individuals	Knowing what is important to people and how they want to be supported tells you what people value, and what is needed to deliver the best support. This is vital information for matching what you have with what you need, for your *business planning*.
'Working/not working from different perspectives'	This can help to clarify what people expect from the service – what is not working tells you where expectations are not being met. This is important for knowing what you need to address in your *business planning*.
Working Together for Change (identifying what success looks like from different perspectives)	This builds on 'Working and not working', and provides vital information about what people want to see in the future – right down to specifying what this 'success' in the future would look like, for your *strategy*.
The Doughnut	The Doughnut can help to clarify what benefits to the people we support are core deliverables for the organisation, what might be areas of judgement and creativity, and what might not be part of the role of the organisation. This is useful in developing *strategy*.
4 Plus 1 questions	This tool is useful in diagnosing some of the potential issues and thinking about 'What have we tried? Learned? Are pleased about? Are concerned about?' It provides another way to appraise progress and inform *strategy*.

Here is an example of how an organisation used 'Working and not working from different perspectives' to decide on its three-year business strategy.

A provider in Northern Ireland, Positive Futures, wanted to involve the people it supported, families, staff and managers in deciding what its strategy for the next three years should be. The organisation had a group of staff and managers who were responsible for the development of person-centred thinking and planning within the organisation. This group facilitated the process of involving everyone. They decided to use the person-centred thinking tool 'Working and not working from different perspectives'. The person-centred planning co-ordinator worked with managers, the self-advocacy groups and parents to enable everyone to think about what was working and not working in their lives.

Each team worked with the people they supported to think about what was working and not working for the people, and for the team. The individuals and team members then chose the top two 'working', and the top two 'not working' items to take forward to the planning day. On the day, everyone brought posters with this detail (from either an individual's perspective, a team's perspective or a family's perspective).

Everyone was then asked to look at all the posters and pull out the top themes. They voted on and prioritised the top seven things that were working for people, and the top seven areas that were not working and needed to change. These were then used to develop strategic actions to build on what was working, and change what was not working.

Jim Collins said that you need the right people on the bus to really achieve your vision and mission.[44] Even with those right people, however, there needs to be ways to ensure that everyone understands the mission, how to deliver it, and how success will be measured. Positive Futures developed a one-page strategy summary (Figure 3.2) to share with everyone, explaining how the person-centred thinking tools directly helped to deliver the organisation's mission, and how this would be measured.

Communicating your strategy – one-page strategy summary

After using 'Working and not working from different perspectives' to develop its vision and overall strategy, Positive Futures wanted a powerful and simple way to communicate it throughout the organisation and they found it in the one-page strategy summary. A representative group of the organisation met to think about what success meant from the perspective of individuals and families, staff and the organisation as a whole. They used the information that had been developed on the vision and strategy days, and turned them into a few bullet statements, describing what success meant from the perspective of people and families, staff and the organisation. The group then consulted on these to check that they fully reflected what people had voted on at the event to determine their vision. The next step was to think about which of the person-centred thinking practices directly enabled staff to fulfill these success statements. Once they had done that, they used a 'logic model' approach to think about what measurements would help them to know how well they were delivering on their success statements.

Success around staff means that the organisation gets and retains great staff and volunteers. Logically, the group thought that, if staff had regular supervision (one-to-ones) based on person-centred principles (person-centred supervision) and their views were sought and acted on, and meetings helped them connect to their purpose and act on it (through Positive and Productive Meetings), then staff may be more likely to stay. If all members of staff were also seen as individuals, and their managers and other members of the team knew what was important to them, and how to support them (person-centred teams), then again, staff may be more likely to want to stay working at Positive Futures. The group decided they would be able to know how well they were doing on this through the retention rates of staff (and volunteers), and how many team plans were in the organisation and being used.

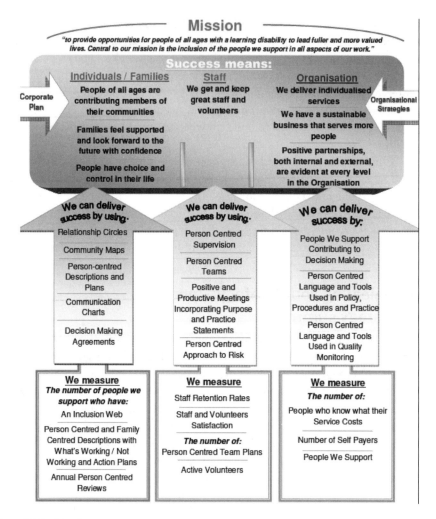

Figure 3.2 Positive Futures one-page strategy

This third stage develops the broad strategies into the objectives, targets, actions and measures for the more immediate future.

The United Response annual operating plan (business plan) incorporates the longer term strategies of the organisation translated into annual objectives, plans and target measures. United Response used a number of the person-centred thinking tools to develop the annual operating plan (business plan) for 2011/12. The person-centred thinking tools used were the following:

- Purpose poster – a visual representation of the purpose of the organisation to clarify and share what the staff were there for – their vision and mission.

- 'Working and not working' – to analyse the current situation from different perspectives and provide a picture of how things are right now in United Response. It clarified what to build on and what to change.

- 4 Plus 1 questions – to look at what they had tried and learnt, and what they were pleased about and concerned about. This helped to focus on what they were learning from their work and projects.

- 'Important to and for' – to sort what was important *to* people from what was important *for* them, so that they could work towards a good balance.

- The Doughnut – to identify specific responsibilities, and clarify roles and expectations.

Developing objectives and targets, and from there to ways of assessing their achievement through measures, milestones and feedback, were also an integral part of this process. We talk more about this in Chapter 11 on measuring and improving quality.

Organisation design and structure can also have an impact on the implementation of those business strategies and plans. In this book we deal with matters of organisation design in Chapter 4 and Chapter 6 discusses aspects of organisation culture, diagnosis and creation in detail, so they will not be discussed here.

We end this chapter with a summary of the typical strategic planning issues or activities, and the potential tools and techniques that can be used to help analyse and understand these – both conventional and person-centred practices. In the appendix of this chapter you will find exercises to help you get started in using person-centred practices around vision, mission, values and strategy.

What do we want to do?	What would be a conventional way of addressing this?	What person-centred practices can I use for this?	Exercise number
Create a vision statement	Visualisation Best case/worst case Visioning	Success from different perspectives Presence to Contribution	1
Create a mission statement	Market and competitor analysis Market research Analysis of customers and products and services	Doughnut Important to/for Presence to Contribution	2
Develop a set of values for the organisation	Cultural diagnosis Stakeholder analysis	Important to/for	3
Strategic planning	Scenario planning Market research Analysis of customers and products and services Organisational architecture SWOT and PEST analysis	Important to/for 4 Plus 1 questions Working/not working Presence to Contribution	4
Business planning	SWOT and PEST analysis Goal setting Organisational design tools	Important to/for 4 Plus 1 questions Working/not working Presence to Contribution	5

Conclusion

A compelling vision and mission, and clear values, set the stage for change and development. Without these, how can you test out decisions and decide what opportunities to take? You cannot know how you are doing unless you know what you were trying to do in the first place.

Person-centred practices provide a different route into exploring these issues, with ways to hear different perspectives about what is working and not working right now, and what people want in the future, as well as reflections on what matters to people, staff and the organisation as a whole. The rest of the book is about being true to these values, and moving forward in line with vision and mission. The next question is, 'Does the way that you are organised and structured create the best context for you to deliver your mission?'

Exercises

Exercise 1: Creating a vision statement

Purpose: To create a vivid description of the future goals and aims of the organisation.

Audience: Usually starting with the senior leadership team, but recommended to have input from as wide a range of perspectives of stakeholders as appropriate and practical.

Typical uses:

- In merger situations, where a joint new vision is required.
- At new business start-ups.
- After significant shifts in business drivers or funding.

How to do it:

Run this exercise at a high level by choosing from the following list of potential tools.

Hopes and dreams – Explore first the hopes and dreams and aspirations of the individuals involved. The discussion can be expanded to test the practicality of these hopes and dreams by exploring where these ideas make sense, who would need to be involved in making them happen, and if the organisation has or can acquire the resources to do it.

Success from Different Perspectives – Create a success poster by asking a range of stakeholders what success looks like to them, and what effects there would be if the organisation was highly successful. It can be done as one group, or by several groups who share and group similar ideas together, and boil them down to a 'critical few' to take the organisation forward.

Presence to Contribution – This tool can help explore the practicality and potential of a vision statement by asking stakeholders to describe what the lower and higher ends of the range of activities or results of the organisation might be.

Exercise 2: Creating a mission statement

Purpose: To describe the journey for the organisation in delivering its services and moving towards the vision, which can be summarised into a succinct statement.

Audience: Usually starting with the senior leadership team, but important to have input from as wide a range of perspectives of stakeholders as appropriate and practical.

Typical uses:

- In merger situations, where a joint new mission is required.

- At new business start-ups.

- After significant shifts in business drivers or funding.

How to do it:

The Doughnut – This tool is useful to formulate a high-level description of how people see the role of the organisation, by exploring what is core to it, where people are happy to see creativity and innovation applied, and what area of business or activity they are not comfortable with being involved in, or are prevented from undertaking for some reason.

'Important to/for' – Use this tool to add detail and understanding to the Doughnut discussion by teasing out those activities and undertakings that people see as the most critical for the organisation to carry out and develop.

Presence to Contribution can be used to describe the range of potential activities of the organisation: 'At the lower end (presence) we are prepared to do *these things*, but at the higher end of our contribution we aim to deliver *this*.'

Again it is sometimes useful to have a set of prompt questions you might want to use to ask people to consider their 'Important to/for' and Doughnut responses concerning, for example:

- The services and support we provide.

- Whom we support/other stakeholders.

- What is unique about us or the people we support?

Exercise 3: Developing a set of values

Purpose: To agree the core values that are essential and enduring principles and beliefs that guide work behaviour, relationships and decision making in the organisation.

Audience: Usually starting with the senior leadership team, but important to have input from as wide a range of perspectives of stakeholders as appropriate and practical.

Typical uses:

- For leadership teams to agree how the organisation will behave at its highest level.

- To engage others in developing the culture of the organisation.

How to do it:

'Important to/for' – Use this to ask people to describe what principles and beliefs that are valued by them either:

- because it makes them feel happy, content or fulfilled, or
- because it makes them feel safe and healthy, or valued by others in the broader context of the organisation.

For this exercise, there are a large number of potential areas for consideration, and the information in Chapter 5 on creating a person-centred culture may help. Some common areas to ask people to think about may include attitudes to the following.

- The focus of activity.
- Change, creativity and innovation.
- Equality and diversity.
- Good practice.
- Community contribution.
- Trust/honesty, and openness.
- Risk enablement.

Exercise 4: Strategic planning

Purpose: To develop the descriptions of the broad activities of the organisation which answer the 'how' we will do it.

Audience: Normally the leadership and senior management teams, but, as in the learning and reflection process used in the Working Together for Change process, can incorporate input from other staff and stakeholders.

Typical uses:

- At agreed intervals to review the alignment of the organisation with its vision, mission and values.
- When changes occur in the operating context of the organisation – for example, from political or environmental drivers.

How to do it:

Presence to Contribution – Use this tool to ask people to describe what broad areas of activity will be important in moving the organisation towards its aims as expressed in the vision and mission, and to describe what the range of these activities might be. At this level, encourage people to use only broad terms and descriptions, rather than the detail of specific tasks. Also encourage them to use qualitative language to describe what the results of the strategies might be.

4 Plus 1 questions and 'Working/not working' – use either or both of these tools to ask people to review current performance and where strategies may need to be introduced or varied to improve performance and move the organisation more positively towards its aims. Working Together for Change is a good way to do this.

Exercise 5: Business planning

Purpose: The process that translates the longer term vision, mission, values and strategies into shorter term achievable results.

Audience: Normally the leadership and senior management teams, but, as in the learning and reflection process used in Working Together for Change, can incorporate input from other staff and stakeholders.

Typical uses:

- As part of an agreed business planning cycle (often annually or as part of a three-year or five-year process); with this being the first year, aim for more detailed description).

- When changes occur in the operating context of the organisation – for example, from political or environmental drivers that demand an immediate response in terms of allocation of resources.

How to do it:

See the tools as used in the United Response example earlier of the annual operating plan (pp.80–81).

Chapter 4

Organisation Design

Every organisation is perfectly designed for the results it gets.

David Hanna[45]

Introduction

The nature of life at work for most people is changing fast and in multiple directions unparalleled since the onset of the Industrial Revolution. Technological advances, economic pressures, regulatory and government interventions affect us all. Most importantly, the legitimate expectations of people we support are also changing as people are more discerning and better informed of the choices available to them than ever before. The same is of course true in other types of business, where the consumer is better informed, has higher expectations and is more selective.

In this context, the way that we have worked and organised in the past will simply not be able to cope in the future. Organisations of all types, shapes and sizes have to look at themselves and ask how they will be able to deliver what is expected of them, cope with the discontinuous but frequent change, and keep staff and other supporters involved and motivated. Part of the answer to these challenging questions lies in a much misunderstood process known as 'organisation design'.

In this chapter, we consider what organisation design means in the context of person-centred organisations and what you might want to change or develop.

We start with a generic description of organisation design and some of its typical characteristics; think about what this means in terms of person-centred organisations; look at how to assess your current organisation and decide how to move forward to achieve the design you want. Throughout we illustrate how person-centred practices can be used, and end with exercises that can help you get started.

What is organisation design, and what does it mean in person-centred organisations?

In the last chapter we focused on vision, mission and values, and the overall process of business strategy development. With these in place, you need to ensure that your organisation is designed to achieve them.

Here are a couple of definitions of organisation design:

- The continual design and alignment of organisational structures, systems, processes and culture to achieve business objectives through people.[46]

- The goal of organisation design is to fashion a set of formal structures and processes that, together with an appropriate informal operating environment, will give people the skills, direction and motivation to do the work necessary to achieve the strategic objective.[47]

In a person-centred organisation, organisation design is the process of focusing the resources of an organisation on achieving its mission. As we saw in the last chapter, this could be expressed in different ways – for example, supporting people to have choice and control in their lives, or to live as citizens in their community; or working with people to achieve their aspirations and what is important to them on a day-to-day basis, and to support them in the way they want to be supported.

When discussing organisation design in this chapter, we are referring to the process of deciding what the following aspects of an organisation need to look and feel like for the mission to be achieved.

- The operating model – by this we mean what defines how an organisation will relate to people it supports, achieve its goals and operationalise its objectives. For example, this might be, 'Do we operate on a supported living model, or some method of supporting people that may not be in their homes?'

- Business processes – this refers to those streams of activity, which may have a base in a corporate function, but which span and flow through the organisation, affecting and engaging multiple departments and people, such as financial, logistics, communications, human resources and procurement processes.

- Organisation structure – this is expressed by organisation charts and departmental or functional descriptions.

- Jobs and roles – the collection of tasks that make up the complete content of a job description, and the part that people play in an organisation as described in their role description – a role not necessarily being a whole job, nor the singular thing that you do for an organisation.

- Tasks – these are individual items of output that are either standalone or collected together to form a whole or part job.

- Span of control – this is the range of people or accountabilities and responsibilities that a person is expected to manage or control.

Let's now look at what this process of design looks like, starting with an example of what it looks like in practice in an organisation whose mission is for people to have control in their lives – United Response.

Changes to the organisation design in United Response to implement person-centred practices

United Response was committed to implementing person-centred practices across the organisation to ensure that people had control in their lives. One of the challenges in this was to ensure that a new way of working and a common language for listening to people and problem solving was consistently used by everyone. To do this, it was important that the organisation design and structure contained mechanisms and processes to drive this change.

While no significant changes were needed to the basic operational management structure, the organisation needed to create new roles and processes to enable person-centred practices to be used throughout the organisation.

This meant changes at *jobs and roles*, and *tasks* levels. It led to the establishment of leadership teams, working alongside the operational management teams in divisions, but specifically charged with the accountability for taking forward the person-centred practices. It also meant expanding the role of managers to be able to coach staff in person-centred practices, and ensuring that they had the skills and support to do this with their staff. This was all supported by a group of divisional trainers who ensured that the (now mandatory) training in person-centred thinking and active support was carried out to the required standards and pace.

More generally, role profiles and competencies for front-line operational staff and their managers were reviewed and updated to reflect person-centred practices. This was done with the engagement of a wide range of staff, and involved people who used the service. The result was a much simplified and novel approach to role profiles, making them far more flexible to what people being supported wanted. Competencies were re-focused on the skills, knowledge and experience required to deliver person-centred practices within the new focused role profiles.

As these organisation design changes at the jobs and roles level were implemented, it was clear that some *business processes* and *organisational structure* changes were required. This resulted in the following changes.

- The way that divisions are managed and led, and the role of people and families in this.

- The way the Board of Trustees governs the organisation and how people supported are involved.

- How business processes such as recruitment are carried out and how people supported are involved in choosing their own staff.

- How learning and development are achieved.

- How the business planning process is carried out, now using Working Together for Change so that this is directed by people supported.

- What fundraising is targeted upon and used for.

- The way that quality is measured and the role of people with disabilities in this.
- The technology needed to carry out the business effectively.

You will hear how this is being achieved in the other chapters of this book.

Reviewing the design of your organisation

We began the chapter with the quote from David Hanna that 'Every organisation is perfectly designed for the results it gets',[48] and so it will be if no attention is paid to organisation design at the right time and in the right circumstances.

Typically, organisation design or re-design is required in the following situations:

1. When those whom we support expect more or something different from us.

2. When organisations merge or de-merge or are taken over.

3. When business processes cease to work effectively.

4. When jobs and roles of individuals change.

5. When new business is acquired or new activities are started.

6. When government or other regulatory requirements demand change.

If we now link this list to the experiences of United Response, earlier we shared how United Response had to change its organisation design to implement person-centred practices to increase the control that people supported had in their lives. This reflects list items 4 and 6 because United Response needed to change jobs and roles to deliver person-centred practice throughout the organisation, and to respond to the personalisation agenda of ensuring that people had choice and control in their lives.

In the last few years, United Response has focused on further organisation design changes to deliver support to people with a personal budget. This means that people supported have control over their budget, and how this is spent. To achieve this, United Response started by using Progress for Providers to assess where it was in all aspects of its service delivery and systems, and what it needed to change (see Appendix 1). The organisation appointed a personalisation lead who played a key role in contributing to the development of Progress for Providers as well as using it internally in United Response and training and supporting other organisations to use it too. The results from Progress for Providers showed where further changes were needed, and this is already influencing the operating model of the organisation in terms of:

- how people supported make decisions about how to spend their budgets
- how staff are deployed to deliver personal budgets
- how services are costed.

A further and most important driver for the organisation design changes in United Response is what people supported want to see changed (list item 1). Every year the organisation uses the Working Together for Change process (internally known as 'learning and reflection days') to drive its annual business planning cycle. Therefore, the design and processes used within United Response have been directly changed through listening to people who use the service through the use of the Working Together for Change process.

One of the problems with any kind of review of organisational design and structure is deciding where to start. An initial assessment of what a person-centred organisation might look like can therefore be useful. We have summarised the aspects of a person-centred organisation that you may want to consider in the checklist that follows, which may help you think about any priority areas that need to be addressed.

How are you doing?

It is the task of the leaders of an organisation to create an environment and a business strategy that enables teams to focus on what is important to the individual being supported without being deflected from this core purpose by excessive concern over compliance with rules and regulations.

The following checklist may help to clarify how this could be achieved. You can use it to rate your own performance using a scale of 1–5, where 1 is very poor, 2 is poor, 3 is fair, 4 is good and 5 is excellent, to give a rough first assessment of the progress of your organisation.

Business process	Key criteria	Rating
Vision, mission and strategy	Are the vision, mission and strategy of the organisation clearly aligned with what matters to the people being supported?	
HR processes	Do HR policies and processes reflect a person-centred and flexible approach to leading and managing staff?	
Financial processes	Do financial processes enable flexibility in the acquisition and allocation of resources?	
Technology	How accessible are IT systems and other modern technology to teams and the people being supported?	
Performance measures and improvement	Are the key performance indicators and critical success factors of the organisation person-centred and do they reinforce successful outcomes for the people being supported?	
Compliance	How far do the organisation's responses to regulatory frameworks and requirement reflect the outcomes for people being supported rather than a strict standard-based approach?	

Reward and recognition	Do reward and recognition processes reinforce the focus on what is important to people being supported and what people want for the future, and do they encourage innovation?
Risk enablement	Is there an enabling, person-centred and pragmatic approach to risk that encourages creativity and innovation in determining how to enable people being supported to be part of community life?
Performance management	How far do the allocation of work and the performance management processes for staff focus on what is important to people being supported rather than the completion of tasks?
Decision making	How far is decision-making authority spread across the organisation, and how flexible is the process? Is there clarity about who makes what decision? Is decision making as close to the person supported as possible?
Structure	Does the structure of the organisation support agility in decision making and activities, or are these hampered by bureaucracy?
Learning and development	Can staff get resources to acquire new or different skills appropriate to the needs of the people being supported?
Leadership and management style	How far does the leadership and management style of the organisation align with the vision and mission?
Communications	How many communications channels are there, and do they offer multiple opportunities to learn and reinforce the vision, mission and values of the organisation?
Equality and diversity	Does the organisation take advantage of diversity to create new opportunities for business, and for learning?

Where are you now? What do you want to do next?

The checklist can be useful here as a series of prompt questions to begin to assess a current organisation. Person-centred thinking tools and practices can help generate a fuller picture of the priority areas of organisation design that you may wish to address. Here is a summary of how the person-centred thinking tools can help.

Person-centred practices	How each practice can inform your understanding of your organisation now or your design structure for the future
'Working/not working from different perspectives'	The information from 'What is working and not working' for people supported can be themed and then linked to the areas of your self-assessment. For example, if what is not working for people is that they are lonely and do not have many friends, what does that tell you about what parts of your organisation you would need to design differently to change that?
Working Together for Change	This process involves 'Working and not working', and includes what is important for people in the future. Working Together for Change includes 'What does success look like from different perspectives?', which can inform your quality strategy and how you both design and evaluate whether your organisation design is supporting where people want to be in the future.
4 Plus 1 questions	This tool is useful in diagnosing some of the potential issues and thinking about 'What have we tried? Learned? Are pleased about? Are concerned about?' It provides another way to evaluate your organisation design.
The Doughnut	This is helpful in deciding what any type of role might look like at individual, team, departmental levels, etc.
Decision-making agreements	To clarify the boundaries of authority, or the processes to be used in reaching decisions and agreements.
Communication charts	To clarify how interfaces between people might work, and what communication methods are appropriate or required.
Matching	Getting the best fit between people and individual or team/ departmental roles and functions.

You can use these person-centred practices with people you already support, and staff, or even with potential 'customers'. A provider in the South East, supporting people who have mental health issues or learning disabilities worked with families who might buy their services in the future. The provider used the Working Together for Change process to learn what these families would want from future services, and the findings informed its organisation design.

Exercise 1 at the end of this chapter explains in more detail how to use these person-centred practices in relation to assessing your organisation design. Now you have a clear sense of where you are – by using the self-assessment and person-centred practices – you can then decide which organisation design model will help you move forward.

Choosing an organisation design model or approach

There are numerous models and tools available for organisation design and, in combination with the tools and approaches we recommend here, they can be very effective in measuring the current design, or indeed in planning a future design. A popular model, which may be suitable for your needs, is the Galbraith STAR Model.[49]

Other popular models include those developed by Nadler and Tushman,[50] and McKinsey.[51] Exercise 2 at the end of this chapter will help you decide on a design model, using person-centred practices. The models differ in their approach and headings, but there are some activities or processes that are often present in any approach to organisation design.

The advantages of using this type of model are:

- their simplicity in giving a succinct picture of an organisation on one page

- flexibility in use across a wide range of circumstances and types of business

- the focus on an organisation acting together as an integrated whole, rather than in a series of disconnected silos.

If you don't want to use an established model like those just mentioned to reflect on organisation design, then there are established components of organisation design that you can consider, which are now discussed. Our process flow diagram (Figure 4.1) also contains most of the components you might want to consider in your organisation design.

Many of these components are discussed in more depth in other chapters of this book but you may want to use the prompt questions here, in conjunction with your use of models such as those mentioned earlier and the person-centred tools, in considering and planning your organisation design.

- Vision – what do you want to be? (see Chapter 3)

- Mission – why are you here and what is your purpose? (see Chapter 3)

- Values – what is important to you and what do you stand for? (see Chapter 3)

- Culture – what sort of place do you want this to be? (see Chapter 6)

- Operating model/principles – what is the basis on which you are going to work with your customers or users of your services? (this chapter)

- Design criteria – what drives the size and scope of parts of the organisation? (this chapter)

- Modus operandi/ways of working – how will the key business processes operate? How is information reported and monitored? (this chapter)

- Organisation structure – what does the organisation chart look like? (this chapter)

- Responsibility charting – what are the key accountabilities and responsibilities for each part of the organisation and each person? (this chapter)

- Jobs – what do people do? (see Chapter 8)

- Interfaces – how does work and information get transferred from one part of the organisation to another, and eventually to the customer? (this chapter)

Next it is worth considering the scale of your design challenge – do you want to make changes at a macro or micro level?

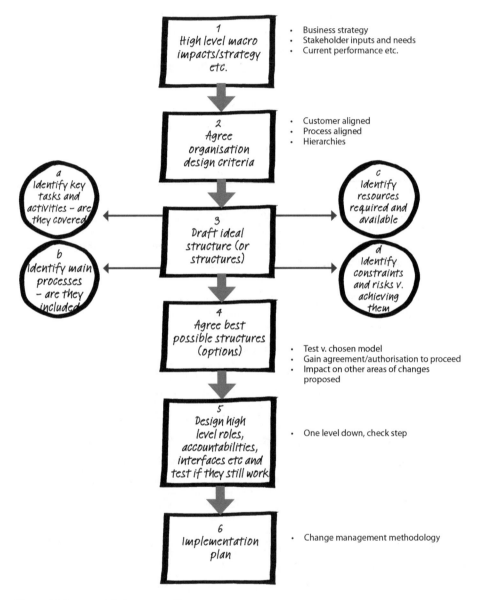

Figure 4.1 Structural design process flow

Deciding on the levels of design that you want to change

There are two levels of changes to your organisation's structure that you can consider. The first we might call the *macro level*, dealing with the bigger strategic issues facing the organisation, and maintaining its existence in a challenging world. Here, an awareness of the external world is important. Listening to the feedback and desires of people you support is vital – for example, through using the Working Together for Change person-centred tools.

The example below shows how starting with a detailed understanding of what is working and not working in a particular area can lead to changes that have wider effects on how the organisation is designed.

Macro changes in an extra care service

A service was commissioned to provide extra care support to six people with physical impairments who had moved out of residential care. Three months after the service was in place, the providers and commissioners agreed to review this using Working Together for Change. Each individual was supported to share their views through a person-centred review. This revealed detailed information of what was working and not working, and what each individual wanted for the future. The people supported, families, staff, provider managers and commissioner spent a day together reviewing the information using the Working Together for Change process. This showed that there were flaws in the organisation design – in *job roles* and *workflow*. It was discovered that staff attended to people who used their call buttons, and that several people felt uncomfortable using them as much as they should, because they thought they would be taking staff time away from people who needed it more.

The commissioners then worked with the provider to re-design the structure of how staff support was delivered by separating out core hours and individual hours. Each individual then had a number of individual hours that they were entitled to, were guaranteed and could choose how to use. Not only was this a fundamental structural change for the organisation, but the commissioners also revised how they commissioned similar services from other providers.

The second level we might call the *micro level*, dealing with the day-to-day issues that people face in completing their daily jobs. Here, a detailed knowledge and analysis of the tasks to be performed is essential in order to enable people who support to achieve their outcomes and be supported themselves in what is important to and for them. Listening to feedback from staff and involving them in the design process is important. At all levels, political agendas, cost pressures and egos are just some of the skew factors that may get in the way.

The following example shows how a similar detailed analysis of what is working and not working can lead to a more specific set of actions focused on an individual and how their service and support is designed.

Micro changes in an older people's residential care home

Sue, the manager in a residential care home, started to use person-centred thinking to explore what structural, process and cultural changes were needed at a team level. She started by working with Sam to use person-centred thinking tools to look at what it would take to implement the principles of individual service funds within the home.[52] She worked out the cost of Sam's service and what this meant in hours. She then looked at which of these hours were 'background hours' to provide the day-to-day support that Sam needed, and which hours he could have individual control over. Sue explained to Sam that he had four individual hours a month and she would help him develop a plan to help him decide about how he wanted to spend those hours. She developed a one-page profile with Sam to ensure that he could use his hours in ways that were important to him. Then Sue and Sam used the person-centred thinking tool 'Working and not working' to think about what Sam wanted to be different in his life, and how using his individual hours could help with this. The main thing that wasn't working for Sam was that his friendships had all been lost after spending three months in hospital and then coming to live in the home four years earlier. He particularly missed his connection with the Crown Green bowling club he had belonged to for a number of years – he had lost all contact with his old mates.

Sam was supported to develop his relationship circle, and he identified the key relationships. He was helped to write to some of his old friends, and as they responded he gained the confidence to think about how he could reconnect with the bowling club, which wasn't far away from the home.

The challenge now was finding the right staff member to support Sam to go to watch the bowling. They needed to match his interests, and how he wanted to use his hours, with staff characteristics and interests. Sue and Sam used the Matching tool to find the right person. They looked at the one-page profiles for staff, which included their hobbies and interests, and found that Greg, a new member of staff, looked the perfect match for Sam because he too was a keen bowler. Sam agreed. Within a month, he and Greg went off to the bowling club together. Sue and Greg used the person-centred thinking tool Presence to Contribution with Sam to help them think about how he could make a contribution. Sam now writes the monthly newsletter for the bowling club. Before retiring, Sam was a keen writer and produced the church newsletter each week, so he feels that he is giving something back.

By using person-centred thinking tools at an individual level, Sue understood what had needed to happen at a micro – or individual – level to change how the service worked for Sam. Working in this way gave her insight into what would be needed within job roles and structures to deliver individual service funds across the organisation, at a macro level.

By now you have thought about:

- what your organisation design is
- whether you want to use an established model like those mentioned earlier, or simply focus on the key headings
- what changes need to be made at a macro and/or micro level.

The next stage is to design your ideal structure.

What would your ideal structure look like?

You should now be in a position to design your ideal or best possible structure.

Here are some questions for you to think about (and go to Exercises 3–6 in the Appendix to help you in practice).

- What are the main tasks and activities that will be carried out within the new structure? (In other words, what will the outputs and/or services be, and how will they be measured?)

- What are the main processes that you have to consider, and that need managing and aligning?

- What resources will you need to carry out your tasks and activities in the new structure (in particular, people, budgets and facilities)?

- What are the main constraints, challenges and risks inherent in going this way? How will these be addressed before moving to the new structure?

Here you need to develop some options and consider what you may be prepared to sacrifice in order to get the best structure you can. This is where the information you collect through looking at what is important to and for the organisation and its stakeholders can aid your decision making.

Figure 4.1 shows this in summary form and a series of steps to be followed.

Any new structure is likely to have consequences and impacts on, for example, business processes, roles, accountabilities, reporting structures, setting objectives, and measuring and maintaining performance. For each situation, a full impact analysis is recommended. You are now in the realm of change management, and we will cover this in Chapter 9.

We end this chapter with a summary of the stages in organisation design, the conventional ways to address these, and the person-centred practices that you could also use. In the Appendix to this chapter you will find exercises to help you get started in using person-centred practices around the organisation design stages.

The table below summarises some of the typical organisation design issues or activities, and the potential tools and techniques that can be used to help analyse and understand these.

What do we want to do? The stage in organisation design	What would be a conventional way of addressing this?	What person-centred tools can I use for this?	Exercise number
Measure the 'as is' situation	SWOT, PEST Diagnostic interviews	Working/not working Working Together for Change 4 Plus 1 questions	1
Choose a design model	Establish design principles Establish design criteria Decide on purpose, vision and design concepts	Important to/for Working/not working from different perspectives 4 Plus 1	2
Design the high-level organisation scope and operating model	Measures of output or performance Boundary management Span of control	The Doughnut Important to/for Success from different perspectives	3
Design organisation Structure	Process or product flows Operating model Business model Span of control Organisation charts	The Doughnut Matching Important to/for	4
Design business processes	Process or product flows Operating model Business model	The Doughnut Matching Important to/for	5
Job design	Task analysis Process analysis Mission critical job design Job descriptions Competencies	The Doughnut Important to/for Decision-making tool Communications chart	6

Conclusion

This chapter poses the question, 'Is your organisation designed to get the results you want, based on your vision, mission and values?' If you don't quite have the perfect fit, person-centred practices could help clarify what you need to make sure everything is orientated to providing the best support for people, in the way people want, with the freedom to make decisions with staff about what matters. Person-centred practices can define the detail of an effective organisation design from the macro level of structure and high-level business processes through to the operational (micro) level of individuals carrying out tasks that truly match the requirements of the people they support. The organisation's structure is the framework for people to work together successfully, the subject of our next chapter.

Exercises

Exercise 1: Measure the 'as is' situation

Title: Is our design working?

Purpose: To establish how well the desired outputs or outcomes of the organisation are being helped or hindered by the current design.

Audience: Leadership teams.

Typical uses:

- In circumstances where an organisation or people are feeling stretched.

- Where business results are starting to fail.

- When new business is taken on or there is diversification.

Tools: 4 Plus 1 questions, 'Working/not working'.

How to do it:

- Use 4 Plus 1 questions to brainstorm the current view of the organisation. The 'What have we tried?' question should be focused on the key aims and objectives that the organisation has tried to achieve. Pay particular attention to understanding the answers to the question, 'What are we concerned about?' Try to answer this question from a range of perspectives of the stakeholders involved, especially the customers and clients. Agree the main headings for any concerns and any immediate action steps that you will take with the information.

- Alternatively, use the 'Working/not working' tool in relation to the current organisation design. Use one of the organisation models mentioned earlier such as Galbraith,[49] Nadler and Tushman,[50] or the process flow diagram on p.94 to give the headings of the design to consider the question under. Group the results into agreed main headings with the detail attached. Prioritise the most important.

- Another option is to use Working Together for Change and to use the information to reflect on what this tells you about the design of the organisation. Group and prioritise the information as above.

Exercise 2: Choosing a design model

Title: What should we base our future design on?

Purpose: To establish the most appropriate operating and business models for the organisation.

Audience: Leadership teams.

Typical uses:

- In merger and acquisition situations.
- Where new business is taken on or there is diversification.
- Where there is a shift in culture and values of the organisation.

Tools: 'Important to/for'.

How to do it:

- Think about what is important to/for the organisation to identify the key values, aims, objectives and targets that it wishes to achieve. 'Important to' aspects are those that the organisation needs to feel are being achieved so that it has a sense of achievement and value in the world. 'Important for' are those financial or compliance aspects of the organisation that must be met in order to ensure ongoing security and stability.

Exercise 3: Design the high-level organisation scope and operating model

Title: What is our new organisation going to achieve?

Purpose: To decide the types of business that the organisation will undertake.

Audience: Leadership teams.

Typical uses:

- In mergers and acquisitions.
- Where new business is taken on or there is diversification.
- Where there is a shift in culture and values of the organisation.

Tools: Success from different perspectives, The Doughnut, 'Important to/for'.

How to do it:

- Think about 'Important to/for' in Exercise 2.
- Use success from different perspectives to define the high level of business results and contribution to other stakeholders (shareholders, clients, people supported, society) that you wish to achieve.
- Use the Doughnut to decide what areas of business activity will be core to achieving those results and contributions; what areas of business activity you might consider to add to those core areas; and those areas that you will definitely not become involved in.

Exercise 4: Design the structure

Title: What does the organisation look like?

Purpose: To design the main departmental/divisional/other main sectional structure of the organisation.

Audience: Leadership teams.

Typical uses:

- In mergers and acquisitions.

- Where new business is taken on or there is diversification.

- In circumstances where an organisation or people are feeling stretched.

- Where business results are starting to fail.

Tools: The Doughnut, Matching, 'Important to/for'.

How to do it:

- This exercise works best in conjunction with one of the organisation design models (see earlier), or the process flow diagram we have included.

- Test your decisions against the person-centred tools. Can you describe clearly for each part of the structure what is its core purpose, where it has freedom to use its creativity and innovation, and what is not in its remit (the Doughnut)? Can you describe for each part of the structure how it meets those items you have identified as important to and for the organisation as in Exercise 2? You can use the Matching tool to help with this part of the exercise.

Exercise 5: Design business processes

Title: How does the organisation work?

Purpose: To decide what the key business processes of the organisation are, and how they will operate.

Audience: Leadership teams.

Typical uses:

- In mergers and acquisitions.

- Where new business is taken on or there is diversification.

- In circumstances where an organisation or people are feeling stretched.

- Where business results are starting to fail.

Tools: The Doughnut, Matching, 'Important to/for'.

How to do it:

- Draw a typical 'customer journey' diagram (see Chapter 12, Change Management) to define the key interfaces with your customers and the expectations they have of those interfaces.

- Decide what business processes need to be in place to make those customer interfaces effective, and the outputs they need to achieve for both the customer and the other stakeholders in the organisation.

- Describe the business process design by using the person-centred tools. For example:

    o   The Doughnut can describe what is the core coverage or scope of each part of the process, where it needs to be flexible to varying demands, and what it will not be designed to do.

    o   Use 'Important to/for' to identify what deliverables the process needs to ensure happen so that the needs of the customer journey are met.

    o   Use the Matching tool to assist in describing the detail of the process so that it will meet the requirements of the items you identified in 'Important to/for'.

Exercise 6: Job design

Title: What are people doing? What do you want them to do?

Purpose: To establish the accountabilities and responsibilities of the people in the organisation.

Audience: Any.

Typical uses: Any situation where a role no longer fits the organisation or works well.

Tools: The Doughnut, 'Important to/for', decision-making agreements, communications charts.

How to do it:

- Through the use of these exercises you can build up a comprehensive picture of the organisation at higher levels of analysis. Exercises 4 and 5 especially will give you a breakdown of the organisation into constituent parts in terms of structure and processes. At this point you need to describe the actual roles that will deliver those results.

- Use some basic parameters of job design in conjunction with the person-centred tools. Again the process flow diagram can help with this analysis.

- Decide upon a set of roles that you consider will meet the needs identified for each part of the structure and describe those roles by testing them against the person-centred thinking tools. For example:

    o   Use the Doughnut to describe the three areas of accountability and responsibility.

    o   Use communication charts to describe the critical areas of the job that require communication and how that happens.

    o   Use the decision-making agreement to clarify what decisions are required in this job and how they will be made.

    o   Use 'Important to/for' to describe the activities and outputs of each role in terms of what is important to and for the customer, the next person in the chain from this role, or the range of people the role interacts/works with.

Chapter 5

Working Together and Engaging Everyone

Coming together is a beginning. Keeping together is progress. Working together is success.

Henry Ford[53]

Introduction

The cornerstone of person-centredness is listening, and acting on what is heard. In a person-centred organisation this happens at an individual level, at a staff team level and at an organisational level, with a range of stakeholders. People who use the service, their families, staff and commissioners all have important contributions to make in the development of person-centred organisations. Change cannot be achieved in isolation and will be weaker in the absence of contributions from other people. There is often some reticence to work in partnership together. It is easy to believe that commissioners are only interested in saving money; that parents will oppose change; that it is too difficult genuinely to involve people supported, and too costly and time intensive fully to involve staff. Person-centred organisations are built on partnership and have a culture of empowerment, where people can work together to create change. In this chapter we look at how the voices of people supported by an organisation, staff and wider stakeholders are heard and acted on through person-centred practices. We also look at what this means for the other actual and potential stakeholders in the organisation, such as families and friends, those who fund the business, the communities in which we work, and others to whom we owe a duty to enact our corporate social responsibility. We will look at the different levels of engagement and what this means for people in whatever relationships they have with the organisation.

What does engaging everyone mean in a person-centred organisation?

There are a range of terms used to refer to ways of working together – for example, engagement, participation, involvement, consultation and co-production. The 'ladder of citizen participation' is one way of describing the different levels of involvement. Developed by Sherry R. Arnstein, this ladder has eight rungs.[54] Figure 5.1 shows that at the bottom of the ladder, the lowest rungs are manipulation, therapy and informing, then consultation, placation, partnership and delegated power, with the top rung being citizen control. Here are what the different terms mean.

Informing – providing people with balanced information to assist them in understanding problems, alternatives, opportunities or solutions.

Consulting – obtaining feedback on ideas, alternatives or decisions.

Involving – working directly with people to ensure that concerns and aspirations are consistently understood and considered – for example, reference groups and service users participating in policy groups.

Collaborating – working in partnership with people on each aspect of the decision, including the development of alternatives and the identification of the preferred solution.

Empowering – placing decision making in the hands of staff, the community or other stakeholders.

Co-production – this straddles collaborating and empowering, and decision making is shared. Effective services need to be designed with and for people and communities – not delivered 'top down' for administrative convenience.[55] Organisations need to work closely with individuals and communities to understand their needs and to maximise talents and resources.

To deliver personalisation and for people to have choice and control in their lives requires going beyond 'consultation' and 'involving people' and focusing on 'co-production' and 'collaboration'. This means that people need comprehensive and clear information about what is possible and what is available to them. We need to know how everyone makes decisions and communicates them, and, where people do not have capacity to make decisions themselves, that we ensure advocacy and that decision making always remains in the best interest of the individual. As well as leading decision making about their own lives, people using services should have opportunities to influence how the organisation develops.

The mantra for involvement in health and social care is 'Nothing about me, without me'. This is a challenge for services, for the following reasons:

- Staff are often unclear about how people with profound learning disabilities, or who have dementia, communicate or can be involved in making decisions.

- Managers could rely on questionnaires, surveys or focus groups to get feedback from people in their services, but these only engage a small number of people with disabilities, and only those who can talk or read, excluding the views of people with communication difficulties.

- Not all services use person-centred thinking, planning or reviews to ensure that people have opportunities to direct their lives and make changes.

- Attempts to involve people in recruiting their own staff in an organisation is often restricted to training a few people who use services across the organisation and including them on interview panels.

- Staff are not involved in decision making at an organisational level.

- Other stakeholders are not seen as partners.

- Organisations do not always see the importance of a relationship with and contribution to the communities they work in.

If these are some of the challenges, what should we be working towards?

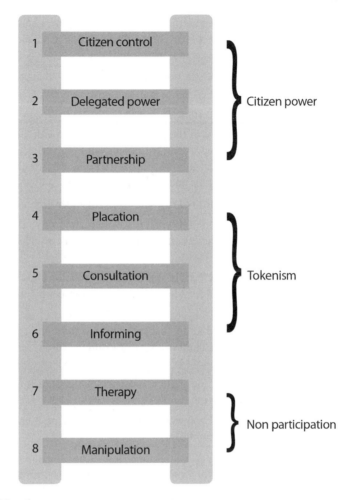

Figure 5.1 The ladder of citizen participation

How are you doing?

The following table is a way to rate what you are doing at the moment in working together and engaging everyone. You can use it to rate your own performance using a scale of 1–5, where 1 is very poor, 2 is poor, 3 is fair, 4 is good and 5 is excellent, to give a rough first assessment of your progress as an organisation.

Measure	Rating (1–5)
We have a statement or charter about how we work together with people to make decisions – at an individual and organisational level.	
Staff know in detail how the person they support communicates and make decisions. We can show how people are being supported to make more decisions in their life, about things that matter to them.	
Staff know exactly how each person wants to be supported – their routines and preferences.	
People choose their own staff to support them.	
People we support are in control of their own budget. We provide detailed costs for each individual we support and for people who may want to buy our service or products. We are clear with people that they can use their money flexibly, and not just to buy hours of support.	
People can buy as much or as little of our service as they want.	
Everyone has an opportunity to tell us what is working and not working about their support and what they want in the future. We act on what people tell us.	
We support people to meet new people and make new relationships and friendships in their community (outside staff and any other people who live with the person).	
We have a specific, measurable plan to enable the person to be fully part of their community, and to make a contribution (for example, through using Presence to Contribution).	
This plan is regularly reviewed and there is evidence that people are becoming part of their community.	
Everyone has an opportunity to contribute their views to shape the way the organisation develops (e.g. business plan).	
As an organisation we have a clear commitment and focus on community and understand the importance of working alongside the entire community to effectively support people to become citizens.	

Working together and engaging with people who use your service

Now that you know how you are doing, we will look at ways that you can further develop how you listen to everyone who uses and works with the organisation, as well as improving relationships with other stakeholders and the community. We think it is important that organisations make a public commitment to how they are going to work together and engage people. Here are a couple of examples, first of all a promise from North Yorkshire County Council.[56]

Our engagement promise

- We will co-ordinate engagement across the Council so that you are not asked the same questions again and again.
- We will not share personal information without asking you, unless required by law.
- We will make sure we tell you about opportunities to have your say.
- We will make sure we give you the opportunity to get involved in making decisions when that is appropriate.
- We will be clear about what can be changed, and if it can't, why not.
- We will feed back to you what has been said and what we are going to do as a result.
- We will use plain English and keep our information jargon free.
- We will offer our information in different formats e.g. on CD or tape where that is appropriate.
- We will make sure we include people who want to be involved, and that everyone has a real opportunity to tell us what they think.

Here is another example from a support provider, Certitude.

Certitude believes that true and proper involvement begins with people being involved in decisions on the most fundamental elements of their support: who, what, how, where and when.

Certitude also believes in the importance of listening, valuing and acting upon what people are telling us through these decisions. The quality of our organisation depends on our ability to listen and shape our services as a result of what people tell us.

How we ensure that everybody we support is involved in decisions about their own life therefore forms the basis of our involvement strategy. Without this, meaningful involvement at any other level is not possible.

Our strategy also seeks to ensure that those who want more involvement in the way the organisation strategically develops have opportunities to do so.

It is an ambitious strategy which we plan to achieve by 2013 and in doing so, we will be able to evidence the following:

- Everybody is involved in decisions about their own life.
- Those who want more involvement in the way the organisation strategically develops have opportunities to do so.

In the next sections we look in detail at different ways that people can be central to decisions about their lives. Everyone supported by an organisation must be able to participate fully in decisions about their own life – this is self-directed support.

In health and social care, we do this through person-centred thinking, planning and reviews. In addition, there must be opportunities for people to be involved in decision making at an organisational level, while recognising that not everyone will choose to be so involved.

In your day-to-day life, when you go to the hairdresser or barber, you expect to explain to the hairdresser exactly what you want, and for this to be delivered. Some people may also be interested in being part of a focus group to look at the 'customer experience' at that hairdresser's, or in testing out a new range of hair products, or being a model for new trainees. Most people will be content to get their hair cut in the way that they want, but others will want more involvement. Involvement in organisations is no different.

Here is a summary of how person-centred practices can contribute to people having choice and control over decisions about their lives, as well as contributing to service change.

Person-centred practices	How each practice can contribute to people having choice and control over decisions about their life, and contribute to service change
Good days and bad days	This person-centred thinking tool can help people have more control over their days. Knowing what a good day is like and what a bad day is like tells you what the person wants their days to be like.
Relationship circles	A relationship circle tells you who people have in their life. You can then have conversations about what this means to the person in relation to their life and support. Do they want to see or be in touch with people more? Do they want more people in their life? Are there people whom they want to have a role in making decisions with them – for example, through a circle of support?
Communication charts	We cannot enable people to have choice and control in their life unless we know how people communicate.
Decision making	This is the most direct person-centred thinking tool for people to have more choice and control in their day-to-day life.
Matching	One of the most significant choices someone makes is who they want to support them, or who, if anyone, they want to live with. This person-centred thinking tool helps to get the best matches.
Person-centred reviews	People have more choice and control in their lives through having opportunities to review what is working and not working for them, and to think together about what needs to change to keep and build on what is working and to change what is not working. In a person-centred review people can talk about what they want in the future and what outcomes they want in their life over the next year, so that they are directing and designing their life and service.

Working Together for Change	Working Together for Change takes the information from person-centred reviews to inform business planning and organisational development. This is the primary way that everyone who uses a service can have their views directly taken into account and acted on at an organisational level.
Person-centred recruitment	Making sure that the person is at the centre of decision making about selecting and recruiting their staff.

The next part of this chapter focuses on what contributing through person-centred practices means for people supported by an organisation, and then staff teams and other stakeholders.

Supporting people to make important decisions

Two of the most significant decisions that people need to be central to in a health and social care context are 'How do I want to live (and be supported)?' and 'Who do I want to provide that support?' We can use person-centred thinking tools with people to understand their answers to these questions. The tools are used with the person, others who know and care about the person (family, friends), staff and professionals.

As you can see from the table, we can use person-centred thinking tools to discover the following.

- What is important to you? What is important for you to be healthy, safe and well? How can we get the best balance between what is important to you and what is important for you?

- How can the amount of choice and control that you have in your life be increased?

- What are the roles and responsibilities of the people who support you?

- What is life like now? What is working and not working for you? How can we change what is not working?

- What else do we need to learn and figure out together?

This information is recorded as:

- What do we appreciate about the person?

- What is important to the person?

- How can we support the person?

What is 'important to' the person is a description of how they want to live.

'How we can support the person' is the mandate for staff, or central to the job description of their role and what they need to deliver. We need to have this information for everyone we support so that people can direct their own lives. Key to directing your life and service is choosing who supports you.

Choosing who I want to support me – person-centred recruitment

Many organisations consider that the answer to person-centred recruitment is simply to have several service users trained and supported to sit on panels. This sends an important message to people coming for interview. It also enables the panel to see firsthand how interviewees respond to and respect people who use the service. It does not, however, address the question of how we enable people we support to choose their staff. This has to start with the description of how the person wants to live, and then the Matching person-centred thinking tool to begin the job description. Here is how Jennie and her mum, Suzie, chose the right staff team for Jennie.

Jennie, her mum Suzie, and her circle of support worked with a provider, Independent Options, to recruit Jennie's staff team. A circle of support is where friends, family and people in the community come together around an individual. The group meets every month or so, for a few hours, and uses person-centred thinking and planning to decide together on what the circle can do to enable the person to live their life fully, in their community. This is how they used person-centred recruitment to keep Jennie at the centre of the process. Jennie does not use speech to communicate, and she has learning disabilities and autism. The family and the circle worked with the provider to keep Jennie central to the process. They started with Jennie's person-centred plan, then developed the Matching information as the person specification and from this the job description.

The job description was split into responsibilities to Jennie, the circle and the organisation. Within each of these the headings from the Doughnut were used to specify core responsibilities and where people could use their creativity and judgement (see Chapter 2). The family and the manager, Joanne, then developed a decision-making agreement so that everyone was clear how decisions were going to be made and that Jennie and the circle would make the final decision on whom to appoint. This included deciding that Suzie would shortlist with Joanne, and Jennie and circle members would meet the shortlisted candidates (doing art together – an important part of Jennie's life) before the formal interviews.

The advert introduced Jennie and used some of what people appreciate about her from her person-centred plan, as well as information from the Matching tool.

The interview questions were based around Jennie's person-centred plan and asked in the order of responsibilities – to Jennie, to the circle and then the organisation. Suzie and another member of the circle were part of the interview panel. Jennie had done her 'interviews' by seeing how people responded to her during the art session. Suzie made the final decisions, with Joanne, about which staff to appoint.

Jennie is very happy with her staff team and Suzie is delighted with how the team is working to support Jennie. Working hard to both get a good match and ensure that Jennie, her family and the circle were central to the process made all the difference.

In Chapter 8 on human resources, you will find a more detailed discussion of the approach to recruitment and resourcing.

Being in control of my money and support – individual service funds

Defining how you want to live and choosing who supports you are examples of co-production in action. People have more power and decision making in their lives when they know what their support costs and can decide how they want to spend the money that is allocated to them – whether they live alone or within a shared service. One option for making this happen is an individual service fund (see Figure 5.2).[57] An individual service fund enables someone to use their personal budget to buy support from a provider who then holds the money for them on their behalf. The person decides how to spend the money and the provider is accountable to them. The provider commits only to spending the individual's budget – the individual service fund – on their individual support and on any management costs they incur directly in organising and delivering the individual support service, and not to put this funding into a general pooled budget.

How we described success in enabling people to take control was rooted in the success standards for individual service funds. These are clear statements about the what, where, who, when and how of real choice and control.

A national provider, Dimensions, wanted to introduce individual service funds across the organisation.[58] The organisation used a range of person-centred thinking tools to achieve this. The staff started with making sure they knew what was important to and for each individual, and, by using 'Working and not working', what people wanted to change in their lives. By looking at community mapping as well, they could then put together an ideal week or month for each person (including what each person wanted to do, where in the community, and when). With this information they were then able to create personalised rotas for each person, and to use an approach to match staff to each individual and what they wanted to do. Using a relationship map (see Chapter 2), they asked all individuals whom they support to think about who they preferred to support them, out of the staff team of 16. Anne-Marie, for example, put four team members in the inner circle of her relationship map, indicating that these were the staff whom she wanted to support her. Then the manager identified the strengths and interests of each of these four staff members, by looking at their one-page profiles, to work out the best fit between them with Anne-Marie's plans for her 'perfect week'. This resulted in substantial changes at a team level in the way that staff were deployed and what was expected of them, and also in the introduction of personalised rotas. From these micro team level changes, the organisation then made design changes at a macro level (see Chapter 4).

Developing an individual service fund with Anne-Marie, and enabling her to choose the staff whom she wanted to deliver her service, are central to her having choice and control in her life. On page 112 is a summary of what the staff needed to learn to deliver an individual service fund for Anne-Marie, and the person-centred thinking tools that helped.

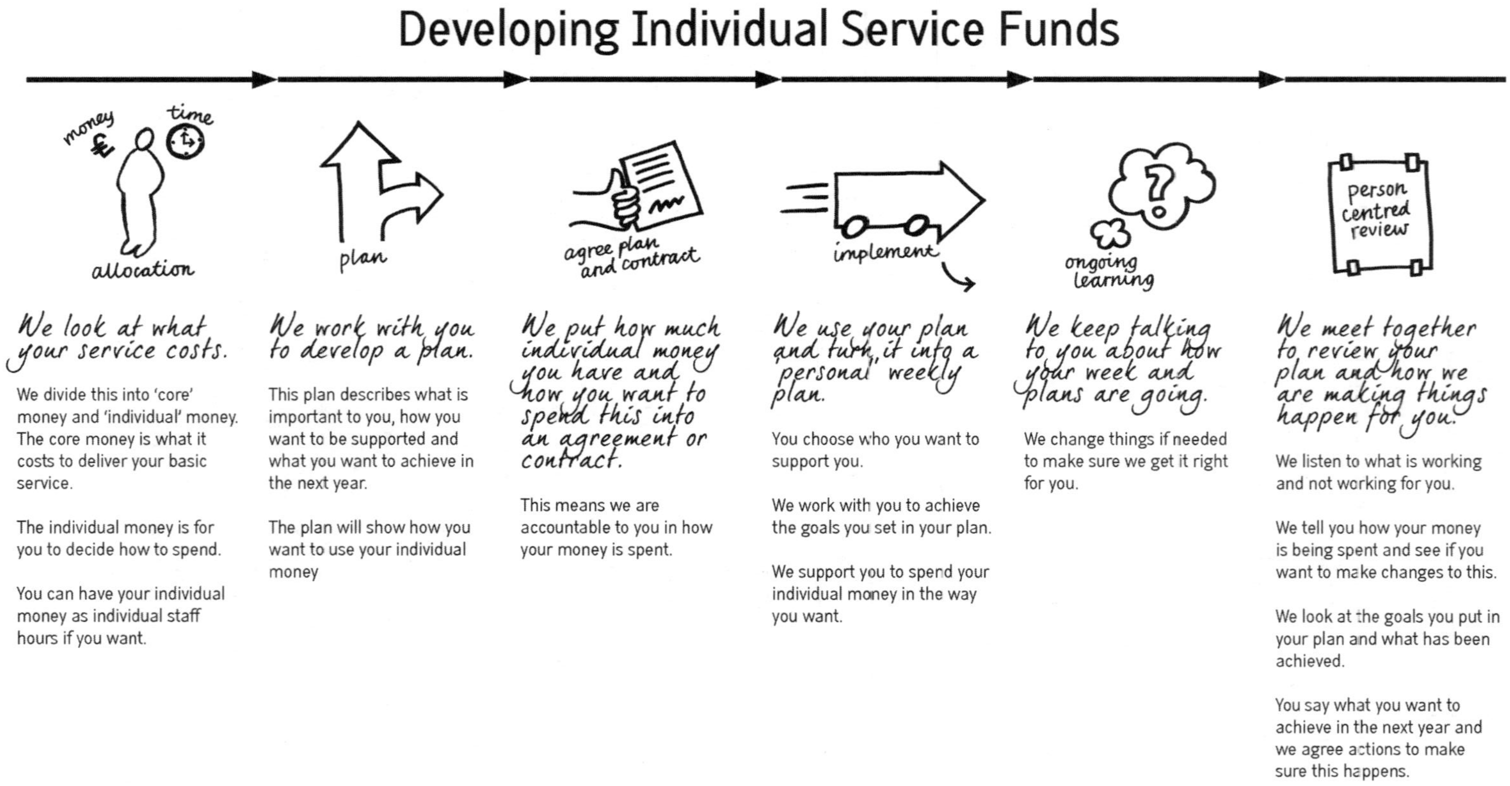

Developing Individual Service Funds

allocation

We look at what your service costs.

We divide this into 'core' money and 'individual' money. The core money is what it costs to deliver your basic service.

The individual money is for you to decide how to spend.

You can have your individual money as individual staff hours if you want.

plan

We work with you to develop a plan.

This plan describes what is important to you, how you want to be supported and what you want to achieve in the next year.

The plan will show how you want to use your individual money

agree plan and contract

We put how much individual money you have and how you want to spend this into an agreement or contract.

This means we are accountable to you in how your money is spent.

implement

We use your plan and turn it into a personal weekly plan.

You choose who you want to support you.

We work with you to achieve the goals you set in your plan.

We support you to spend your individual money in the way you want.

ongoing learning

We keep talking to you about how your week and plans are going.

We change things if needed to make sure we get it right for you.

person centred review

We meet together to review your plan and how we are making things happen for you.

We listen to what is working and not working for you.

We tell you how your money is being spent and see if you want to make changes to this.

We look at the goals you put in your plan and what has been achieved.

You say what you want to achieve in the next year and we agree actions to make sure this happens.

Figure 5.2 Developing individual service funds

What we needed to learn for an individual service fund	The person-centred thinking tool that can help gather that information
What is important to Anne-Marie/what good support looks like to her (we summarised this into a one-page profile) What this looks like in a week (we called this a 'perfect week')	Relationship map (a way to learn who is important). 'Good days and bad days' (a way to learn what is important and what good support looks like). Morning routine (a way to learn what is important and what good support looks like).
Where are the important places for Anne-Marie?	My places in the community (community mapping – to learn where the things that are important to Anne-Marie take place and where she wants to spend her time).
Where Anne-Marie wants to be in a year's time (these are her outcomes)	'What is working and not working' (a way to think about what needs to change to build on what is working and change what is not working). Hopes and dreams for the future (a way to imagine a better future, based on what matters to Anne-Marie). My gifts and contributions (identifying Anne-Marie's gifts, strengths and talents to build on and share in the future).
Co-production – ensuring that Anne-Marie has as much choice and control as possible	Decision-making agreement (a way to know what decisions Anne-Marie makes in her life and how staff support this). Communication charts.

Reflecting on how things are going and making change – person-centred reviews

A person-centred review is a meeting that combines two person-centred thinking skills and tools: an understanding of the balance between 'important to' and 'important for' the person, with what is working and not working. Person-centred reviews can kick-start the development of a person-centred description, or add detail to this information. The purpose is to create shared actions for change, based on a reflection and analysis of what is working and not working for the person and others. A person-centred review brings together people who are providing support from different roles or places, with family and friends. It places the person who is being supported firmly at the centre.

The person-centred review process is illustrated in Figure 5.3. It naturally begins with introductions, and then people are invited to share positive information about the characteristics or contribution of the focus person. This reflects that underpinning value of focusing on capacities in person-centred practice. The facilitator works to 'pitch this' so that it feels empowering, not patronising. More than anything, it begins a meeting with a clear sense of its being different from traditional ones. This feels very different for individuals who are more used to attending meetings that focus on what is wrong in their life. It also helps to remind those at such meetings to think about the people concerned beyond their diagnoses and see them as individuals with capacities, gifts and contributions.

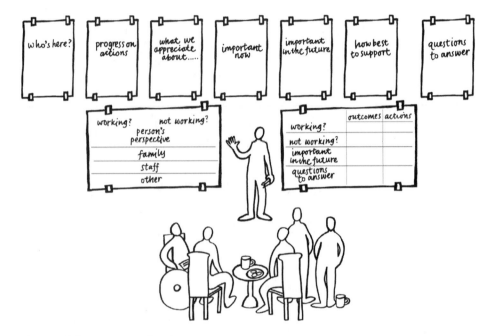

Figure 5.3 The person-centred review

At this stage, a typical review would involve social workers and professionals reading their reports. However, in a person-centred review, the person shares their own perspective, and then everyone adds their information (including family and friends). So, rather than sitting formally around a table, information is shared and collected together. Sometimes flip chart paper is pinned on the walls in the room and everyone is given a pen so that they can write their thoughts on each in a more relaxed way. Another way to do this is on a table, with A4 sheets of blank paper and a question written on the top of each sheet. These are circulated around the table for people to add their information. The way that information is shared is decided with the person, taking into account the number of people coming to the review and where it will be held. The aim is to create a comfortable atmosphere that gives everyone an equal opportunity to have a say, and for this information to be recorded.

Information is recorded around the following types of questions:

- What do we appreciate about the person?

- What is important to (the person) now?

- What is important to (the person) for the future?

- What does (the person) need to stay healthy and safe, and supported well?

- What questions do we need to answer?

- What is working and not working from different perspectives?

The 'What questions do we need to answer?' sheet is where people ensure statutory requirements are addressed. It is also a place to record any questions or issues that the people concerned or their supporters want to work on or work out.

Once the information has been recorded and shared, the next stage is to use it to explore any differences in opinion and generate actions based on what is working and not working for people and moving towards their desired future. In this way, the person-centred review makes it more likely that the people concerned will have what is important to them in their life and move towards the future they want. Actions are agreed that keep what is working happening and change what is not working. This person-centred information is also used to build detailed person-centred descriptions.

The questions that the facilitator may ask of a person in this part of the review are as follows.

- What needs to happen to make sure that what is working in your life keeps happening?

- What needs to happen to change what is not working for you?

- How can we address each of the 'questions to answer'? What else do we need to learn?

- What can we do together to enable you to move towards what is important in the future?

The next part of the process is to think about solutions and develop actions. With what is working for the person (and others), you simply ensure that this continues. You may be able to address what is not working for people within the current service and resources. You may need to use person-centred thinking skills to find out what you need to do differently.

This process is also used with 'What else we need to learn?', by looking at the 'questions to answer' and then thinking about any person-centred thinking tools that could help address them.

When there are areas of a person's life that are not working and not within the sphere of influence of the people in the room, then other people need to be involved to figure out solutions. For example, this could include working with people from the housing department if the person wants to move, or finding a supported employment service if the person wants to change or find a job. All this should lead to detailed actions that change what is not working for the person, add to your learning and keep improving how you are delivering personalised services that truly offer choice and control.

One action from a person-centred review is likely to be for someone to take the information and learning and either work with the person to create a one-page profile or add it to an existing profile to create a more detailed person-centred description.

DENNIS'S PERSON-CENTRED REVIEW

Dennis is 74 and lives by himself in the South of England. He received domiciliary support and has a personal budget. At his person-centred review, he talked to Lucy, his care manager, about the support he received. When asked 'What is working?', Dennis talked about his friendship with his neighbour, and visits from his family. When asked 'What is not working?', Dennis said 'Staff talk over my head – I feel like a package and not a person' and that he got cold when he had a wash (he was washed in a cold bathroom because his carer got too hot). In the future, Dennis wants to take up his steam train hobby, get the monthly steam train magazine, and visit his daughter in Weymouth. Lucy and Dennis thought together about what needed to happen to change things, and came up with a list of actions including talking to the manager of the service before looking at using his budget to purchase different support. Another action was writing in detail how he wanted to be supported, in a one-page profile, so that all the staff who supported him could use it and support him with consistency.

So far we have looked at how people you support can direct their life and service through individual service funds, choosing their staff and person-centred reviews to keep making necessary changes. Another way that people can influence how their service is delivered is by giving feedback to managers about the staff who support them:

The Inclusion Co-ordinator in United Response did a small piece of research with people who were supported in Lancashire and Merseyside.[59] She interviewed people about their experience of reviews – previous traditional reviews and person-centred reviews. People clearly preferred person-centred reviews – in terms of their involvement and the outcomes in their lives.

Influencing changes in my service – contributing to one-to-ones (supervision) and 360-degree appraisals

Another important way that people supported can share information, contribute to decisions and influence their service is through one-to-ones (supervision) and 360-degree appraisals of the staff who support them. It is important that in social care managers seek contributions from the people staff members support to inform one-to-ones. Managers can use the person-centred thinking tool 'Working and not working' from the perspective of the person being supported, and add this to what is working and not working from the manager's perspective.

Earlier we shared the story about Jennie and her mum, Suzie, recruiting staff. This is how Jennie and Suzie worked together with the manager, Joanne, in the end of probationary period review (see Figure 5.4).

> After three months, Suzie shared her views with Joanne, the manager, for the end of probationary period review. She gave Joanne her perspective on the relationship that different team members had with Jennie – the most important issue as far as the circle was concerned. Then Suzie used the job description, and went through what was working and not working for each item. Joanne did the same, and in the review asked each individual what they thought was working and not working. Therefore, like a 360-degree appraisal, the review was based on information about each person's relationship with Jennie, and what was working and not working against the job description from the perspectives of Suzie, Joanne and the team member themselves.

Finally, in this section, we show how Working Together for Change is a process for everyone who uses services to influence how the organisation changes and develops.

Making my contribution to how the organisation changes and develops – Working Together for Change

Working Together for Change is the central process for people to contribute to how an organisation changes and develops.[60] It is a simple, systematic process using person-centred information from reviews and support plans to drive strategic change in commissioning with and for older people. It collates and analyses person-centred information to provide powerful insights into what works and doesn't work in people's lives, as well as their aspirations for the future. The Department of Health's 'Putting People First' programme worked with HSA and four councils in early 2009 to test and refine this method.[61] The experience has shown the approach to be flexible, transferable and effective. Here we describe the process and why it is important through the story of Dennis, 74, who lives alone and has carers who support him every day from a domiciliary agency.

The Working Together for Change process begins with person-centred information: a person-centred plan or person-centred review. These lead to actions based on what is working in the older person's life, addressing what is not working and moving towards what the person wants in the future.

Earlier we described Dennis's person-centred review. At the end of his review, Lucy asked Dennis for his top two 'working', his top two 'not working' and his top two ideas for 'what he wanted in the future'. She fed this information into the two-day Working Together for Change workshop.

Clustering information from Dennis's and other reviews

On the left is the individual person-centred review, resulting in 'actions for individual change'. These will change what is not working for the person and respond to what

End of Probation Appraisal
Senior Support Worker

Name: Date:

Responsibilities to Jennie

Core responsibilities	What is going well?	What needs to be improved?
1. To communicate well with Jennie. This means knowing how to communicate with Jennie and how Jennie communicates, and to use her communication system and visual cues daily (described in detail in her Person Centred Plan). To support Jennie in her decision-making, so that Jennie increases the amount of choice and control that she has in her life.		
2. Support Jennie in her relationships (for example, arranging for Jennie to meet up with her friends, supporting Jennie to send birthday cards) and enable her to be part of her local community.		
3. Support Jennie in all the activities on her weekly timetable and discuss any suggested changes with Suzie (Jennie's Mum).		
4. Work in a person-centred way with Jennie, going at her pace, supporting her to develop her interests. This may include practical assistance, support, teaching, advice, role modelling, encouragement and positive feedback.		
5. Support Jennie to eat healthily and stay safe (there is detailed information about this in her person-centred plan).		
6. Support Jennie a respectful, dignified way. Her personal care routines are described in her person-centred plan.		

Figure 5.4 Contributing to an appraisal

Working Together for Change Process

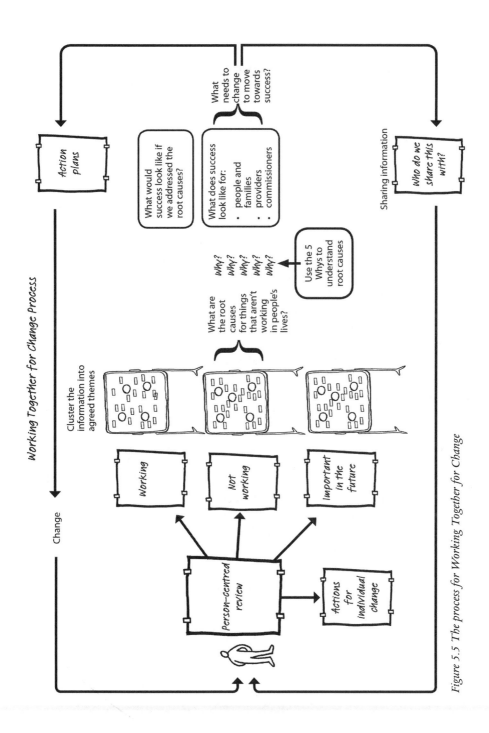

Figure 5.5 The process for Working Together for Change

they have identified as important for the future. At the same time, the person is asked to prioritise information from their review to take into the Working Together for Change process. This information, combined with other people's reviews, is thematically clustered during a workshop. These clusters are analysed so the group develops an understanding of what is working and can be built upon; what is not working and needs to change; and the things that will guide future changes. This information informs changes in local action planning (blue line) and changes in strategic commissioning (green line) where the information can be used alongside other information sources, such as the Joint Strategic Needs Assessment (JSNA).

Anonymous information from Dennis's and 15 other people's reviews was shared at the first one-day workshop with commissioners, members of the Older People's Association, care managers and providers. All the information was aggregated and written onto cards – red for what was not working, green for what was working, and blue for what people wanted in the future.

The facilitator read out each of the green 'working' cards and the group decided which cards were similar, and then what to call each theme. Everyone then had a chance to comment. There was a wide range of positive, encouraging themes, suggesting areas that were working well for people. They repeated the exercise with the red cards. There were several other cards with similar issues to Dennis's. For example: 'Agency carers…there are too many of them…men and women thinking they can do it. I will do it myself.' and 'I am not allowed to use a wheelchair to push myself around the house due to the risk of scraping my knuckles on the door jamb.' The group decided to call this cluster, 'I am not treated with respect or as an individual by my paid carers.' There were four other clusters of what was not going well for people. The group said this information was not new but felt more powerful seeing it all together, in the older people's own words.

Finally, the group clustered the blue cards that looked at what people wanted in the future and found people did not want extraordinary things, but more everyday experiences such as going out, meeting people, taking a holiday or starting a hobby. The group analysed the 'not working' clusters. People worked in teams of older people, commissioners, providers and care managers and discussed possible root causes. Lucy was part of the group looking at the 'I am not treated with respect or as an individual by my paid carers' cluster. Their list for why people might not be treated with respect included the following observations.

- Paid carers are too task focused and not outcome focused.
- Paid carers are not matched to older people.
- Paid carers get poor-quality training and supervision.
- Information is not recorded for carers to use.

What success would look like – from different perspectives

Lucy's group shared their observations with the other groups and thought about what success would be like for older people, staff and managers if they could address these issues. What would people say if they changed things for the better?

The group decided that older people would say:

- 'My carers listen to me and understand what is important to me.'

- 'I look forward to my carer visiting me.'

The staff supporting older people and their managers would say:

- 'I get good training and support.'

- 'It is easier to respect others when you are respected yourself.'

- 'I have all the information I need – we have written information about what matters to the person and how best to support them.'

Each group did the same process for their 'not working' cluster and wrote it up on a poster called 'What would success look like?'

Making changes to deliver this success

The participants then looked at the roles of commissioners, providers, care managers and the Older People's Association and asked what each could do to work towards this success. The Older People's Association offered to work with providers in the recruitment and training of staff. The providers looked at what they could influence, and thought about possibilities with the care managers. They committed to things such as recruiting staff more locally, having people working a wider range of hours and matching staff to older people by developing one-page profiles to describe what matters and how people want to be supported. They would then use the Matching tool to get better matches for personality characteristics, hobbies, interests and skills. Staff could use their one-page profiles to introduce themselves to the people they supported. The providers also committed to reviewing how they supervise and support staff and individuals, and to re-evaluating the training they provide for carers.

The commissioners took their information to a further meeting and put it alongside data from the JSNA and other sources.

The commissioners decided to:

- further analyse review data to determine best practice if and where people have reported that relationships with their care staff are working particularly well, and to encourage replication by other providers

- develop individual service funds for domiciliary care services to empower individuals to design their own support and express preferences regarding care staff

- use this and other priority areas identified through Working Together for Change to set the overarching outcomes for an outcomes-based approach to commissioning for all future older people's services

- commission specific direct payments services for older people, offering specific support with employment, legal and HR issues

- consider designing or commissioning a web-based database for personal assistants or care workers that supports person-to-person transactions whereby individuals can build networks of care staff and choose between them.

Lucy shared with Dennis what had happened on the day. The individual actions agreed at his review were having an impact. He was warm in the bathroom now. He enjoyed working with Lucy to put together his one-page profile, and could tell that staff had read it and that some were using it to think about how they supported him. It was hoped that the actions the providers agreed to would change things in the short term for him and others in a similar position. The commissioners' actions should mean people will be less likely to receive a service in which they are not treated with respect and as an individual.

Dennis's story shows how person-centred information can drive strategic change in organisations and effect improvements in commissioning. Working Together for Change is a tried and tested tool councils can use to ensure the current changes in adult social care are co-developed and co-produced with older people and families. As well as helping those undertaking JSNAs, it can provide a way to understand and measure the outcomes of personalisation by generating and analysing qualitative data for commissioning, thereby improving the links between strategic decision makers and the people they serve.

Involvement and co-production at an organisational level

Everyone who uses a service must have their voice heard in informing organisational change – and using person-centred reviews to inform the Working Together for Change process is a powerful way to do this. Additionally, some people may want to take a more active role in influencing organisational development and change. In United Response the two main ways that this takes place are through the quality checkers' team (described in Chapter 11) who report to the Trustees, and through leadership teams that include people who use the service and family members, so that people contribute to each division's strategic planning. Here are some other examples of how this happens in United Response:

- Being part of the Working Together for Change facilitation group.

- Being part of short-life task groups with staff looking at particular issues – for example, a group of staff and people who use the service developed the competencies for staff.

- Forums where people who use services set their own agenda and report their thinking/ideas/questions/concerns to the CEO and senior leadership. This happens through the divisional and area leadership teams, where people supported and their families take an active role in decision making for the organisation at regular meetings with management and other staff.

- Being involved in delivering training. Two people who use services and two managers deliver training to trainee doctors and nurses about how to support people with learning disabilities. Each trainer has a one-page profile that includes how to best support them in training. The trainers use these to know how to support each other.

- Making sure that people and their families are heard by other stakeholders. The presence of family members or other close supporters at meetings with procurement staff or commissioners has been encouraged very successfully to influence the understanding of needs, and therefore the funding decision, which otherwise may have been less helpful to the people supported.

Involving people who use the service in decisions about their life and service is central to a person-centred organisation. Engaging staff in decision making about how they work, and how the teams operate and influence the organisation, is also key to how a person-centred organisation operates.

Working together in engaging staff, families and stakeholders

Involving staff and making sure that their views are heard and taken into account brings out the best of all the resources that an organisation has, to enable it to be as effective as possible. In this section we begin with staff, and then look at working in partnership with families and other stakeholders.

Here is a summary of the person-centred practices that can be useful in engaging staff, families and stakeholders.

Person-centred practices	How person-centred practices can be useful in engaging staff, families and stakeholders
One-page profiles	One-page profiles enable us to know what is important to staff about their life and work, and how to support them in their role. One-page profiles are important in matching people to roles and people supported to ensure the best match on both sides.
'Working and not working from different perspectives'	This person-centred thinking tool is a way to hear what staff think about what is going well, and what is not working from their perspective. This could be about the support they are delivering (for example, in a person-centred review around an individual), about the support they are getting (for example, in a one-to-one or supervision session) or about how the organisation works. Using the 'Working/not working' tool can help you to understand why a relationship with a particular stakeholder or stakeholders is not as effective as it might be.
Positive and Productive Meetings	This is a process that ensures that everyone's voice and contribution are heard in meetings, and that roles within meetings are shared between people and matched with strengths.

cont.

Person-centred practices	How person-centred practices can be useful in engaging staff, families and stakeholders
Person-centred supervision	This process means that one-to-ones and supervision are two-way, and opportunities for staff to get feedback on their work, think about problems and solutions, and reflect on what they are learning and their role. It includes clear, shared accountability for actions and decisions.
Working Together for Change	When an organisation asks staff what is working and not working for them (for example, in supervision or one-to-ones), Working Together for Change can turn this information into actions and inform business planning and organisational development. Working Together for Change is a way to involve all stakeholders, together with people supported and staff, in organisational change.
Presence to Contribution	This enables you to look at whether or not you are optimising the opportunities for working together with the other stakeholders in your business. This person-centred thinking tool can help assess how you want to participate at local level, in your sector, or at national level. It can cover the range of activities from collaboration and partnership (perhaps with the local community), right through to corporate social responsibility (for example, United Response collaborated with a well-known bank to provide additional resources to help people with their banking needs).
The Doughnut	This is a way to enable staff to know exactly what is expected of them, and the areas in which they can make decisions without having to check back for permission. If relationships with external stakeholders need to be clarified, or perhaps become more formal, then the Doughnut tool can be used to detail the respective roles of each party.
Decision-making agreements	Decision-making charts can help you to clarify what decisions need to be your own, or taken by an external party, or are shared – around an individual, in a team or as an organisation. This helps staff to know which decisions in the organisation they can make themselves, and which they will be consulted on.

Working together in a person-centred organisation means looking at the typical processes – how people meet together, how individual supervision takes place – and seeing how these could be re-designed as ways for people genuinely to listen to each other, and think together.

Nancy Kline developed the concept of a 'thinking environment' and describes ten components that have to be in place for staff to think well for themselves.[62] These include ensuring that people give each other proper attention; focusing on equality and equal turns; appreciation; full information; excellent, incisive questions; freedom from being rushed; and focusing on the environment. You can see these components in practice in a person-centred approach to meetings and one-to-ones (supervision), and other ways of engaging staff fully in delivering the organisation's vision, mission and values.

Listening and acting on what matters to people – one-page profiles

Working together has to start with listening to people and learning what matters to them. This information can be recorded on one-page profiles.

Many organisations, like United Response, are now expecting all staff to have a one-page profile. Aisling Duffy, Chief Executive of Certitude, explains why, in an email to all staff:

> We believe that the more we understand about our colleagues the better we are in our jobs. This is why we are committed to supporting everyone in Certitude to develop their own one-page profile and share these with their team colleagues. I know many of you already have one-page profiles or are working on them as part of our commitment as a person-centred organisation, which is great. Tools, such as these, do not in themselves create a person-centred organisation but alongside our unwavering commitment to a culture of openness and communication go a long way in creating the conditions where being truly person-centred is business as usual at Certitude.

One of the important decisions for staff members are whom they support, and we explore 'matching' based on one-page profiles in Chapter 8.

Another national organisation, which also expects all its staff to have one-page profiles, set up a new project team to look at developing individual service funds across the organisation. The chair of the meeting, a director, asked everyone to bring their one-page profiles to the meeting. She started the meeting by asking everyone to introduce themselves using their one-page profile, and to share something that was important to them. She also asked everyone to share something from the support section that would be helpful for others to know, so that everyone would know how to support each other in the project.

One-page profiles are a way to evaluate whether people are getting the support they need in the way that they need it, as described in the following example:

> At an HSA team meeting we looked at our one-page profiles to think about how well we were doing in supporting each other. Individually we chose our top five 'What is important to me?' and top five 'How best to support me'. Then for these ten items we rated each one to say how much each one was present (5, always present; 1, never or rarely). This gave us a score out of 50, which is a way of knowing how well what is important to us and how well we are supported is actually present in our work lives. We then set actions for what we can do as individuals to improve this, and then what we can do together as a team. Using this approach (and thank you to Mary Lou Bourne for sharing this with us) we can have a 'quality of work' number that we can revisit regularly, to see if it goes up (or down!). In this way, you can use one-page profiles to create actions for you individually, as well as for the team.

One way to find out how much people work together and support each other is to take a look at their meetings.

A different way to think about meetings – Positive and Productive Meetings

Positive and Productive Meetings is a collaborative approach that creates a respectful and supportive environment that enables people to think clearly and therefore do their best work. The process reflects person-centred principles – for example, making sure people are listened to, and that they have an opportunity to use their skills in meetings. Aisling Duffy, Chief Executive of Certitude, describes the difference that using Positive and Productive Meetings has had on the leadership team:

> Our leadership team has been using Positive and Productive Meetings for eight months. Undoubtedly our meetings are more productive as the outcome we are seeking from each agenda item is clear to everyone from the outset – the result being meetings which are much more focused and where we achieve a lot more in the time available. The positive framework has also helped to create the conditions within our meetings for complex and sensitive issues to be discussed in depth and constructively addressed. Participation is excellent and the added focus on team development has been a great benefit to us all. I would wholly recommend Positive and Productive Meetings.

Positive Futures has its own trained, accredited trainer in Positive and Productive Meetings and has included the principles and practices into its policy on meetings. We explore Positive and Productive Meetings in detail in Chapter 9.

One-to-ones and appraisals

Not many staff look forward to traditional supervision sessions, often seeing them as punitive, or a waste of time at best. In person-centred organisations, one-to-one sessions are an important opportunity for people to think well together, problem solve, share successes and demonstrate accountability. This was certainly the experience in Hull City Council, as Tracy Meyerhoff, Assistant Head of Services, explains:

> Supervision in Hull had always been management-led and although it was meant to be a two-way process, many staff and supervisors turned up unprepared for monthly supervision. Staff would often avoid or make excuses not to attend.

> By using 'What is working and what is not working from different perspectives' we were able to establish that the main issue with supervision in Hull was the lack of trust between staff and supervisor.

> Most staff told us that the agenda for supervision was dominated by the supervisor and was often used as a means to 'tell them off'.

> There was no clear purpose, no preparation and very often it was cancelled so staff saw supervision as having no real value to their role.

s were

Voice'
– and
sity.

ed on:
eas or

ionary
d yet?'
ently?'
d this
to use

quality
ement

on-centred supervision in Hull and we now have our
it' that identifies our core responsibilities for supervision,
nt and creativity and what is not our responsibility. We now
odel and found that staff value the opportunity to agree the
tems are for information and what is going to be discussed.
for us was to include the appreciation round as this was
t previously paid good attention to. Feedback from staff was
the biggest improvements to supervision, as it really made
respected.

iew 'what's working and what's not working' in supervision.
at staff now feel supervision is important to be able to do
re not afraid to ask questions or seek support. They feel
ommitment from their supervisor and that supervision is
tive. In each supervision an action plan is agreed giving
ity as to who is going to do what and when.

it has really helped us focus our thinking on developing a
re. If we want our staff to develop and use person-centred
actices with people they support, then we must first ensure
pport our staff through person-centred supervision.

of a person-centred approach to one-to-ones in Chapter 8
le of the way this is done in United Response using a process
lence'.

three-
vhat is
future
as the
usiness

ership
eading
with
a 'T'
st-line
gether
ll read

n their
)-ones
ation.
overall

team days

ribute their perspective to organisational decision making is
er than their normal team meetings. These could be regular
get together, where they set the agenda and then share the
s, or specific short-life groups that address a particular issue
nt to explore.
an be ways to get staff together either to look at issues or
organisation, or for staff to develop their own agenda to feed

the regular learning and reflection days are an example of this
ther for Change process, and other person-centred practices. In
nths, the operations support and development team in United
s working and not working around a key theme. One example
s. Staff and the managers all contributed their perceptions of
not working from their perspective. As a result of looking at
ing 'Working and not working' the quality manager took the
process and content of the visual performance indicators used
to measure performance. This also involves people supported,

and an example considered was a review of the way recruitment process
designed and carried out, and what role the HR team should play in that.

Examples of consultative mechanisms in United Response include 'Unitec
– a forum for consultation with staff on the full range of employment matter
'Diverse Voices', focused on the progression of excellence in equality and dive

Other approaches

Here are some other ways that staff views and suggestions can be heard and a

- Staff satisfaction questionnaires that have opportunities to share i
  examples of good practice.

- The CEO getting together people at the time of their three-month proba
  period and asking them, 'What do you know that I may not have notic
  and 'If you were me, what would you be doing more of, or doing diffe

- Hotline to the CEO – in United Response, Su Sayer has a hotline a
  number is in the front of the staff handbook with an invitation for a▮
  it to contribute.

- Continuous improvement groups (what may have been known as
  circles') using tools such as the 4 Plus 1 questions to generate impro
  on a day-to-day basis.

Staff and working together for change

The Working Together for Change process can also be used with staff. Over ▮
month period, every manager in one-to-ones could ask each staff member
working and not working from their perspective, and what they want for the
in the organisation. This information could be used in exactly the same wa〉
Working Together for Change process described earlier to feed into the b
plan.

Working Together for Change and being members of development or lea▮
groups enable staff to be involved in generating ideas and decision making. In
change in United Response, each division had a leadership group charge
ensuring change and embedding person-centred practices. These groups we〉
slice of the organisation – large numbers of senior managers, working with f
managers and staff. These groups co-produced the outcomes for their work t
– success statements – and also decided how they could measure these. You ▮
more about this in Chapter 6.

As you can see, there is a range of ways to enable staff to be fully involved
own sphere of influence and work – through making sure that meetings, one-
and appraisals are opportunities for thinking together and not just sharing infor▮
There are also many ways to ensure that staff are able to contribute to the

direction and change within the organisation, at an individual level, in forums and working groups, and through Working Together for Change.

Family and friends are usually very important in people's lives, and some people will want to have their families heavily involved in their decision making while others may not. A person-centred organisation seeks to work in partnership with families who are involved in people's lives.

Working together with families, friends and circles

Working together with families will happen to different degrees depending on what a person wants, and whether there are capacity and communication issues. In addition, some families will want to get involved at an organisational level.

At an individual level, families often have expertise and important insights about what matters to a person and how best to support them. This will inform one-page profiles and families will usually be invited by the person to be involved in their person-centred review. Circles of support are another way that families and friends can be involved in working together with the individual and service.[63] Earlier in the book we have shared stories about Jennie and her circle of support. Provider organisations could be involved in circles of support in different ways. The first is actively encouraging people they support to think about circles of support, and finding ways that these could be independently facilitated. Another way is to enable staff to be part of circles of support for other people not supported by the organisation. Providing paid services to circles of support – for example, book-keeping or training – is also a possibility. Yet another, where there is a circle of support, is making sure that the manager and staff feed back and report to the circle, as the person and the circle require.

> IAS, a provider based in the North West, actively supports staff and managers to be involved in circles of support. They worked with a family-led organisation to train circle facilitators, and make these available to local families who wanted to set up a circle around their son or daughter. As well as this, they brought together local established circles in the area to ask what would help more circles develop. One of the issues that came from that was how hard it can be for circles to manage the 'business' side of employing and supporting staff. IAS responded to this by developing a costed 'offer' to circles and people who have personal budgets that lists the support they can offer. This includes management support for circles, where a manager supports the staff on behalf of the circle, or mentors an existing manager.

Working together with families at an organisational level

There are different ways that families and relatives can work with organisations. In United Response, for example, families are invited to be involved in leadership teams at area and divisional level, and at national level learning and reflection days. This engagement allows direct input of perhaps unknown information and expertise to the organisation. There are several approaches here: first, involving families in the leadership of the organisation at a Trustee or leadership team level; second, establishing groups where families can feed back and contribute in either ongoing forums or specific focus groups; third, getting information from a wide range of families through surveys, or using Working Together for Change from a families' perspective, looking at what is working and not working for them. Here are some examples of what this looks like in practice.

IAS established relatives' forums that met directly with the CEO to give feedback on the organisation from their perspective. This informed the work that the organisation did on their statement of purpose (described in Chapter 3). The CEO was accountable for addressing their concerns, and also making sure that the feedback he got about what was working well from a relatives' perspective was shared within the organisation. Similarly, Dimensions employs family members to work with the organisation to ensure that the voices of family members are heard. Dimensions has a specific, ongoing group drawn from families, and has projects that actively explore what families want and need from the organisation.

Tim Jones, one of the divisional directors at United Response, took a different approach to ensuring that families' and individuals' voices were heard in the organisation. Here he describes what he did:

> Jim Collins talks about the importance of getting the right people on the bus.[64] In United Response, we realised that we had to expand the people on the bus – the leadership team – to be able to deliver the divisional purpose. Change normally happens because things are broken and need fixing. When I replaced the divisional management team (DMT) with the divisional leadership team (DLT) it was for reasons other than this. In fact, my senior operational colleagues were a good bunch of people who were pretty efficient and effective. They still are. We were a good team.
>
> But it started to slowly dawn on me that we were missing something. A paid perspective on what and how we were doing in leading and managing the business of the division was there in abundance. But that was it. There was no other 'take' on the matters we were discussing. Now, you might think the idea of those with executive power (in this context, DMT members) involving others – those we support, parents, families, carers, advocates, more junior managerial, administrative and support worker colleagues – in sharing the responsibility for getting right the support we provide to individuals would encounter some resistance. Not a word of it. There was none. Instead, there were those who, like me, wanted to rush headlong into it. There were others who wanted to focus on the planning process to make it happen, while the remainder could see the pitfalls to avoid. I could not have asked for a healthier, more balanced and positive response to doing things differently; and so, with everyone on board, we began our journey in September 2008.
>
> The obvious people to approach first were those we support and, in particular, the four who had undergone training earlier in the year to become quality checkers

[described in Chapter 11]. These 'experts by experience' took no persuading to join the DLT, quickly seeing the benefits of being part of a forum that would receive their quality check reports. However, their contribution would be more than this, for they would be assisting the DLT in getting right every aspect of its business.

The first DLT meeting took place in January 2009 and was attended by former DMT colleagues, the four quality checkers, managerial and support worker colleagues. It was a large group of people coming together for the first time and the focus was on familiarising ourselves not only with each other but this new inclusive way of overseeing and improving the division's performance. Forget the classic 'forming-storming-norming-performing' sequence that new teams undergo. At the end of the first meeting I was asked by members if they could get stuck into a 'meaty' subject when we next met. 'Of course,' was my response, 'What are you thinking of?' The answer came back, 'Money. How it's spent and if it's wasted!'

What a challenge for my Finance Manager colleague – an inclusive 'Finance is Fun' presentation! But, like the rest of my colleagues, he was up for it and duly delivered what some of my senior operational colleagues went on to describe as the 'easiest-to-understand presentation' he'd ever given! On the back of some really piercing questions from non-paid members of the team, the discussion focused on the use and cost of agency personnel, recruitment strategies and the expense associated with suspensions. What a start! Helping United Response do the business has become the norm for members of the DLT. This year it has produced the divisional plan and approved both the divisional learning and development plan and the new work strategy. An added dimension has been brought to all three. Indeed, the breadth, depth and quality of all our discussions have been greatly enhanced.

And so, by the summer of 2009 our thoughts were turning to the local area management team meetings that my senior operational colleagues were chairing – and had chaired for many years – back in their patches with their front-line managerial colleagues. Changing the membership to model the DLT's was not an issue...it wasn't the subject of debate...it just happened because people knew it was the right, logical next step! So we now have local leadership teams involving local people – those we support, quality checkers, parents, families, carers, coaches, managerial and support colleagues – in helping us get it right for those who rely on us, their nearest-and-dearest and those who are paid by United Response to deliver high-quality support services. What's more, the DLT's agenda reflects the local issues, challenges and successes, comprising, as it does, a minimum of two representatives from each of the local leadership teams. It's often said that meetings are held at the expense of doing the business! In our case, involving many more people in meetings that are purposeful and relevant drives activity, commitment, responsibility and accountability. It's also so much more fulfilling and rewarding as it means our chances of getting things right for people are greatly enhanced.

Working together with other stakeholders

In times of change, the impact of external stakeholders on your organisation is overlooked at your peril. More importantly, external stakeholders are a huge potential resource to the organisation. A person-centred organisation, therefore, does not look narrowly at what people it supports wants and needs, and seeks to satisfy them purely from internal resources. It seeks to take advantage of help and support from wherever it can be gained, always with the values of the organisation in mind of course, but with the primary goal of fulfilling its mission and ensuring that people have control in their lives, and can contribute as citizens.

At one level, this can mean benefiting from others' ideas and good practice. At another level, it can mean putting energy into scouring the community to utilise free resources, or to make sure that universal services are taken up. In a person-centred organisation this is a two-way street. In other words, it is OK to take from others, but you have to give something as well. So, contributing to the local community and carrying out activities that demonstrate corporate social responsibility at a broader level also matter.

Working together with suppliers and vendors

This is perhaps an underutilised source of working together, although it has been more to the fore in the procurement world. It may be surprising how much providers may be prepared to contribute, or improve the quality of their product or service if there is a match of what is important to and for them with what you hold dear in your organisation.

The Presence to Contribution tool can be used to establish the depth and breadth to which providers are linked to your organisation. The Doughnut can be used to clarify the expectations of you and your providers. A regular review using the 'Working and not working' tool can be helpful in maintaining the relationship and quality of the product or service both you and your provider are supplying.

Some organisations in other business sectors have worked hard at this aspect of the business. The close links between some high-volume car manufacturers and their suppliers might be a good example. There is obviously some scope for this in health and social care where common goals often exist.

Funders and commissioners

Again, in the social care world public authorities are the decision-makers in funding a service, or may influence a purchasing decision that may be made by the holder of a personal budget. They therefore have a direct interest in the quality of the service, and the value for money aspects of that. A person-centred organisation must of course look at the value for money aspects within the context of what is important to and for people it supports. Working together with funders and commissioners on the cost versus quality equation is therefore extremely important, rather than focusing entirely on the cost aspects. Again, sharing information about what is important to (and for) each party, the clarification of roles and responsibilities using the Doughnut, and regular review, either through the person-centred review process, or using the 4 Plus 1 questions tool, can all be value-adding activities in this area.

Working together with the local community

Community is important to person-centred organisations – both in supporting people to be part of and contribute to their neighbourhood, and in being connected and contributing as an organisation. The role of communities is even more significant in times of national economic constraint, because services contract and people seek opportunities for people to support each other in different ways.

This is where the concept of timebanking developed from, where people give and take according to their skills and opportunities. The critical aspect of this is that there is equality of value of the contributions. United Response has been working with people living in Newsome to develop a timebank that naturally includes some of the people United Response supports. This is how their involvement started:

> Instead of starting with problems and trying to fix them, we started with what we have and what's important to us, and we tried to build on that first. So we started with the idea that
>
> 'We don't know what we need if we don't know what we have.'
>
> Secondly, instead of seeing some people as the volunteers and others as needy, or some of us as delivering services to customers with nothing to offer of interest except money, we tried to share and develop the opportunities that we can create for all of us to contribute and benefit – by exploring the principle of giving and taking.[65]

David explains what this means to him:

> I am a member of Newsome timebanking. I live in my own flat in Newsome supported by United Response. This is my experience of timebanking.
>
> In August 2008 I helped Steven move home, I helped load the car which was supplied by another timebanker. This was my first experience of timebanking and it got me out and about meeting new people.
>
> In the summer of 2009 I lived in Halifax and was waiting to move to a flat in Huddersfield. I travelled over from Halifax to do timebanking as this was a good way to get to know people in Huddersfield.
>
> I cut an overgrown hedge for a lady called Catherine after she'd had an operation. This was the first time I'd ever cut a hedge and as you can see from my smile I enjoyed it. Catherine gave us coffee and biscuits. I think she enjoyed chatting to us as much as she appreciated our hard work. At first Catherine and I didn't know each other very well. I was a bit nervous at first but now I have done various timebanking jobs I have got to know her well and become friends.

In 2010 I also started to help at luncheon club. This occurs every two weeks on a Thursday. We prepare food, set up tables and wash up. I have learnt how to cook new dishes...and all about food hygiene, as you can see from my hat! I have met lots of new people here and they are very friendly.

In autumn I swept up the leaves at Newsome Church, hard work but good experience. This makes a difference at church. It looks good in the spring when the flowers come out.

I work at the allotments which are part of Growing Newsome. This encourages people to grow their own vegetables and promotes healthy eating. On the allotment I've helped build a greenhouse. I have done digging, planting, putting wood chippings down and got a lot of experience doing this. I enjoy watching things grow and eating them! Through my work at the allotments with Growing Newsome I attended the mayor's food festival at the town hall. I was quite chuffed as we won a community award for the mayor's local food initiative.

Timebanking has got me out and about meeting lots of people. I've been able to try lots of things and gain new experience. I am much more confident meeting new people. I have really enjoyed it and hope it will help me get a job in the future.

Another approach, again used in United Response, is to use part of the service premises or office accommodation as a community 'hub'. So, in Kent, part of the area office happens to be a shopfront on a high street, and lends itself well to providing a varied kind of drop-in centre for people from the local community both to access and contribute services and items of value to them. Both these ideas require some kind of pump-priming and facilitation, but can sustain themselves with minimum effort, once the idea takes hold in a community.

Corporate social responsibility

Many organisations now recognise that corporate social responsibility is an essential part of their efforts and expenditure. This is another way to describe making a community contribution. While obviously being the 'right thing to do', and aligning the organisation more with its stated values and mission, it is once again really just about doing good business. Identifying those aspects of products and services that can contribute to the wider good, and making them available to those who need them, bears a cost but also brings value and recognition of quality.

In United Response, such activities have included the production of guidance for people with disabilities to help with using banking services, and with exercising the right to vote. It has also brought the provision of learning and development in learning disabilities for trainee doctors and experienced nurses. In these examples, there were other parties too, who supported the activity because for them it represented the right thing to do, but also good business sense.

Conclusion

Person-centred organisations are all about people – and how they work together is vital. Primarily, it has to centre on the people supported, and expanding their sphere of decision making in their life as far as it can go. This has to include what people do, when, where, who supports them, how they are supported, and how they want their life to change in the future. These are the hallmark of successful individual service funds. 'Nothing about me, without me' extends to staff, and the range of ways that staff voices can be heard in an organisation – from meetings and one-to-ones to using 'Working and not working' with their managers in appraisals, and this information being used through Working Together for Change to inform business planning.

We see relationships and working together as broader than people, families and staff, and look at what this means for other stakeholders and the community. This reflects the modern world, where information flows rapidly and is wide ranging; where no individual or organisation can work in isolation; and indeed where everyone is expected to listen to the views and influence of stakeholders outside as well as inside the organisation. The level to which an organisation pursues working together demonstrates the true nature of person-centredness in that organisation. Person-centred organisations are community focused, and look for opportunities for contribution at individual, staff and organisational levels. Working together is about practice as well as culture, and in the next chapter we look more deeply at what a person-centred culture means.

Chapter 6

Creating a Person-Centred Culture

The changes that are sweeping through our corporate organisations allow people to be who they really are… Heart, feelings, truth, values, spirit, giving, and even love are no longer dirty words at work. People like that. In fact, they have been starving for it.

Jeanne M. Plas[66]

Introduction

To deliver personalisation requires a person-centred culture, where everyone is focused on ensuring that people who are supported have control over their life, and are living the way they choose. This is where you can see the shared values and beliefs we talked about in Chapter 2 in practice, day by day, everywhere. Culture is 'simply the way we do things around here' and, fundamentally, that has to be person-centred.[67] In a person-centred culture you see trust, empowerment and accountability. You hear a common language, and find person-centred practices used fluently and consistently throughout the organisation. A person-centred culture expects people to be who they really are, as Jeanne Plas says, and to bring 'their whole selves' to work to support people well. This is not a return to a staff-centric way of working, but a celebration of the talents, interests and relationships that staff have, and seeing these as opportunities to enhance the support they offer.

This chapter looks at the characteristics and manifestations of a person-centred culture, where person-centred practice is a day-to-day habit, embedded everywhere. In this chapter, we cover some of the critical areas to consider in building such a person-centred culture, and we will describe what we mean by a person-centred culture; the role of person-centred practices; how to assess your current culture, how to decide what you want to build on or change, and ways to make person-centred practices a habit.

What does culture mean in a person-centred organisation?

The defining characteristics of culture, for many authors, are values and behaviours. Others add more ethereal things such as symbols and unwritten rules, or the history of why things are done in a certain way. For example, Hofstede and Hofstede (2005) link culture with thinking in their definition of culture: 'Organizational culture: the collective programming of the mind which distinguishes the members of one organization from another.'[68]

The emphasis that Nehru makes on shared language in relation to culture eloquently describes why understanding what is important to staff and an organisation is key to understanding culture:

> In order to understand people, we have to understand their way of life and approach. If we wish to convince them, we have to use their language in the narrow sense of the mind. Something that goes even much further than that is not the appeal to logic and reason, but some kind of emotional awareness of the other people. (Jawaharlal Nehru, *Visit to America*)

At its most simple, culture is 'the way we do things around here'.[69] Culture defines the way that people behave and the habits they adopt in the way they go about their work. It is the way that an organisation sees the world, and differs across organisations in the same way that each of us as individuals see the world differently from our neighbours and colleagues.

Authors on culture such as Hofstede and Hofstede, Schein and others include areas such as values and beliefs, behaviours, assumptions, stories and myths, rituals and routines, symbols, artifacts and unwritten rules in their descriptions of the aspects of culture.[70, 71]

In the following table we give our interpretation of the meaning of some of these areas and look at what all this might mean within a person-centred culture.

Cultural aspect	What this means in a person-centred culture
Values – the driving force, and the element that many people will hold out for to the last	People supported are at the core of everything we do – enabling people to live their life the way they choose, with whatever support they want from us to do this. You can see this in the way that our services are designed around individuals, and how everyone works.
	Relationships are central – in how we support people, how we appreciate each other and how we work together. Staff and managers know what is expected of them, and are trusted and accountable to deliver this.
	Diversity is celebrated.
	We value creativity, seeking and creating opportunities, and enabling risks.
	We value partnership and working together, ensuring everyone has a voice in how we work.
	We value ongoing learning and development, never standing still, always improving what we do.

cont.

Cultural aspect	What this means in a person-centred culture
Beliefs – those things that create an emotional, but not necessarily rational, understanding of the world for most people	We see people positively, recognising their capacities and contributions, and paying attention to their dreams for the future.
	Everyone has the capacity to contribute – to others' lives and to the neighbourhood where they live.
	We believe we are better working and living together, and we celebrate diversity in our workplace and communities.
	People have positive intent in what they do – we trust people to do their best with no malice or wrongful motivation, aiming for win-win outcomes rather than win-lose.
Behaviours – the acceptable or unacceptable things that people do	Treat people with respect and dignity in all areas of their life.
	Demonstrate careful listening and acting on what has been heard (according to how the person communicates).
	Ensure that people are supported to make decisions and choices, with decision making as close to the person receiving the service as possible.
	Reflect what matters to people and how they want to be supported.
	Respect people's human rights.
	Demonstrate accountability – people do what they say they will do, when and where.
	Reflect on what is being learned and act on new learning.
	Providing just the right level of support – just enough, not too much or too little.
	Just enough paperwork – as little red tape as possible.
	Person-centred thinking tools and practices used as a habit at all levels of the organisation.

Assumptions – those things that we think that others will find acceptable or unacceptable, and on which we base our decisions and actions	People will understand what our values are because of what they see us doing.
	That people want to work in partnership with us. If we take a risk that is properly thought through, then we will be supported even if something goes wrong.
	We see each person we support as an individual and appreciate their gifts and qualities.
	People will seek to understand actions before criticising them.
	That help will be given if it is needed.
Stories and myths – the anecdotal evidence that supports our values and beliefs and explains why we think and act the way we do	Firsthand stories – told by the person themselves.
	Stories about the achievements, contributions and aspirations of the people we support.
	Stories of great support by staff in enabling people to be in control of their lives.
	Stories about support for taking thoughtful risks, trying new things and pushing boundaries.
	Stories of when we have tried something, and have learnt from it (even when it has not gone well).
	Stories about how people we support have been poorly treated or had poor quality of life in the past, and how unacceptable that is.
Rituals and routines – perhaps the ways in which we express our fear of not thinking and acting in line with our chosen culture	Being tenacious about engaging people we support in decisions about their life – day-to-day and in person-centred reviews.
	Working Together for Change as an annual or bi-annual routine to inform business planning.
	Routinely using 'Working and not working from different perspectives' to review and improve organisational processes.
Symbols – the overt signs to others of our values and beliefs	Posters and displays of people we support achieving and contributing.
	Information about how the organisation works – for example, the 'Way We Work' poster.
	Inspiring and uplifting quotes and pictures.
	Photos from celebrations.
	Disabled people employed by the organisation.

cont.

Cultural aspect	What this means in a person-centred culture
Unwritten rules – the things that you only know if you are part of the culture, and that make you feel that you belong, or don't belong	Respectful and enabling language. How people dress – casually, but recognising when some occasions require more formal clothes. We include people we support and other stakeholders as equal parties as a matter of course, and are open and honest with them in all our interactions.
Language – the facilitator of effective communication and inclusiveness	Respectful, inclusive and enabling language. People understand the terms used in person-centred practices and these are routinely used as part of the organisational language. Communication is by many methods, and is matched to the recipient.

The issue of language is particularly important within person-centred organisations. One of the instant ways to assess the person-centredness of an organisation is to listening to how the staff refer to people: 'Language is how we activate our values' (Mary Lou Bourne, quoted by Michael Smull).[72] Michael Smull suggests that we need to look at the language we use to see how it supports our values and helps us move toward our vision.

Among the values that are central to person-centredness is to have a culture of mutual respect where there is 'power with' and not 'power over'. We need to use language that supports the values. Mutual respect begins with how we refer to each other. Having 'power with' builds on the foundation of mutual respect and requires language that is inclusive, that refers to people as participants in a process rather than objects of a process. For example, this means talking about helping someone eat rather than feeding someone, and not using the term 'allow' because this suggests we have power over the person, and can decide whether they do something or not.

If we consider some of the aspects of a shared vision for a person-centred organisation, it is one where people:

- have positive control over the lives they have chosen for themselves

- are recognised and valued for their contributions (current and potential) to their communities

- are supported in a web of relationships, both natural and paid, within their communities.

Having positive control requires language that empowers people and reflects the expectation of asking, listening and acting on what we hear. Relationships that last begin with and are sustained by the contributions that we make to each other. How we think about each other is reflected in how we talk about each other, and act towards each other.

There is some language that we want to avoid:

- Language that makes people feel or be portrayed as different from us.
- Language that makes people the object of what we do rather than a participant in it.
- Language that diminishes people or their contributions.

When we teach and demonstrate the person-centred thinking tools, the language we use either reinforces what we are trying to convey or undermines the message. It is hard to overstate the importance of language. How we use language matters, and it matters as much as how we use the tools that we teach.

At the same time, expecting people always to talk in ways that they see as 'politically correct' creates resistance and doesn't change how people think. We want to encourage and deepen understanding, and to be careful in walking the thin line between encouragement and coercion. We also need to keep in mind that people who use language that conflicts with our own values or vision can still be deeply committed to the people they support, while coming from a different background, culture or training. We also need to monitor our own language, and ask others to challenge or remind us when we make the inevitable mistake; and then we must respond without defensiveness, and keep on trying to get it right.

With the nine aspects of culture, the question is, of course, the following: Is the culture of your organisation as stated in your mission, vision and values, or does it depart from that in different ways that you may not be aware of? What are the 'unwritten rules' (if any) about the culture of your organisation?

It goes without saying that culture has a direct influence on the outcomes any organisation achieves and how successful it is. That's why everybody blames culture for the problems of an organisation, and there is much talk about 'changing the culture' to overcome those problems. Typically a non-person-centred culture could be perceived as professionally driven, or with a structure that is consultant driven, or hierarchical (such as some aspects of public sector operations, perhaps); or focused on profit and lacking in social responsibility (such as some private and commercial organisations); or there to serve staff, with decision making by staff, avoiding risk or having a blame culture that does not support creativity or initiative (such as some social care organisations).

Many organisations look at these problems internally, and try to change things, particularly when going through mergers and acquisitions, or other times of change. Many use financial difficulty as a lever to bring about cultural change, and see re-organisations as a way to do this. In the next sections we look at how to assess your organisation's current culture, and how to build on and develop what you learn from this assessment. Person-centred practices are important as ways of both assessing and changing the culture of an organisation.

Here is a summary of the person-centred practices that can be useful.

Person-centred practices	How each practice can contribute to assessing your current culture and creating a more person-centred culture
'Working/ not working from different perspectives'	Using this person-centred thinking tool to gain a range of perspectives is a powerful way of exposing real feelings about the nature of an organisation, and also the assumptions we may have about how others view us and what we do. In the social care context, this would mean carrying out this exercise with, or at least from the perspective of, people we support, their families and other circles of support, staff members delivering the support, managers and technical staff supporting that delivery, and also, potentially, external bodies such as funders and regulatory authorities.
Working Together for Change	'What is working and not working' tells you a lot about the culture of the organisation. Working Together for Change also includes 'what people want in the future'. You can use this information to think about the culture you will need in the future to deliver what people want.
Praise and Trouble	People need to be and feel appreciated, and how much they feel appreciated will give important information about culture – for example, whether there is a strong blame culture. Ideally the balance between appreciation and criticism is 5:1.
The Doughnut	People need to be absolutely clear what is expected of them, so that they can be accountable in their work and know where they can be creative and experiment.
Meetings – how positive and productive are they?	Meetings are a microcosm of the culture of an organisation. How meetings are run, what is discussed and how decisions are made will tell you a lot about the culture of the organisation. Are they positive and productive with everyone contributing and sharing responsibility for meetings going well? Are the decisions made at meetings shared and do the actions happen and make a difference to the organisation? Is information about what is going well shared at meetings?
Person-centred one-to-ones/ supervision	These can be used to reinforce the vision and values of the organisation; to check understanding of person-centred practices, and to demonstrate them; to carry out practice leadership and feedback on observations of good and poor practice; and to identify any needs that staff may have – what is important to and for them, as well as the people supported.
'Important to/ for'	A detailed knowledge of what is important to and for people supported, staff and other stakeholders can ensure that the culture continues to align with the needs and desires of all those engaged with the organisation, and so maintain that engagement.
4 Plus 1 questions	Provides useful monitoring and review knowledge about the progress and alignment of culture that informs the decision making and action planning process.

What you will see in the culture of a person-centred organisation, therefore, is an almost obsessive focus on the person being supported, and delivering the very best support, exactly the way the person wants it, with the person in control. The organisation will be characterised by relationships built on trust and partnership; accountability and appreciation; and everyone is driven to keep learning, developing and improving. Given that, how are you doing?

Where are you now? How do you assess your culture?

This is often described as assessing the 'as is', or the 'current reality'. However you describe it, there is some value in putting some kind of quasi-objective measure on where you are. The following table gives some more detailed examples of excellence in operating in a person-centred culture.

Aspect of culture	What this means in a person-centred organisation	Rating (1–5)
Values	There is an agreed way of working that reflects values.	
	It is easy to see that the values of the organisation are lived out in all that we do – for example, managers demonstrate enabling people supported to have as much choice and control as possible in their lives; staff work in a consistently person-centred way, proactively and competently using person-centred thinking tools in all areas of the work.	
	Staff know and demonstrate the importance of relationships – with the person they support and with each other in the team.	
Beliefs	We have a strong culture where we appreciate each others' gifts and strengths and use that in our work wherever we can.	
Behaviours	Person-centred thinking tools and practices used as a habit at all levels of the organisation.	
	Decisions are made as close to the person supported as possible.	
Assumptions	We see talents and capability in all those we work with and support.	
	People rightly assume that they will be supported to take thoughtful risks.	
Stories and myths	Widespread storytelling fuels the process of knowledge sharing with all the stakeholders in the organisation.	
	We can explain our actions and progress through stories of our successes.	
Rituals and routines	Reflection and review of what we do is habitual across the organisation.	
	People we support and their families are always listened to before we take decisions that may affect them.	

cont.

Aspect of culture	What this means in a person-centred organisation	Rating (1–5)
Symbols	Our visual communications convey the importance to us of the people we support. Contribution is recognised by a range of visible celebrations and signals.	
Unwritten rules	Everyone has a strong sense of what is good and bad practice. There are no barriers to feedback on poor practice, regardless of status or hierarchy.	
Language	Our language and written communication is respectful – for example, we don't abbreviate people we support to 'PWS'. We use 'people first' language. The effectiveness of our communications, knowledge sharing and activities is facilitated by a shared understanding of the common language person-centred practices.	

You can use this self-assessment combined with person-centred thinking tools to learn about your culture. You could use 'Working and not working from different perspectives' either generally or around each of the aspects of culture, or 'Praise and Trouble' (see example in this section and the exercises in the Appendix to this chapter).

You could also look at assessing the current culture and deciding on the future desired culture by looking at more tangible characteristics – perhaps those that you would describe as things you can touch and see around the organisation. Here are some questions that could help you to think about some of the important characteristics of culture in a person-centred organisation:

- What information do the visible symbols of your organisation convey?

- What do your organisation design, business processes and structure focus on – the people supported, or something else? Are they simple to understand or complicated?

- What is driving the organisation and where is it going next in terms of strategy?

- Is the language or jargon of the organisation inclusive or exclusive? Simple or complex?

- How do people know they are doing a good job? How is success celebrated and praised?

- How willing is the organisation and its people to do things differently?

- How highly does excellent support to people supported rank in people's priorities?

- What do managers spend most of their time doing? Is it ensuring outcomes for people, or doing administration tasks?

- What are the mechanisms in place for staff to get feedback on how they are doing, and to raise problems with their boss?
- What opportunities do people get to learn? How much is invested in learning and development?
- Is there a set of standards for quality management? Do they involve people you support and other stakeholders?
- How do you approach risk, and what does this tell you about your culture?

One of the key issues that demonstrate a person-centred culture is the attitude towards risk. Is it enabling and encouraging, or are risks to be avoided at all costs? At the end of this chapter we share how United Response wanted to change their culture around risk, and we devote a chapter to risk – Chapter 10 – because it is so important in relation to the amount of choice and control people have in their lives.

Thinking about what is important to people about each of the aspects of culture described earlier can help inform your analysis of the culture in your organisation. So the questions for people could be: 'What do you think are the key things around here that people seem to value, and which motivate them to work here?' You could also use 'Working and not working' around the earlier list of the more tangible indications of culture – for example, what is working and not working from a managers' perspective about how they spend their time?

Here are some examples of what the tangible aspects of culture can tell you:

- What would you think of a charity for disabled people that had no disabled access to its offices?
- If you visit a disabled person being supported in their own home, and you are told that one room is the staff area, what message does that convey about what is important around there?

There are also less tangible aspects of culture – perhaps those that might be implied in things that you hear or feel, or you intuitively know are there. Here the context questions might be:

- How do people talk to each other, work together and respect each other?
- Are there 'unwritten rules' about the ways certain things *must* be done, but which are not necessarily logical or related to the objectives of the organisation or the people supported?
- How far do people go to help each other?
- Do people know what they need to know about the organisation and its values and aims to do their job and be ambassadors for the organisation?
- Disagreement – how frequent is there conflict of views and how is this resolved?
- Will people stick with the values of the organisation if difficulties arise?
- Do people talk freely about how they value and enjoy their work?

- Can staff take decisions and act if they need to?

- Are there diverse people and views, and are they heard and accepted?

'Praise and Trouble' is an exercise developed by Michael Smull that clearly identifies the culture of an organisation based on what people get praised for, and what they get into trouble for.

Using 'Praise and Trouble' to assess culture

A consultant was asked to do a review of an NHS community team. One of the aspects of the service that she wanted to learn about was the culture of the team. She asked for a meeting with the 12 team members (without the manager present), and asked them to think about the last month, with two questions in mind.

The first question was: 'What have you got praise for over the last month?' She defined 'praise' as anything that their manager had said or done that had given them the impression that she would like them to do more of this.

The second question was: 'What have you got into trouble for over the last month?' She defined 'trouble' as anything that the manager had done or said that had given them the impression that she was displeased, or wanted them not to do or to do less of that.

Everyone had a sheet of paper split into two, with 'praise' on the left side and 'trouble' on the right. The team wrote down their answers.

The consultant wanted to learn three things:

1. How much feedback were people getting?

2. What was the proportion of positive to negative?

3. What were they getting feedback on, and was this consistent with the mission of the organisation and the purpose of the team?

The consultant learnt that a few team members were getting very little feedback. Three people could only list two or three things on their sheets. When the consultant gently probed about this, it turned out that they rarely saw their manager from week to week. Other people, who happened to be based in the same office as their manager, all had six to eight items on their list.

Everyone had more negatives than positives, by a 2:1 ratio. In a truly person-centred culture you are looking for a ratio of 5 positives for every 1 negative. Finally, when the consultant asked people what they were praised for, the answer was overwhelmingly based on accuracy with paperwork and delivering it on time. The manager was rewarding great paperwork, not staff being person-centred with people the organisation supported, or enabling people to make changes in their lives.

For more information on exercises to assess the culture of your organisation, see Exercises 1 and 2 at the end of this chapter.

Creating a person-centred culture

So, where do you start in making culture change? Again, there are many offerings in the market place on how to define your future culture. In essence, most contain the following steps:

- Identify all the key people and types of service or offerings that are important to or for your business.

- Decide how you want to position yourself in relation to these – what relationship do you want to have with them?

- Decide on the cultural characteristics that you need to have in these relationships, and to deliver your mission, vision and values.

Following this initial assessment of what you want to change, it can be helpful to describe this in relation to where you are now, and where you want to be. One way to do this is to create a summary table to describe where you are now (call this 'From') and where you want to be (call this 'To'). You can see examples of this 'From – To' table in Chapters 1 and 10. From this you can establish a gap analysis of the scale of the difference between where you are and where you want to be. This can be a good starting point for further detailed discussions and use of the exercises in the Appendix to this chapter.

Exercises 1, 2 and 3 explain the use of the Praise and Trouble, 'Important to and for', 'Working and not working', 4 Plus 1 questions and matching person-centred thinking tools to explore these areas more fully.

Here are three ways that you could start to move towards a more person-centred culture. The first is around the behaviours you would expect to see in a person-centred organisation and managers making person-centred thinking a habit within their teams; the second is around signs that communicate the culture; and the third is about culture change via a planned programme of change.

Making person-centred thinking a habit

To really make a difference to people's lives – and to ensure they have more choice and control – staff supporting or providing services to them need to participate in an ongoing loop of listening, learning and action. This can be done through habitually using person-centred thinking tools. These are the foundations of change and they can help staff to learn what matters to individuals; what good support and service provision looks like; and how individuals communicate their choices and make decisions. By using person-centred thinking, staff can think about their role in individuals' lives and how they can bring about action. They can analyse what life is like now for the people concerned, what is working and now working for them, and what needs to change. Then staff can continue to learn about what is important to and for each individual and how to balance the two.

In this section we offer seven different ways to build good habits that can help achieve the outcomes or changes that people want to see in their lives.

Let's start by thinking about your own life and experiences. Many of us have tried to create new habits such as eating healthily, exercising more and daily meditation; or to change old habits such as stopping smoking or drinking less. We are more likely to succeed in changing habits in the following circumstances.

1. You know your starting point, so that you can see future progress
This equates to establishing the 'as is' situation mentioned previously. If you joined a weight loss group, one of the first things that would happen is that you would be weighed to know where you are starting from.

2. You have a plan
If you wanted to stop smoking, you would think about how to avoid situations where you were more likely to want to smoke, and how many cigarettes you wanted to cut back on within the next month. Writing your plan down is also a good discipline.

3. You make a public commitment
If you are changing your eating habits to become a vegetarian, then telling people that this is what you are doing is an important way to embed the change. Weight loss groups have been shown to be more effective than people trying to lose weight individually. This is because of the support available, and also because people are making a public commitment by demonstrating by attending the class that they want to lose weight.

4. You have ways to remind yourself of what you want to change
One approach used in neuro-linguistic programming (NLP) is to have a stone or marble in your pocket. Every time you put your hand in your pocket and touch the stone, you remember what you are trying to change. A more direct approach for people who want to lose weight is for them to have a picture of themselves at the size they want to be and to put this in a prominent place such as on the fridge.

5. You are supported by an individual or group
You are more likely to be successful if you are getting support, either from a buddy or a group, such as quit smoking or weight loss groups.

6. You record and report back on progress
The other side of making a commitment, and telling people about it, is letting them know how you are getting on. At the very least it is important to review and 'report back' to yourself, if nobody else.

7. There is recognition or rewards for improvements and success
It is encouraging to see how you are making progress in your new habit or changing an old one. This might be watching your weight decrease on a chart or a jar fill up with the money otherwise spent on cigarettes. Positive reinforcement of your efforts is very effective. How many tennis players do we see using a clenched fist signal to reinforce a great shot?

Name	What person-centred thinking tools have you tried?									
	important to/for	doughnut	matching staff	relationship circle	comm. chart	working/ not working	learning log	4+1 questions	dreaming	positive and productive meetings

Scale

1 not using

2 just started still learning how and when

3 have learned how

4 competent & confident but need to remind myself to use it

5 habit

Figure 6.1 What person-centred tools have you tried?

We have taken these seven ways to create or change a habit and applied them to making person-centred thinking a habit. It is important to keep in mind that success here is not tools being used as a habit, but people having the lives that make sense to them. Using person-centred thinking as 'business as usual' is one way to make this more likely. For each of the seven ways, a resource is suggested, which are available as free downloads (http://www.helensandersonassociates.co.uk/reading-room/how/person-centred-thinking/habits-for-highly-effective-staff.aspx).

Resources and tools

1. You know your starting point so that you can see progress
The Learning Community for Person-Centred Practices developed a way of rating your current competence in using person-centred thinking tools. Figure 6.1 is an adapted version of this rating scale. There are other versions that also look at what opportunities you may have to use a particular tool. This rating scale can be used for individual self-reflection or as part of one-to-ones or team meetings.

2. You have a plan
Being able to rate your existing level of competence can help you think about areas that you want to improve, or tools that you want to try. This can be captured in a simple action planning format. If you can also establish targets or milestones along the way, then your plan will become more achievable. Progress against plans can be measured very well using the 4 Plus 1 questions tool.

In one organisation implementing person-centred thinking, all members of staff and managers used an action planning template that stated what they wanted to try to improve and what support they needed. Both the staff members and their managers then signed them.

You could also look at whole-team actions or even whole-organisation actions to focus on or improve competence in a particular tool. Some teams have a 'person-centred thinking tool of the week' or month (see Figure 6.2), which they display on notice boards and make an agenda item in team meetings and individual supervision sessions. When this is done across a locality or organisation, you can have email reminders and even text reminders of that week's or month's person-centred thinking tool.

3. You make a public commitment
You can make a personal, private plan to use a particular person-centred thinking tool or develop your skill in using it, or you can go public (see the example in Figure 6.3). For most people, going public increases the likelihood that it will happen.

At an individual level, commitments to use a particular tool could be shared at 'a round' in a team meeting. If recorded in the minutes, it could then be a standing agenda item where people feed back their progress. At a team level, a postcard of the tool that the whole team is focusing on could go on the team notice board, in the newsletter or pasted into electronic diaries. At a leadership level, senior people modelling the right values and behaviours is important in this respect.

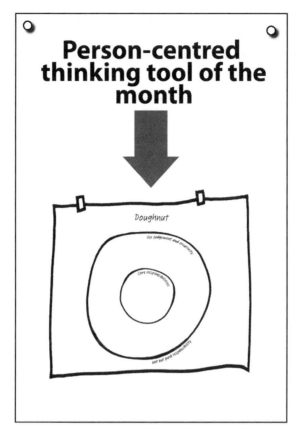

Figure 6.2 Person-centred tool of the month

4. You have ways to remind yourself of what you want to change

There are several ways that you can have both discreet and more public reminders to use person-centred thinking tools. One possibility is to use stickers in diaries, notebooks or on desks (see Figures 6.4a and b). You can have these for forward planning or retrospective reflection.

We are used to seeing inspirational posters and postcards in offices. Another possibility is to have postcards and posters or even cartoons that reflect the person-centred thinking tools. These can be used in many ways, for example:

- on notice boards
- to show the 'person-centred thinking tool of the month'
- in team meetings – people can choose a card and share a success they have had using that particular person-centred thinking tool.

Many people have found the person-centred thinking minibook a useful reminder and quick reference to help them use the tools on a day-to-day basis.[73] A variation of this and building on NLP techniques is to use a picture book of your desired outcomes and goals, which you read at regular times each day.

Action plan

The priority person-centred thinking tools for me to develop my skills are

1   Why?

2   Why?

3   Why?

What opportunities could I have to use them?

What support will I need to use them?

How can I get/ask for this support?

My next steps are

1   Target date

2   Target date

3   Target date

How will I know I have been successful?

Figure 6.3 Action plan

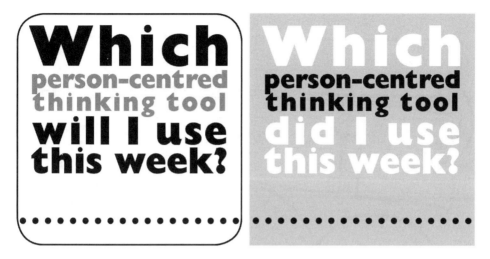

Figure 6.4a Person-centred thinking tool reminder   Figure 6.4b Person-centred thinking tool reminder

5. You are supported by an individual or group

Getting support is crucial in building good habits and making changes. This could be your manager, a peer who is at the same level of learning and trying as you are, or a more experienced staff member who acts as a coach. You could book regular 'check-ins' with the person or agree to call each other if either of you are stuck.

Change may be even more likely if your whole team is working on this together. Here are some ideas of how to integrate person-centred thinking in team meetings:

- Use the person-centred thinking postcards (each has a different tool on it). Put them face up on the table or floor or 'deal' them out. Ask everyone in turn to talk about a situation last week when they could have used that person-centred thinking tool or tell a story of when they did.

- Use opening rounds where people are asked to share something that is going well specifically in how they are using person-centred thinking.

- Practise crafting and sharing stories about using person-centred thinking and practise for an event or celebration when the team can share.

- Use the 'Achievement exercise' (developed by Max Neill; see Figure 6.5) focused on person-centred thinking in pairs and then share with the whole group.

6. You record and report back on progress

Recording progress is both encouraging (when you are doing well) and a learning opportunity (when you are not doing as well as you had hoped).

There are different ways to record progress and reflect. Some people find a person-centred thinking journal useful. Several organisations are using person-centred thinking portfolios when people have blank copies of templates and ways to record their progress, achievements and learning. In United Response, for example, all members of

Figure 6.5 Achievement exercise

staff are provided with a learning and development portfolio to record their progress. Of course, there are person-centred thinking tools that are designed for reflecting on progress and you could use 'Working and not working' and 4 Plus 1 questions, and adapt the 'learning log' for this purpose. You can use a small pad of tear-off pages – one a week – to record seven days' worth of effort in using person-centred thinking. This is called a person-centred thinking habits chart (see Figure 6.6).

Person-centred Thinking Habits Chart

Person-centred thinking tool	M	T	W	T	F	S	S	Notes

Figure 6.6 Person-centred thinking habits chart

7. There is recognition or rewards for improvements and success

One possibility is to look at the existing recognition and reward schemes that already exist within the organisation and see if these can be adapted to focus directly on skill and persistence in using person-centred thinking. For example:

- Have certificates of competence for each person-centred thinking tool – given when someone has produced three 'best practice' examples of a tool (for instance, three Doughnuts for different people or situations, with a filled-in template and 'story' that explains why it was used and the difference made). The anonymised examples and stories can then be shared in training or on the intranet.

- A local person-centred thinking 'awards ceremony' or celebration every six months where people can share their successes in using person-centred thinking with people to change their lives.

- In United Response, taking part in a learning and reflection day is a very public recognition of the contribution that people are making to the ongoing planning and strategy of the organisation.

These seven approaches are examples of ways that managers can embed person-centred thinking tools within their day-to-day work and support staff in using them to create a person-centred culture. Here is how Dimensions is supporting its managers to embed person-centred thinking and practices as a habit within the organisation.

> The senior managers in Dimensions are committed to all staff using person-centred thinking as a habit in the organisation as the foundation for delivering personalisation through individual service funds. They had learned how difficult it was to implement individual service funds without staff being fluent in person-centred thinking tools, and for managers to be consistently using Positive and Productive Meetings and person-centred supervision.[74] Managers are absolutely key to the culture and practices in an organisation, so Dimensions decided to invest in their first-line managers, so that they were both competent and confident in using person-centred thinking tools, and were able to support and coach their team to use them.
>
> The first thing Dimensions did was to find out what the current reality was, and they used Progress for Providers for Managers (Appendix 2) with all their managers, to establish the baseline of competence in person-centred thinking tools and practices. Where there were already examples of good practice (people scoring 4's and 5's) the senior managers worked with managers to write up these examples to share through the intranet and to use in training. They recorded the results on a spreadsheet that clearly demonstrated areas for development, and they used this information to design a learning programme for managers. In addition to the learning programme, they worked with their performance coaches so that managers had a local 'expert' in person-centred thinking (skilled to an accredited trainer level) to support them in implementing what they had learnt. The programme started with all managers participating in the two-day person-centred thinking training, and then doing further training in how to make person-centred thinking a habit within their team. This training introduced the seven approaches described earlier as a menu for managers to choose from. They also received training and support in using Positive and Productive Meetings, and person-centred supervision, and how to use person-centred thinking tools in meetings and supervision sessions. Managers are expected to be able to demonstrate their own competence in using person-centred thinking tools in their role as managers, and to develop person-centred teams, as well as being able to coach and support their staff in habitually using person-centred thinking tools. Dimensions is introducing an online testing process to enable managers and staff to check their competence in using person-centred practices, and is providing e-learning as well as coaching to help people develop their practices to make person-centred thinking a habit in the organisation.

Signs that communicate a person-centred culture

A second way to influence culture is through the signs around the organisation that communicate the current culture. In United Response, the values, expected behaviours

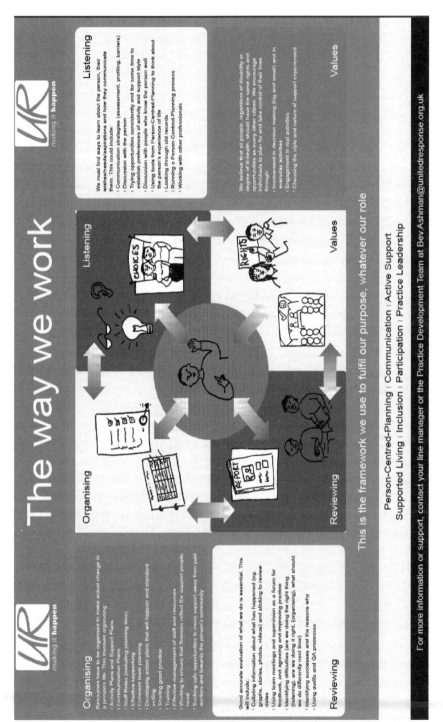

Figure 6.7 The Way We Work

and how person-centred thinking tools can deliver these values are powerfully communicated through following the Way We Work diagram (Figure 6.7).

On one page, this diagram encapsulates an image of the culture of the organisation. In the quadrant concerned with listening, you will see an articulation of how the people in the organisation are expected to relate to others. Staff are expected to find out and understand in detail what is 'important to' and 'important for' people they support when planning support (organising).

The main features of the success of this approach are:

- *Clarity* – the framework has four specific areas, prominently displayed, with the subtext giving examples.

- *Direction* – the title of the framework presents this way of working as the default option for United Response.

- *Accessibility* – the central part can be used with people supported, so that they can understand and get involved in the process.

- *Permission* – this is not a manual. It prescribes *what* needs to be done, and the person-centred practices that can help, but it does not prescribe *how these are used*, leaving individuals and teams free to explore their own ways of achieving organisational expectations and, more importantly, those of the people supported.

- *Brand* – the picture became one of the most recognisable features of United Response's work to internal staff, and was also used effectively with external agencies. It is still a prominent internal symbol.

Initially the framework was sent out as a paper document, but this did not have sufficient impact. So, a Way We Work poster was developed as part of a strong re-launch with a clear and directive message about its application. This was much more successful.

Real Life Options use their one-page profiles as a way to demonstrate developing a person-centred culture. If you visit the offices of Real Life Options, you will see a printed folder on the table at reception that introduces all the head office staff through their one-page profiles. Upstairs, where the offices are, the directors' one-page profiles are framed on the walls.

Making person-centred practices a habit in an organisation, and paying attention to signs that communicate a person-centred culture, are two ways to move forward. Next we share a programme to manage cultural change in a organisation, demonstrating how United Response approached this.

A planned programme to change the culture

Chapter 12 of this book discusses the approaches and person-centred practices for managing change in more detail. Here we consider some of the principles relating to culture change.

Again, much of the thinking around culture change in the past has been about creating mass dissatisfaction and radical adjustment to culture, often through the charismatic leadership of a powerful leader or leadership team.

The premise we put forward here is that this previous wisdom *can* be successful, but if it is solely based on that drive then it often doesn't work, and if it is successful it can be short term. This is borne out by most major studies of the success of change management projects.

Culture change that sticks, we believe, has some critical characteristics:

- Strong sponsorship and personal belief by the leader or leaders of an organisation are very important. The power and influence of leaders on how others in an organisation behave is well observed and documented in many authoritative leadership books and articles. The 'shadow of the leader' has real meaning in determining what other staff believe to be the reality of a culture. Leaders are observed by their staff all the time. Why? Because they are looking for congruence between what the leader says and does, and that gives them the confidence to follow the expressed values of the leaders and the organisation.

- Michael Smull describes 'optimistic discontent' as powerful in change. Again it is well documented that in order for people to do something differently there must be a sense of at least discomfort, if not dissatisfaction, with their current reality. Michael cleverly couples this with the other prime driver of desire to change – that of the powerful feeling or vision that there has to be a better way. So the gradual spread and building of both aspects into a body of opinion works better.

- Adjustments to behaviour that are pulled through an organisation from the bottom up are more effective than top down-driven re-alignment of roles and responsibilities. This aligns very much with the more recent approaches to change in using learning and development to promote new ways of working through an organisation. Understanding what is important to and for people supported is fundamental. So is a strong belief that the best people to understand this are those who directly support individuals. When the people providing direct support have the freedom to act on what is working and not working for people, supported by their managers, this is a powerful way to create change. There is not usually enough energy in management and leadership alone to make all that happen. We talk more about this in Chapter 12.

Developing a person-centred culture in United Response

In 2005 the directors were concerned that some people in the organisation, including some high-performing people, perceived there to be a 'big message' from the organisation and its leadership about being cautious, and a negative message around risk (in other words – don't take any risks). This bore little or no relation to what the directors' team really aspired to, so it was important to begin to change this aspect of the culture.

A staff consultation exercise carried out later in the year confirmed that, despite much complimentary feedback about the organisation's culture, there was a concern that the organisation was over-focused on the potential negative consequences of risk taking. The approach to risk is in our view a critical area in determining the culture of an organisation, and it is one of the prime drivers of how people behave within a culture.

The directors decided that building on the Way We Work framework was imperative, but that in itself this was insufficient to generate a climate in which permission, risk taking and supporting judgement would become the organisational norm and a characteristic of its culture. They agreed an ambitious programme of change, based on introducing person-centred thinking tools and practices, to create a person-centred culture that would support risk taking and enable people to have more control in their lives.

All divisional directors showed an interest in piloting the programme in their division, but one, Nick Rogers, showed particular enthusiasm for piloting the programme in the North West. His division was selected on the basis of this enthusiasm and Nick's skill in leading and developing the work would prove to be pivotal to the success of the pilot.

Bob Tindall met with Helen Sanderson and Michael Smull and together they explored a 'breadth' and 'depth' approach. This kind of culture change had not been tried before in United Response and it inevitably created some issues that needed to be considered particularly carefully. Essentially these were that, if learning was spread too thinly, it would not penetrate into the division, and, if the learning was focused too heavily on particular services, there would not be the impact in terms of making a real change across the division. Both these dangers created potential problems for organisational learning, in addition to those for the division itself.

Nick Rogers, the lead director on the work in the North West division, summarises his view of the challenges and progress as follows.

> The initial response to the idea of using person-centred practices was concern over how we would find the time to do this – to make the changes in thinking and practice that the process implied. The next response was a feeling from many people that, given the amount of time that seemed to be needed, were we not already person-centred? After all, we said we were person-centred all the time.
>
> The time we spent on an initial two-day person-centred thinking training with Michael Smull, followed by leadership sessions with Helen Sanderson and Julie Bray, helped us realise that we could be better than we were and that the time had to be found. This time with Michael and Helen helped us see two things:
>
> 1. That there was much more we could do to ensure that person-centredness was thoroughly embedded across the division.
> 2. That the tasks necessary to achieve this were what we already did anyway. The change was in how we approached them – it was about doing differently not doing more.

Central to the approach was the idea of breadth and depth.

The breadth was working across the division to ensure the message and the change were going forward everywhere. We skilled everyone up to deliver the changes by training people in using person-centred thinking tools. Depth was in having the front-line managers as coaches who would deliver in-depth support and lead by example in using person-centred practices. The depth programme was developed in the leadership team, to look at what needed to change in terms of local practices, policies or procedures to embed person-centred practice and change the approach people had to risk. The leadership team met each month, and with the support of HSA they reviewed their project plan, the breadth of coverage across the division and listened to feedback from the coaches about what was working and what was blocking implementation or person-centred practices that the leadership team needed to address and change within the division. The leadership team was coached to use Positive and Productive Meetings, and storytelling to communicate changes. Coaches were given additional help in developing the depth of their knowledge and skills in using person-centred practices and how they could help staff 'make person-centred thinking a habit'.

Initially we had tried to make the leadership team too large in order to achieve the breadth we were seeking. After about nine months we slimmed the team down. We increased the number of coaches so that all managers were expected to now be coaches. Every six months we had a review, a learning and reflection day to capture learning and stories; identify and address challenges; and update the project plan to reflect this. As the work moved from the North West to national, we decided to move to local leadership teams and end the divisional one, so bringing the focus closer to the people we support and front-line staff.

As Nick started to lead his division in this change, one of the priorities was to make a visible show of support (sponsorship) for the programme and to emphasise its connection with active support. Bob Tindall, the Managing Director, took part in the initial two-day person-centred thinking training (attended by a hundred people), and had a ten-minute slot in it to emphasise the sponsorship of the leadership of the organisation for this activity. The risk in this was that, by doing so, Bob was committing the organisation to corporate implementation of the change programme, by creating a sense of expectation in other divisions for the same support in person-centred practices, which would, at a later date, have to be satisfied in terms of additional resources to implement the programme. This did, however, very much strengthen the vision and sponsorship for the change. People could see that the work was happening in depth in the North West, but that they were expected to start to use person-centred thinking tools across the organisation. Bob also demonstrated his active sponsorship by using the person-centred thinking tools in his role, and attending the six-monthly learning and reflection days in the North West region.

To strengthen the communication around the change across United Response, the Way We Work poster was redesigned to include some of the new person-centred thinking tools. The poster kept the same format in order to drive home the point – loudly and clearly – that the change programme was building on things already achieved, rather than 'the latest initiative'. This was a theme that continued to be emphasised throughout the early stages of the change process, and also at the point when it was decided to roll it out to the rest of the organisation.

One of Nick's biggest achievements was persuading people that the time that needed to be carved out for the programme was achievable within existing workloads. It was also organised very well. The initial person-centred thinking training, as indicated previously, involved getting over 100 people together – the biggest event held in the organisation for a number of years. As implementation developed and positive changes began to happen, the programme began to gather momentum, and North West division's six-monthly learning and reflection days were important opportunities for learning and celebration that then influenced how the change was rolled out nationally.

The culture definitely changed, and stories and examples (some of which are shared in this book) illustrated the changes for individuals and for staff. The attitude to risk was noticeably different, and people could share stories that illustrated this (we cover this in more depth in Chapter 10). In addition, United Response won the National Training Award for changes to both individual and staff lives. Among tangible results, the North West division saw a distinct improvement in staff turnover when benchmarked against other areas not using person-centred practices yet. Turnover is a critical measure for people supported, because it is known (from asking them) that consistency in staff who support them is one of the most important satisfaction factors for them. From a financial perspective, it is also known (from correlating the statistics) that turnover is the key driver of high cost for temporary agency staff (much more so than, for example, the impact of sickness absence). Consequently, the North West division had an improving performance in this area too and consistently achieved lower levels than other divisions.

The key elements from United Response's story about creating a more person-centred culture are:

- Understanding the change that the organisation wanted to make – building a culture that enabled risk-taking so that people could have more choices, greater control and a better life.

- Being able to see this in the context of the mission and values of the organisation – absolute clarity on what its 'higher purpose' of the organisation is: nothing is superior to doing the right thing for the people supported.

- Public expression of the way things are done, the culture and what that means in practice on a day-to-day basis – the Way We Work poster.

- Active leadership commitment, shown by modelling and reinforcing the practices that the directors wanted to see – for example, by using Positive and Productive Meetings, using the person-centred thinking tools in learning and reflection days, sharing stories about risk, and using the person-centred thinking tools and in their leadership role.

- Giving all managers the skills and in-depth knowledge to lead, demonstrate and coach others in the change – for example, by the investment of managers as coaches and supporting them to be able to 'make person-centred thinking a habit' in their teams.

- Identifying what is getting in the way, through the coaches sharing this with the leadership team, and acting on it to make changes.

- Clear sponsorship from the top of the charity – for example, Bob Tindall attending the North West learning and reflection days, and using the person-centred thinking skills himself.

Summary of tools and techniques

The following table summarises areas to consider when thinking about culture, and potential tools and techniques – both conventional approaches and person-centred practices that can be used to help analyse and understand these.

The Appendices give more detail as to how the person-centred thinking tools can be used to address specific issues. This book does not explain in detail how the more conventional tools can be used, but this is readily available elsewhere, or can be obtained from the authors if needed.

What do we want to do?	What would be a conventional way of addressing this?	What person-centred tools can I use for this?	Exercise number
Uncovering the covert aspects of culture	Figuring out unwritten rules 'As is' diagnostics – interviews, questionnaires, etc.	Praise and Trouble Working/not working	1
Find out what the current culture is like	Diagnostic tools assessing cultural dimensions Focus groups Diagnostic interviews	Working/not working 4 Plus 1 questions Praise and Trouble	2
Find out which areas of our culture we want to change or improve	Diagnostic tools assessing cultural dimensions that measure the strengths and weaknesses of defined dimensions of culture From/to tool Culture mapping	Working/not working Praise and Trouble Matching tool	1, 2
Visioning the future culture	Establishing core values, competencies, value propositions and competitive advantages	Doughnut Important to/for One-page team profile One-page strategy	3

cont.

What do we want to do?	What would be a conventional way of addressing this?	What person-centred tools can I use for this?	Exercise number
Encourage culture change	Encouraging dissatisfaction Communicating a new vision/mission	Working/not working Important to/for Success poster	4
Plan implementation of culture changes	Culture surveys Culture mapping	Important to/for 4 Plus 1 questions	5
Maintain cultural change	Culture surveys Leadership strengths and weakness analysis	Working/not working 4 Plus 1 questions	6

Conclusion

Culture takes us back to vision and values. The culture of an organisation is really what its values look like on an hour-by-hour basis. Knowing what your culture is like now (as is), and what you want it to look like, is the start of cultural change. The culture around risk is key – the degree to which people are comfortable and encouraged to take thoughtful risks will tell you a lot about your culture. Don't accept person-centred paperwork as evidence of embedding person-centred practices and changing culture – it is staff behaviour and relationships that are the most important. Having one-page profiles for people and staff are a good start, but it is how they are used that is crucial. One senior manager said: 'Staff have a one-page profile, but they are not sure why they have one or what to do with it next.'

To avoid the nightmare of creating good paperwork in an organisation but little change, we must keep coming back to purpose – what are we trying to achieve? If we think about one-page profiles for staff, the purpose of them is to share knowledge, to inform action, to 'match' to people or tasks, and to begin a person-centred team plan (Chapter 9). It is not a new work profile that goes on a staff member's file and that's it. These deep, far-reaching changes in culture and practice require leaders at all levels of the organisation who demonstrate the values of the organisation.

Exercises

Exercise 1: Understanding organisational culture

Title: Discovering unwritten rules.

Purpose: This is an activity that can be done with a group or several groups to uncover the implied culture or working practices within an organisation. The focus can be the whole culture or particular aspects of it (e.g. the leadership style).

Audience: Can be done with groups at any level.

Typical uses:

- To stimulate thinking about the culture/working practices of the organisation or a particular area.

- As a diagnostic tool, to describe how the organisation is currently operating.

- As an activity for a leadership team to look at the organisational context for leadership.

- With teams to help understand what culture and organisation development are.

How to do it:

There are options around how to run it.

Exercise 1a: As a facilitated discussion session using prompt questions. For example, what are the explicit messages around how you are expected to do things around here and then what are the 'real' messages – implied and unwritten? The aim is to get these out, explore the differences, consider any tensions, and to challenge any issues as appropriate.

Exercise 1b: Another approach is to ask people why they are proud to work for your organisation, and what they are not so proud of. Praise and Trouble can be used in this context.

Exercise 2: Assessing organisation culture

Title: Diagnosing the 'as is' culture.

Purpose: Finding out what the current culture of an organisation is like, and how things are done around here.

Audience: Colleagues at all levels in an organisation.

Typical uses:

- To stimulate thinking about the culture/working practices of the organisation or a particular area.

- As a diagnostic tool to describe how the organisation is currently operating.

- As an activity for a leadership team to look at the organisational context for the level of change required to move towards a new culture.

How to do it:

Decide on what dimensions of culture you want to use and then use 'Working/ not working from different perspectives', the 4 Plus 1 questions or Praise and Trouble to establish what your culture is like.

Use the definitions of cultural aspects and characteristics and the questions about them on pp.137–141 and 144 to prompt thinking here.

Put the output into groups of typical cultural characteristics and agree the analysis of the culture with the audience. Again use the list of cultural aspects and characteristics for this grouping as a list of possible headings, and to prompt thinking when using other tools.

Exercise 3: Planning the future

Title: Visioning the future culture.

Purpose: This is an exercise that should be done first with the leadership team of an organisation, then perhaps repeated in other sections of the organisation to interpret and expand upon the desired future or to-be cultural aspects that the organisation desires or needs to move towards.

Audience: Leadership teams.

Typical uses:

- To stimulate thinking about the culture/working practices of the organisation, or a particular area that will be required to meet the needs of a new business operating model or context.

- As a diagnostic tool together with diagnosing the 'as is', to describe the gap between how we are currently and how we want to be.

- As an activity for a leadership team to look at the organisational context for leadership and priority actions towards a new culture.

- With teams to help understand what culture and organisation development are and plan for change.

How to do it:

Use the Doughnut to define the boundaries of the organisation. Use the definitions of cultural aspects and characteristics and the questions about them to think with people about what you want your culture to be – what is important to you, and what might be important for you.

Group the output and agree the analysis with the audience.

Finalise the definition of the desired culture and decide how to communicate it – for example, informing a one-page strategy, or a one-page team profile for the leadership group that reflects the culture.

Check that the definition of the desired culture aligns with the overall vision of the organisation.

Exercise 4: Creating the energy for culture change

Title: Optimistic discontent.

Purpose: To confirm that colleagues accept the need for change in the culture and are willing to make some commitment to helping to make the changes required.

Audience: Colleagues at all levels in an organisation, but starting with the key leadership teams and then cascading sponsorship for the proposed culture through the organisation.

Typical uses:

- To on-board colleagues with the need for culture change.

- To uncover potential sources of resistance to change.

- To check and confirm that culture change is needed.

How to do it:

Use 'Working/not working from different perspectives' to establish how people see the cultural aspects of the organisation. Use the definitions of cultural aspects and characteristics and the questions about them as an aid.

Use the 'Important to/for' tool to ask people what aspects of culture are key to them to change for the future, or retain if they are currently working. Ask colleagues to brainstorm what is important to/for them and the people supported/clients/families/stakeholders/customers in order to get several perspectives on the issues.

Ask how far do we meet what is important to people with the current culture and ways of working – quantify using a chosen scale, say marks out of ten or a star rating.

Ask what specifically is not working for the areas where needs are not being met. Ask what could be done to meet the needs better.

Use a success poster as an aid to summarising what this might look like for people.

Exercise 5: Planning the cultural change

Title: Prioritisation and implementation.

Purpose: To establish the prioritisation of implementation of actions to move towards a new culture.

Audience: Any team engaged in the implementation of culture change.

Typical uses: Planning of a culture change programme.

How to do it:

It is required to have already completed an analysis of the 'as is' and to-be culture so that the desired cultural aspects and the gap between the 'as is' and to-be culture are known.

Use the 'Important to/for' tool to work through each aspect of the desired culture and identify actions that it will be necessary to take to close the gap between the 'as is' and to-be cultures.

Prioritise these actions using a rating scale (e.g. a -5 score against the level of importance or a two by two matrix which allows the comparison of two criteria (or chai square) – importance versus risk, importance versus cost, importance versus urgency, etc.)

Use the 4 Plus 1 questions tool as an aid for establishing another level of detail of the plans and checking practicality. Take each proposed action and test against the 4 Plus 1 questions.

Finalise the project plan and review frequently using the 4 Plus1 questions tool.

Exercise 6: Maintaining the energy for culture change

Title: Learning and reflection.

Purpose: The learning and reflection tools (4 Plus 1, learning log) are used on a regular basis with different groups of colleagues to gather knowledge of what has been working and not working during the course of a culture change, and develop this into a part of the ongoing business planning process.

Audience: Can be used with any groups of colleagues who have shared similar experiences and learning as part of a culture change.

Typical uses:

- To inform business planning or leadership actions to take forward a culture change.

- To ensure that staff colleagues are fully engaged in the process and progression of a new culture.

How to do it:

Start by asking people to draw out a route map of where the culture was two to three years ago, what it is like now, and what it should be like in the next two to three years given the progress being made. This can also be done at the end of the exercise if people are not sure, or repeated at the end of the exercise as a check against what has been learnt in the day.

Use the 'Working/not working' tool to establish what the key areas people feel need attention or are going well.

Group the output.

Root cause the reasons why these aspects are not working. To do this you can use the conventional five whys, or fishbone analysis tools, in combination with the 'Working/not working' tool. This gives more detail to the action planning process.

Ask people to vote on the top three to five aspects of the not working and root cause information output that need to be taken forward for action. An alternative is to ask people to vote on them all and prioritise them into an overall action list.

A Café-To-Go or World Café process can be used as an alternative to the root-causing process in order to fill out the detail of the not working aspects. This is where key questions about what is not working are placed on a series of tables, and groups of people move around the tables and comment on each question. Each table has a facilitator who stays with the table and collates the information and passes it on to each group to build on.

Chapter 7

Leadership

Management is efficiency in climbing the ladder of success; leadership determines whether the ladder is leaning against the right wall.

Stephen Covey[75]

Introduction

It takes leadership to work together, and to create a person-centred culture to deliver your mission, vision and values. Person-centred leaders stand out – they embody the values of the organisation. In this chapter we explore what person-centred leadership looks like, and what this means for relationships and behaviours. Congruence and consistency are key. Nothing breeds cynicism in an organisation faster than inconsistency or lack of congruence in the behaviour of the leaders in relation to the organisation's values.

Traditionally, there may be a view that leadership is the responsibility of those in more senior positions, but as the epigraph above suggests, leadership is about clarity of vision and direction. In person-centred organisations we expect to see leadership at all levels, regardless of whether you are a senior leader, a team manager, or an administrator working on your own. That traditional view of leadership as a mark of status or hierarchical position is also inconsistent with the person-centred ethos of finding and supporting the contribution of every individual.

We start this chapter by looking at person-centred leadership and the contribution of person-centred practices.

What does leadership look like in a person-centred organisation?

Creating a person-centred organisation requires people who are skilled in leading, managing and coaching. Like Stephen Covey, in the epigraph, we see leadership and management as different:

- Leadership is about providing inspiration, guidance and direction.

- Management is about ensuring the process and procedures of the organisation are upheld, and delivering results.

Coaching is about releasing the human potential of the organisation.

In this chapter we focus on leadership, and we cover management and coaching in the chapter on person-centred teamwork. Much of the writing on leadership focuses on the more senior levels of leaders in an organisation, or those with accountability for directing other people's work.

The research of Kouzes and Posner,[76] has led them to argue that leadership occurs at multiple levels in an organisation. This is an expectation we would have for a person-centred organisation. There is also work emerging on person-centred leadership. Jeanne Plas and Susan Lewis emphasise how person-centred leadership requires an inversion of the traditional view of the organisational chart with the leadership at the top:[77]

> Inverted organisation charts guide communication and decision-making. Executives and managers know that the front-line worker makes or breaks the company and that senior leaders are there to serve. Theirs is a facilitative role, rather than a dictatorial role.

This captures the orientation of leaders in a person-centred organisation to the people the organisation supports, and therefore how the staff providing the direct support and the manager who supports them are arguably the most important people in the organisation. The other academic texts that we think closely align to our understanding of person-centred leadership are Stephen Covey's *Principle Centred Leadership*[78] and Charles Handy's 'Rules of Trust'.[79]

Covey describes principle centred leaders as:

- continually learning

- service orientated

- radiating positive energy

- believing in other people

- leading balanced lives

- seeing life as an adventure

- being synergistic

- exercising for renewal on all four dimensions of human personality – physical, mental, emotional and spiritual.

These qualities resonate with person-centred leadership because they extend to how someone lives their life (leading balanced lives, seeing life as an adventure, exercising for renewal) and not just behaviours that you would expect to see at work. The focus on relationships and believing in people is central to what you would expect to see in a person-centred leader. Developing relationships is based on trust, and Handy's and Covey's work on trust is important for leadership.

Trust – the key ingredient

> Trust is the glue of life. It's the most essential ingredient in effective communication. It's the foundational principle that holds all relationships. (Covey, Merrill and Merrill)[80]

If we are seeking to create person-centred cultures based on trust, empowerment and accountability, then Charles Handy's rules of trust are important. Building trust is perhaps one of the most difficult aspects of leadership and relationship creation. Charles Handy discusses the 'Rules of Trust' in relation to the growth of virtual organisations, and managing people whom you cannot see or who you do not meet.[81] There are many parallels to this in health and social care, with a highly dispersed workforce and an expectation of high levels of accountability for front-line staff to deliver what the people supported desire and need. This is of course overlaid by regulation and legislation covering most aspects of people's work – so trust becomes critical. Handy is clear that trust requires leadership, and the table that follows identifies his rules and how person-centred practices can help to put these into practice in an organisation.

Handy's Rules of Trust	How person-centred practices can help to build trust
'Trust is not blind'	You need to know people reasonably well, and have some confidence that they are committed to your same goals.
	Knowing people can start with a one-page profile, to capture what matters to them and what good support means to them.
	People contributing to their team's 'purpose' or 'success' poster is a way to have conversations about the alignment of values.
	Continually reviewing practice using 'Working and not working', the 4 Plus 1 questions and learning logs are good ways to deepen knowledge of people and their practice.
	Discovering what people's hopes and dreams are for the future helps us know what people value in their lives.
'Trust needs boundaries'	This is all about setting the rules and goals for an individual or team and then letting them get on with it.
	The first boundaries are the vision, mission and values of the organisation. This sets its overall direction and boundaries. The next boundary is set by the person supported, in understanding what matters to them, how they want to be supported, and what they want for the future. This may be recorded in their one-page profile, the outcomes they want to achieve over the next year, and how they want their week to look to reflect this.
	To deliver the vision, mission and values within the context of how the person wants their service requires that staff are clear about what they are responsible for, and where they can try new things and use their judgement. The Doughnut is the ideal person-centred thinking tool for this. Staff and teams need to

cont.

Handy's Rules of Trust	How person-centred practices can help to build trust
	keep learning and reflecting on their understanding of their boundaries – for example, by using 'Working and not working from different perspectives' (crucially including the person supported and the manager) or the 4 Plus 1 questions.
'Trust demands learning'	This rule of trust emphasises the aspects of a person-centred culture concerned with regular review of what has worked and not worked, learning using the 4 Plus 1 questions for review after action, the use of learning logs and making changes as necessary.
	This can happen in individual coaching on the job; in one-to-one sessions; in team meetings and across the whole organisation through Working Together for Change.
	Meetings should be opportunities to share learning – for example, in Positive and Productive Meetings.
	The person-centred supervision process has learning and accountability at its heart.
'Trust is tough'	This toughness keeps at its heart the organisation's mission, and will not tolerate practice that is outside the values of the organisation. This means that leaders need to act immediately when they see or hear behaviour that is not consistent with the values. One of the litmus tests of a person-centred organisation is how it responds to poor performance. Were people clear what the values of the organisation were? Were people clear about what was expected of them (the Doughnut)? Were the consequences of not delivering that clear? Have we given consistent, clear feedback on what the person is doing well and what needs to change? Have we done everything we can to support the person to deliver (according to how they want to be supported as described in their one-page profile)? Person-centred one-to-ones (supervision) are where clarifying expectations, giving feedback and ensuring accountability happen on a regular basis. Despite everything that we may do to recruit well and manage people properly, there may still be occasions when someone needs to part company with an organisation, and nobody should avoid that possibility. The key is to deal with it in a way that continues to demonstrate person-centred values towards the individuals concerned.
'Trust needs bonding'	'Trust needs touch' – Opportunities to connect, to appreciate each other, to celebrate achievements. Bonding takes place when we share about ourselves in a deeper way. In Positive and Productive Meetings people share something that is going well for them at work, and something that is going well for them at home at the beginning of meetings. Sharing (as much or as little as people feel comfortable with) about your life outside work is a way to learn about each other in a different way, and this can be a bonding experience.

From this, reviewing the work of Kouzes and Posner, and Covey, and the wealth of information on leadership, we summarise what we see as the four key characteristics of person-centred leadership. You will see person-centred leaders doing the following.

1. Authentically living the organisation's values

The hallmark of a person-centred leader is how they live the values of the organisation in all areas of their work and life. You can see this in what they say; what they do; how they recognise and reward others who demonstrate the values; and what happens when people do not. You would be able to see most of this just being in a meeting with a person-centred leader.

Person-centred leaders stay focused on what really matters – keeping the people supported by the organisation at the heart of everything they do. A person-centred leader is continually learning, experimenting and taking risks themselves. Michael Smull encourages people to share their 'most successful failures'. These are 'good tries' or risks that people took, that did not have the desired outcome, but were still 'successful' because of what the person learnt as a result. When leaders share what they have tried but did not work out in the way they had hoped, and what they learned from that, they send a powerful message about encouraging and supporting new ideas, initiatives and risks, continual learning and humility.

2. Enthusing others with the vision and its possibilities

Person-centred leaders 'radiate positive energy', enthuse others about the vision and keep stretching the notion of what is possible. This does not mean that all person-centred leaders are loud, charismatic people. They are people who can help others see further, and imagine better, and this may be in very unobtrusive ways, as the Chinese philosopher, Lao-tzu, suggests:

> As for the best leaders, the people do not notice their existence. The next best, people honor and praise. The next, the people fear and the next, the people hate. When the best leader's work is done, the people say, 'We did it ourselves.'

3. Paying attention to relationships, building trust and working together

Relationships are central to a person-centred leader. Person-centred leaders are present and mindful in their relationships with others; they believe in the best in people, and bring out the best in people. Person-centred leaders show appreciation, in the ways that work for people.

> When I worked in services in Manchester I worked with a team using person-centred planning with the two people that they support. The team did some excellent work in providing very person-centred support, with two people who did not use words to speak. As well as telling them directly, I wanted their efforts and success to be rewarded and acknowledged. I thought that the best way to do this was to get the CEO to write to them to express her appreciation. The next time I spent time with the team, I was surprised that they had not seemed very interested in the letter. Disappointed, I asked them 'What does appreciation

look like to you?' They told me that what they would really like would be able to share what they had tried and learned with their peers. We arranged for two of the team to talk at the next staff development forum to do this. I learned an important lesson about not assuming that what would have felt like appreciation to me (being recognised by the CEO) is what being appreciated feels like to other people. The adage 'treat people in the way you would like to be treated' does not work in a person-centred organisation. You need to find out how people want to be treated and not assume that it is the same as you. (Helen Sanderson)

Here is how a team leader addressed this issue:

Kim asked each member of her team what being appreciated looked like and sounded like. She did this by asking each person in their one-to-one to talk about a time when they really felt valued and appreciated. From that they talked about the key elements of this, and then decided on the top three ways that they as individuals felt appreciated. This was summarised for each team member onto one page in the person-centred team plan.

4. Demonstrating person-centred practices in all their roles

If we expect to see person-centred practices throughout a person-centred organisation, then we also expect this to be led and demonstrated by the leader.

There are some behaviours and ways of working that everyone in an organisation, whether they be the lowest graded staff member or the CEO, can adopt to make person-centred working a reality across the organisation. Again, it is important not to differentiate in the overall approach to people, whether they be colleagues, people served and supported, regulators, or other key stakeholders. All meetings throughout the organisation should be seen as positive and productive, and as offering opportunities for everyone to contribute their views and think together. Finance officers, admin teams and the CEO can use the person-centred thinking tools in their roles.

A few months after United Response had started to introduce person-centred thinking, Bob Tindall was invited to speak at a conference on safeguarding. He used the 4 Plus 1 questions to frame his presentation. This sent a powerful message to the organisation that he was both competent in using person-centred thinking, and actually using the tools in his role. The fact that the United Response business plan is framed using the person-centred thinking tools sends the same message to staff and stakeholders – 'person-centred practices are how we do business here'.

Here, Su Sayer OBE, Chief Executive of United Response, sums up her experiences of learning from leading a growing organisation and maintaining the focus on the people supported.

I have learnt that it is really important to know when to helicopter and look at the organisation as a whole. At other times it's really important to focus in on the detail. Time after time when I've done that, I've managed to help people simplify the process and get rid of some of those log jams (focusing on what really matters).

No one likes a leader who takes all the credit for themselves. So even if it was your idea in the first place, there are bound to have been lots of other people involved. Make sure that they get the praise (humility). Play to a person's strengths, and give them control over what they do. Of course you want to minimise someone's weaknesses, but if you want to get the best out of someone play to their strengths and make them part of a team where they're paired with someone with complementary strengths (appreciation).

Use the personal touch, for example sending anniversary letters, making yourself available on a hotline, adding your personal touch to standard HR-type letters, by making phone calls to people or even an email (being present). If you've got the courage to apologise if you've made a mistake it makes it a lot easier for other people to do the same (humility).

Be absolutely passionate about what you're doing, radiate enthusiasm. People love enthusiastic people (enthusing others).

Don't be afraid to ask for help (humility). I've had to ask so many times. I've written to people out of the blue. When we were expanding very fast at one stage, I wrote to the eminent management consultant Professor Charles Handy and explained that I had read his book over and over, and I still couldn't quite understand a particular concept. On receipt of my letter I had a telephone call and that evening I was sitting by his fireside with a glass of wine whilst he explained to me how to do it. How amazing was that?

Emphasise the outcomes achieved, and not the process of getting there – focus on doing the right things rather than doing things right (strengthening values and behaviours). This is fundamental to ensuring that individual needs and desires are met (commitment to values).

Leadership of an organisation – how are you doing?

The table that follows gives some examples of excellence in leadership in a person-centred way. You can use it to rate the performance of your organisation's leadership team or to assess person-centred leadership competence across the organisation generally, using a scale of 1–5, where 1 is very poor, 2 is poor, 3 is fair, 4 is good and 5 is excellent, to give a rough first assessment of your progress as an organisation. You could argue that most of the self-assessments in the book are about leadership and change, so in this one we have just highlighted behaviours that relate to the four key characteristics of person-centred leadership described earlier.

	Rating 1–5
Authentically living the organisation's values	We/I put people at the centre of everything we/I do, in all areas of my work.
	We/I make sure that we stay focused on what matters.
	We/I ensure that people are always described positively, and as specific individuals, and encourage others to do the same.
	We/I do not tolerate disempowering language.
	We/I continually learn, and share what we/I learn with colleagues.
	We/I take risks where they are carefully thought through.
	In meetings we/I keep focused on our vision and values, and what this means in practice in our thinking and decision making.
	We/I hold ourselves and other people accountable for how they live the values of the organisation.
Enthusing others with the vision and its possibilities	We/I communicate positively and in an upbeat manner about our future as an organisation.
	We/I encourage others to extend what we think is possible, and to keep trying and learning so we continually improve.
Paying attention to relationships, building trust and working together	We/I know our staff well – what matters to them and how they want to be supported. We/I ensure they each have a one-page profile that summarises this information.
	We/I plan and implement actions to make sure our staff feel appreciated, trusted and valued.
	We/I ensure that meetings are opportunities for deepening relationships and thinking and working effectively together, by taking advantage of each others' gifts.
	We/I give people feedback and reward and recognise behaviour that is in line with our values and vision.
	We/I address behaviour that does not reflect our values, and support others to do the same.

		Rating 1–5
Demonstrating person-centred practices in all their roles	We/I have a one-page profile and use this with staff and colleagues to share information about each other.	
	We/I demonstrate and support colleagues in using person-centred practices, and proactively and competently using person-centred thinking tools in all areas of our work.	
	We/I ensure that everyone can describe at least five person-centred thinking tools (why and how you can use them and the benefits to the person) and talk about their experience of using them and the outcomes doing so achieved.	
	We/I consistently demonstrate enabling people supported to have as much choice and control as possible in their lives through working with them in a person-centred way.	

Developing further as a person-centred leader

Now that you have had a look at your own leadership, here are some ideas that could be useful to develop further.

Authentically living the organisation's values

Living the values of the organisation is about staying focused on what matters. How often have you found that a problem or a debate is not actually about the subject or the person you thought it was? A useful question to keep asking when difficulties arise, and things are not working, is 'Who is this about?' More often than not, if the answer is not that it is about people being supported, then there is room for action and improvement. This is no more than the usual leadership action of focusing on the vision, mission, purpose and values of the organisation, and continually reinforcing those in your interactions with people.

Assuming positive intent is another important way to live the values of a person-centred organisation. We see this as so important, and make no apology for repeating it here (it is also discussed in Chapter 8), but we recognise that it is very difficult to do. Many of us are raised to be suspicious of others and their motives. Indeed our life experiences can confirm that we are right to be suspicious. Assuming positive intent does not necessarily mean ignoring that upbringing and experience. It does mean asking the right questions and listening carefully to the answers before forming your final judgement. It also means searching hard for the information that someone might feel unable to give you, to explain their own actions or questions.

It also means being prepared to be disappointed sometimes.

Authentically living the values of the organisation means spending time with and listening to people who use your service. Visiting and meeting people are also opportunities for showing interest in staff who have innovative ideas, and recognising creative contributions. In United Response, questions have also been used in staff satisfaction surveys to see if staff have noticed senior people visiting the service, and how they have come across. Richard Williams, CEO of Options, sets clear expectations of how much time he expects his managers to spend directly with people supported. Another approach is for each manager to be connected (matched) to an individual who uses the service, whom they spend time with each month. This gives an opportunity to see the organisation's work through another pair of eyes (the most important pair of eyes – the person using the service) and to see the impact of decisions that are made in the organisation on people's lives. Some leaders prefer to see this as a consultancy role, and pay someone who uses the service to spend a couple of hours a month with them, and for the leader to use that time to help inform their practice and decision making. Other leaders do this by being involved in someone's life (not necessarily someone whom the organisation supports) through being an active member of their circle of support.

Continuing to learn and develop personally is also a way to demonstrate the values of the organisation. This could be through a coach or mentor. In United Response, a number of senior managers decided that they would benefit from a coach or mentor to support their development via the organisation's Developing Excellence process, and these were provided. There is a vast range of resources for this now, including senior people from various industries and sectors who give up part of their time to provide this service for not-for-profit organisations free of charge. Being part of action learning sets, networking, and membership of representative groups in your sector are other ways to keep learning and developing.

Enthusing others with the vision and its possibilities

A key part of enthusing others to see what is possible concerns sharing knowledge and information. A common feature of businesses that are unsuccessful or successful only for the short term is that knowledge is treated in a selfish way (given of course the boundaries of essential protection of intellectual property). It can often be seen as a trait of those in or seeking positions of power (leadership in one way) that they follow this road, and there are of course examples of people who have been very successful by doing so. We hope that you can see, in the content of this book alone, that our approach is different. The regular sharing of knowledge and good practice across an organisation (and even sometimes with its competitors) builds trust in each other, inevitably produces better results, and helps people get a clearer sense of what is possible.

What is possible in the future will inevitably involve taking risks. This is required in being able to enthuse others about the vision of the organisation, but it is also central to living its values. We discuss in Chapter 10 the detailed approach to risk taking. People very quickly learn what 'Praise and Trouble' means in an organisation, and risk taking is one of the prime areas that they pay attention to. Getting the message across that risk taking is OK, if it is done in a thoughtful way and with the best interests of the customer at the forefront, is a complex and critical part of leadership in a person-centred organisation. It is vital for people to know the boundaries of risk taking, and that they will be supported by their managers if they stay within those boundaries, or indeed can explain why exceeding the boundaries was the right thing to do.

Paying attention to relationships, building trust and working together

> Wise men speak because they have something to say; fools because they have to say something. (Plato)

This is colloquially translated from the Latin as 'just shut up and listen'. A key skill of person-centred leaders is being able to listen out for and hear what is important to and for others, or what is working and not working for them. This is about the process of active listening, as it is carried through into action to do something in response to an expression of what is important to or for someone, or what is working and not working for them. Aligned with this is the act of giving someone your absolute attention, even if it is for a very short period of time. If someone knows and feels that they are the only thing that matters to you at that moment in time, it is incredibly powerful. Giving full attention is one of Nancy Kline's components of a thinking environment; it is also linked with mindfulness and being present. It is not uncommon for organisations to include training and support in mindfulness, to enable people to be genuinely present for one another (and recognising the benefits this provides in managing stress). The use of communication charts can be very helpful here in understanding the nature and requirements of the people you are listening to.

In Chapter 8 we will introduce an organisational process for equality and diversity based on individual behaviour that treats everyone with dignity and respect, regardless of who they are. Here the behaviour is all about acting decently towards people rather than trying to adapt to a complex set of largely unknown rules and standards. Once again it is the common theme of the person-centred approach that we look at issues or situations, or indeed people, from a range of different perspectives, and are not misled by a narrow view. This is an extension of the 'Frame of Reference' (FOR) approach common in conventional thinking about relationship building. This approach recognises that both talker and listener have their own FORs, which are created by, for example, differences in intelligence, knowledge, beliefs, experiences, expectations, and so on. The key is to look for that joint area within the FORs where there is common understanding and empathy. So we argue that showing high levels of respect for another's FOR heightens the possibility of being better able to understand and communicate.

One area of critical importance is the use of language. There is insufficient space here to detail the many aspects of this, but some useful approaches you may care to investigate further include the following.

- The use of precision language patterns as used in NLP approaches, for example, which help to clarify exactly what a person is saying to you.

- The empathetic approach of the learning styles classification of VARK (verbal, auditory, read/write, kinaesthetic),[82] which seeks to listen for and mirror the style of the person presenting themselves to you.

Again, the particular person-centred thinking tool that can be used here is the communication chart, which helps to focus on people's communication, whether they use words or not, and especially where behaviour communicates more clearly than words.

In the last chapter on culture, we introduced Michael Smull's exercise called 'Praise and Trouble', which emphasises the importance of giving people feedback, and feedback on what matters in relation to the organisation's values and mission. A concept that came originally from the thinking of *The One Minute Manager* is 'catch someone doing something right'.[83] Good leaders spend more of their time catching people doing the right things than the wrong things. Note here that we talk about the right things being done right, not the wrong things being done right. Many problems are caused by misguided staff doing completely the wrong thing, but executing it perfectly. At the same time, good managers let staff know very quickly and straightforwardly when something is not working. This concept again comes first from *The One Minute Manager* in the form of the one minute reprimand. It is an essential part of our approach, because the risks of tolerating poor practice and conduct are too high. The rules of good feedback apply, of course. So, be sure of your facts; be specific about the behaviour you are criticising; and be clear as to what you think the other person should do differently. At the same time, remember to consider what the feedback says about you and your values, or code of personal conduct. This is your leadership accountability for acting consistently with the organisation's declared vision, mission and values. This is where the value of good coaching techniques comes to the fore. In Chapter 9, we explain further the role of coaching in this context.

Forgiveness is the attribute of the strong. (Mahatma Gandhi)[84]

Many of us are quick to judge and condemn what we perceive as bad behaviour. The person-centred approach is to explore why things happen the way they do; be tolerant of idiosyncrasy; and get as much learning from a situation as possible. It is about being clear as to what is poor practice, exploring why it happens and then responding appropriately. You would deal with a situation differently if poor practice was a result of lack of clarity and understanding about what good means, and the person was unclear of their roles and responsibilities in a situation, as opposed to poor practice that reflects values that are inconsistent with those held by the organisation. Here, the 4 Plus 1 questions can help in reflecting on poor practice. Remember that feedback is a two-way process, so be prepared to abide by the rules here too. If you are given feedback, listen and clarify rather than react. Try to learn more about any concerns the other person is raising, what specific conduct or behaviour, or what effects it has on them. Always play back and include any feedback in your summary of the agreed actions to improve. If the other person has made what you think is a good point, then check out with others how they feel about it too.

Demonstrating person-centred practices in all their roles

Finally, in a person-centred organisation, you would expect to see person-centred practices being used fluently and consistently, and for this to be obvious in the leaders' approach and behaviour.

The table that follows gives some illustrations of how you can do this.

Issue	Person-centred thinking tool that could help	What you can do
Understanding why a person is not performing to their best, and what you might do to help or coach them	Good days and bad days	Discuss what helps an individual have good days and what doesn't, and how this might manifest itself in behaviour.
Understanding why problems occur in working together, and what you can do to avoid or resolve them	One-page profiles	Write down and share these for you and your team or colleagues.
Understanding why someone places different emphasis on things than you do, or prioritises certain activities	Important to/for	Discuss with another person what the priorities are for the way they want to conduct their life and what this means for them at work.
Understand why you may get a poor reaction to your behaviour, or people won't do what you want them to do	Praise and Trouble	Discuss what you give feedback on and how much feedback you give and the person's perceptions of this.
Whether people understand what a good contribution looks like, and if they understand how to do it	Presence to Contribution	Discuss with your team or colleague what the range of outputs or outcomes from their work can be, and what is less and more acceptable.
Clarifying roles and responsibilities	The Doughnut	Discuss what people see as their main responsibilities and what they feel they can take decisions about.

Conclusion

The whole of this book is essentially about leadership manifesting in different ways. In this chapter, we have tried to describe what is different about leading a person-centred organisation – a focus on living the values of the organisation; an ability to get alongside people and motivate and enthuse them with the vision and its possibilities; a consistent focus on relationships and working together; and using person-centred practices in day-to-day work. Meetings look and feel different when a person-centred leader is present. Here is a summary of some of the difference we have explored in this chapter.

Conventional behaviour	A person-centred approach
Being suspicious of others	Assuming positive intent
Focus on outputs	Focus on outcomes
Arranging work to suit the worker	Work is arranged to suit the people we support
People contribute in the same way	We make use of skills, knowledge and interests and match to roles
Must be busy	Must be present
Hesitate before bringing up a difficult issue	Raise a concern about something that is not working as soon as possible
Discipline someone	Discuss why they did what they did, and what the consequences are
Assume people are the same	Value everyone as different

Chapter 8

Human Resource Management

I believe in the adage: 'hire people smarter than you and get out of their way'.
Howard Schultze, CEO of coffee chain Starbucks (1994)[85]

Introduction

Our success in living our values and fulfilling our mission requires working closely together. Human resources (HR) is about bringing the best out of the organisation's most valued assets – the people who work there – and ensuring that their individual and collective contributions come together to achieve the mission.[86] This combination of tools and techniques also goes under the names of personnel management, people management or people development, but essentially makes up all the ways that we have of dealing with the relationship between an organisation and the people who work for it.

One simple definition is that human resource management is the process of matching individual staff and their contributions to the people supported and the organisation. The person-centred thinking Matching tool has a powerful contribution to make here. Getting the right staff to support people, well matched in relation to the support the person needs, their personality characteristics and ideally shared interests, is key to great human resource management.

This chapter demonstrates how an integrated approach using person-centred practices with established human resources approaches can ensure that the talents and commitment of staff make a difference to the people supported.

What does human resource management mean in a person-centred organisation?

> The soft stuff is always harder than the hard stuff. (Roger Enrico, Vice Chairman of PepsiCo, referring to areas such as HRM as opposed to quantitative factors in *Fortune*, 27 November 1995)[87]

It depends on what you define as hard and soft, but we would tend to agree that dealing with the myriad of diverse people we come into contact with is much harder than measuring widgets, and just as hard to know when you are actually getting it right. Too often we stifle talent and creativity, or even just contribution, by being too prescriptive about what we do and how we do it. When we talk about human resources management (HRM) in this chapter, we mean both what first-line and other managers do, as well as what an HR team may be responsible for. In keeping with the value of decision making happening as close to the person supported as possible, most of the recruiting process and certainly the selection decision for new staff would take place at an individual level – with the person and the manager of their service, not done by a central HR team. The HR team's role here is in establishing a flexible, person-centred framework and processes that reflect the values of the organisation, and in taking the administrative and transactional burden away from managers so that they can focus on the quality of the selection decision.

A person-centred approach to HR means that we will be getting the right people in the organisation. 'Right' means people who fit with the values of the organisation, and who are passionate about its mission and vision. We then get the best possible match with either people supported or their role in the organisation. People supported will choose their own staff, and we can use the Matching tool to help this to happen. Great matches reflect the skills or experience required to do the job and the personality characteristics needed. If our matches involve individuals supported, then great matches will include shared interests. Once people are employed, knowing what matters to people and how they want to be supported is vital. People will have clear expectations and know absolutely what they need to do and where they can try new things and experiment. Ongoing support and development, keeping staff motivated, and thinking and problem solving together is important. Recognition and rewards that reflect the values and mission of the organisation and fit with what is important to the person are also key to good HRM.

Here is a summary of how some of the person-centred practices can help.

Functions of HRM	How person-centred practices can help
Recruitment and selection	Person-centred recruitment involves using person-centred information, and the Matching tool to develop the person specification and job description. This means using one-page profiles, person-centred plans or detailed support plans. The decision-making agreement is important to clarify the roles of different people in decision making, and this is where we think about how to keep the person absolutely at the centre of the process. Some organisations introduce one-page profiles for staff at this stage (see the example from Dimensions in Chapter 2).
Supporting, supervising and appraising staff	One-page profiles of staff inform the supervision process both to match actions closely to what is important to the staff member, and to review whether they are getting the support they need. 'Working/not working from different perspectives' identifies what is going well and development needs. The Doughnut can help to clarify accountabilities. 4 Plus 1 or learning logs are used to review learning and progress.

Workforce development	Using 'Working and not working from different perspectives' at an individual, team and organisational level will provide important information about what the workforce development issues are. Working Together for Change is another important way to co-produce this information, and develop objectives and actions for workforce development. Using 4 Plus 1 at a team and organisational level can inform workforce development (for example, the 4 Plus 1 example in Chapter 2 led to identifying learning development needs).
Policies and procedures	'Working and not working' and the 4 Plus 1 questions can be used to review the effectiveness of policies and procedures.

How are you doing?

The following table gives some examples of excellence in operating in a person-centred way in HRM. You can use this table to rate your own performance using a scale of 1–5, where 1 is very poor, 2 is poor, 3 is fair, 4 is good and 5 is excellent, to give a rough first assessment of your progress as an organisation.

Criteria	Measure	Rating
Selecting and recruiting direct support workers	Each job advert and person specification is individualised to the people who are supported using person-centred information and the matching process.	
	Adverts are placed locally in a range of ways (Post Office, local radio, etc.) and we actively recruit local direct support staff.	
	Direct support staff are always recruited for an individual person (not to a pool of staff employed by the organisation).	
Supporting, supervising and appraising staff	We use person-centred information about what matters to the person and how they want to be supported as the foundation of how we support and supervise direct support workers.	
	Before supervision and appraisal, we ask the person (their family or other stakeholders) about how the support worker is doing and ensure that supervision and appraisals focus on how we can deliver the best service to the people we support.	
	Supervision sessions also recognise what is important to and for staff, and are opportunities to consider what is working and not working and to think and problem solve together.	

cont.

Criteria	Measure	Rating
	We have a way of feeding back to people and families positively. Listening to individuals and families forms part of our performance management system.	
Supporting team members individually	Each staff member has a regularly reviewed individual development plan that includes how they are developing their competence in using the person-centred thinking tools and approaches.	
Workforce development	We have developed a detailed workforce strategy and training programme based on input, ideas and involvement of staff, individuals and their family (or other stakeholders).	
Learning and development	The strategy includes what will need to change about the way we train, support and deploy our staff, and the way we organise and govern ourselves if we are to be a truly person-centred organisation.	
HR policies and procedures	Our policies and procedures are person-centred and actively promote enabling people to have choice and control in their lives. We work with people who use services, families and staff to develop these, and they are presented in a way that is easy to read and understand. There are as few of them as possible.	
Reward and recognition	We have a range of ways of rewarding and recognising good practice and contributions, which reflect what is important to and for the people we support, staff and other stakeholders.	
Equality and diversity	Equality and diversity aspects are reflected in all our policies, procedures and ways of working.	
Staff consultation	We have processes in place to ensure that colleagues are well informed about the status of the organisation, and the voice of staff is heard in relation to all matters that affect their life at work.	
Supporting team members individually	We ensure that each team member reflects on their own practice and is accountable for this. This includes celebrating successes and problem solving difficulties. We use a range of ways to ensure each team member has individual support in using person-centred thinking tools and approaches (for example, peer support, mentoring and person-centred thinking, as a standing agenda item for supervision).	

Support and development as a team	We have a strong culture of reflective practice around our experience of using person-centred thinking tools and practices. In the team we have a variety of ways (for example, standing agenda item in team meetings, sharing best practices and problem solving, practice groups, person-centred thinking tool of the month) to support team members to develop their skills in using person-centred thinking and approaches.	
Staff know what is expected of them	Staff know what is expected of them – they are clear about their core responsibilities and where they can try new ideas in their day-to-day work. Staff are clear about their role in people's lives and know what they must do in their work around the people they support, and any team, admin or finance responsibilities. Roles and responsibilities are clearly recorded (for example, in a Doughnut) and this is reflected in job descriptions. Staff know how to use person-centred thinking to deliver their core responsibilities.	
Staff are thoughtfully matched to people and rotas are personalised to people who are supported	Decisions about who works with whom are based on whom the person supported wants to support them, and include thinking about the best match.	

Making all HRM person-centred – what can you do next?

In summary, what we are trying to do is support a culture of being person-centred by embedding the approaches and language of person-centred practice into as many of the ways of working with people as we can.

The full list of areas where we suggest you can use person-centred practices and make an impact are resourcing; performance management; flexible working; learning and development; competencies; disciplinary, capability and grievance handling; absence management; reward and recognition; equality and diversity; staff consultation; the back office; and policies and procedures.

Recruitment, selection and resourcing

We include here all those activities associated with placing the right people in the right roles and jobs. Traditionally staff are recruited to an organisation and then allocated to a team. Sometimes people whom the organisation supports are trained to take part in interview panels. The team leader then develops the rota for the team and allocates different staff members to shifts where they support people or carry out their tasks. This looks very different in a person-centred organisation, because decision making about who to employ is made as close to the person as possible, and by the person. The person specification and job description will be developed directly from the individual's person-centred description. The person themselves (or their family) will be involved in the recruitment process as much as they want, in the ways that make sense to them, including the decision about whom to employ. The staff rota will then be developed around what the person wants to do and the support they need, and staff will be matched to the different competencies or personal characteristics this may require.

The key tool we use here is Matching. This uses information – for example, from the one-page profile of a person being supported – and identifies the personality characteristics, support and skills needed in a staff member or team. It also identifies interests that the person being supported may have, so that recruiters can explore if any suitable candidates share these – watching a particular football club, or going fishing perhaps. Other approaches include the engagement of prospective staff in social events with the people they will support, and in workshops with their prospective team-mates. This might take the form, for example, of an exercise to consider what is important to and for each team member in their daily work, and an assessment of the compatibility of that information with each other and with the people to be supported.

In Chapter 2 we shared a summary of a person-centred recruitment process using one-page profiles, matching, decision-making agreements and 'Working and not working from different perspectives', and in Chapter 5 you may remember the story of Jennie and Suzie, who used the person-centred recruitment process. Person-centred information, and in this case the one-page profile format, can also be used in recruiting for other posts in the organisation. Figure 8.1 shows the one-page profile that was used in part of the recruitment process for a business administrator for HSA.

This person-centred approach does not rule out the assistance of appropriate technology, and detailed monitoring and measurement that you would find in other environments.

In United Response, for example, you will find the use of online recruitment, and social networking such as Twitter, Facebook and blogging.

The organisation knows this is important because the resourcing process is measured in as many ways as the staff can think of. It is clear that the main source of recruits is via word of mouth. In the modern world, this includes social networking capability. The second biggest source of recruits is via the Internet, so of course online recruitment and wide exposure to jobsites are critical.

Additional measures include the rate of involvement of people supported in recruitment, turnover and stability, vacancy rates, time to fill, and ethnicity comparisons at application, interview and appointment stages. United Response strives to achieve matching rates of ethnicity at each of these stages, as evidence of achievement of its equality and diversity goals. Using person-centred practices together with these efforts have contributed to a reduction in the rate of turnover of staff, and the

Business Administrator for HSA

Could this be you?

What people like and admire about you

- Your positive 'can-do' attitude.
- Your excellent customer service - you see every contact with customers as an opportunity to demonstrate our values.
- Your friendly, positive, calm and helpful telephone manner.
- You're a great 'completer finisher'; someone who gets things done.
- Your excellent problem solving skills.
- Sense of humour.
- Team worker and methodical.
- Great integrity.
- Flexible and trustworthy.
- You meet deadlines.

What is important to you

- To deliver the very best service to customers.
- To get things done and see the difference that my work makes.
- To work in a quiet office environment, sometimes by myself.
- A tidy, organised and clutter free office.
- Working with people who are committed to making a difference in people's lives.
- Having a good working relationship with team members whom I speak to on a regular basis.
- Being able to use my initiative at work.
- Being trusted by the team.
- Being on time.
- Clear understanding of expectations.
- Being organised and having an efficient filing system so I know where everything is.

How we will support you

- Being part of an excellent, energetic and passionate team.
- Weekly meeting with Helen to review the week's tasks.
- Longer meeting every six weeks for support and supervision.
- Close working relationships Andy (HSA Press) and Jan (HSA finance officer) who share the adjacent office and Charlotte (HSA director).
- Develop a one page profile within the first six weeks of you joining us so that we know what is important to you and how to support you.
- Looking at what is working and not working about your role in HSA.
- Learn about your dreams for the future and see if we can support you to move forward with them in this role.

Figure 8.1 Recruitment information based on a one-page profile

consequent savings on resourcing and training costs. Staff turnover had previously been competitive and in line with industry norms. However, at the time of writing in December 2011, the rate of staff turnover had reduced by 41 per cent, relative to the baseline rate taken in March 2006 when the change programme to introduce person-centred practices first began.

The importance of getting the right feel to the recruitment experience cannot be underestimated. First impressions are very important. So, if you walk into the reception at United Response Head Office, you will see pictures of the people supported and their achievements. You may well be helped to find your way, or enjoy your stay, by a paid member of staff who also has a learning disability. The culture of the organisation is conveyed immediately to people who are applying for jobs within it.

Stephen (one of the authors) tells the story of his recruitment as HR Director:

Here's how the process went for me:

- Saw an advertisement in a professional magazine – a conventional approach but giving the flavour of what the organisation is about.

- Interviewed by the people who would be my direct reports – an immediate impression that congruence between manager and managed is important round here, and an opportunity to assess if my values and ways of working will chime with my prospective team.

- Called back the next day for a second round of interviews. I wasn't told this might happen, but if I was truly interested I had to 'make it happen'. So I did.

- Interviewed by the CEO and MD – conventional, but an opportunity to test the congruence between the behaviours of the leaders of the organisation, the managers I had met so far, and the material I had read and seen.

- Final interview with a panel of people supported by United Response and their support workers. There was no doubt in my mind that this was the most important of them all, and if I failed here then the job was not mine. This was the most challenging interview of my life. All the questions were asked by the people we support, and included some really tough ones such as, 'If you get the job what will you do for us?' and the best of all, 'Can you tell us a joke?'

- When I was asked afterwards what I thought of all this, my response was immediate – I was left in no doubt that this is an organisation that really lives its professed values in the way it works.

This recruitment activity is mirrored across the organisation through the matching staff process, and innovative ways of involving the people supported in the process. It often surprises people, but leaves them in no doubt about the nature of the organisation.

Psychometric testing and recruitment – the MacIntyre Profile

Bill Mumford describes how MacIntyre has been exploring psychometric testing as another approach to getting the best fit between staff and people.

There is a well-established link between personality or character traits and people's behaviour and attitudes towards others. Our personality will influence our personal and working lives and is apparent in the way we interact with other people. Recruiters use psychometric tests to gain an insight into how the personal traits of a potential recruit are likely to impact on their performance at work.

MacIntyre uses the Rapid Personality Questionnaire (RPQ) which is a widely used psychometric test designed to give '…a reliable, valid, quick and simple to use general purpose profile…with a work setting'. We use a version that is particularly suited for non-graduate level applicants. It has a theoretical basis founded on the 'Big Five' aspects of personality which various researchers have refined over many decades. Within the RPQ these are defined as: extraversion/introversion, confidence/caution, structural/non-structural, tough-mindedness/benevolence and conformity/non-conformity. Respondents are asked a series of 80 questions such as 'How do you think others see you at work?' and are given a range of options which they need to rate on a scale from 1, 'Not at all like me' to 5, 'Very much like me'. Each dimension is scored on a scale between 1 and 19 with the average, on a normal distribution of people, being the midpoint.

When MacIntyre asked a group of over 30 so-called 'natural' support workers, those highly thought of by colleagues, families and individuals, to complete the RPQ the findings were unexpected. The individuals' collective scores were average when compared with the general population except for them being statistically more benevolent than average (perhaps not surprising) but what was unexpected was a significant bias towards introversion. The latter was particularly surprising as these colleagues were not thought of as shy and retiring types but rather on a matter of principle they could be very challenging of authority! On further analysis and reflection the apparent contradiction became more understandable when one defines introversion more as being facilitative towards others than self-regarding and so colleagues were skilled at putting others first rather than themselves and were intuitive and confident about doing this. Exactly the same findings were replicated when MacIntyre repeated the survey with another 100 senior practitioner colleagues. The findings were too significant to ignore (especially knowing that an interview process tends to favour extroverts) and so an idealised personality profile has been created, known as the MacIntyre Profile, and is used for all recruitment for front-line and senior practitioner roles.

Besides knowing what personal traits are best suited to the workplace employers also want to know the knowledge, skills, judgements and actions that people need to perform a role effectively. The use of a Competency Framework is a way of linking the goals of an organisation to individual performance, in particular the desired behaviours. By discovering what these are and making them explicit it has significant benefit in a formal selection process and also helping workers to understand the kind of behaviours the organisation values.

With support from the HR specialists Kenexa and with the full involvement of front-line colleagues, combined with observation of work in practice, MacIntyre has created its own set of competency frameworks. These have been incorporated in job descriptions, supervision and appraisal and are used at interview. Examples include 'Listens to and checks their understanding of others' views, ideas and feelings' as opposed to 'Assumes they understand the views, ideas and feelings of others without listening or asking'. Also 'Expresses confidence and self-belief in the ability or success of others by providing encouragement and praise' rather than 'Focuses on risks/difficulties/problems/obstacles facing others during the task'.

This is a well-established practice in most sectors but virtually unheard of in social care – in particular for front-line workers. MacIntyre combines this recruitment methodology with the development of facilitation skills (we term 'Great Interactions') and person-centred approaches. It is a total organisational approach and therefore when evaluating the outcomes of recruiting in this way it is hard to disentangle. However, there is considerable evidence building up, across the organisation, to support the belief that there are positive effects on core workforce performance indicators. There has been a marked improvement in workforce retention, less sickness and absence, a greater take up of formal learning opportunities and significantly less low-level performance management issues. The staff members themselves have reported positively about the recruitment process and have found the profile offers insight into themselves and, for those new to social care, their ability to adapt into the role. They also report that the process seems to affirm 'status' to their role, that is, it is important enough for such apparently advanced recruitment techniques to be used.

It has been difficult to evaluate objectively from the perspective of the person being supported. However, there has been some take up from individuals and families who wish to employ personal assistants; they have reported that the process has increased their confidence to take on the responsibility of self-directing their support. Likewise front-line managers across MacIntyre, once they have mastered the process, report a similar increase in confidence in their decision making. For many the evaluation has been indirect from families and others close to the individuals who have made various positive observations. It is safe to conclude that recruiting people to a proven profile with a carefully constructed competency framework is unlikely to lead to worse decision making!

Flexible working

This is an area where legislation requires that flexible working is available and consequently it is often seen by some organisations as a necessary evil. On the contrary, we see it as a positive business advantage, especially in a world where competition for high-quality staff is strong and relatively low salaries mean that entry and exit are frequent at relatively low differentiating factors. So what may be seen as a relatively small increase in pay can cause someone to move between companies.

In that environment, it is the other differentiators of an organisation that become important, and flexible working is one of those, along with other benefits and the quality of management. So we recommend it, despite the fact that your HR and payroll staff will tell you that it is an administrative nightmare. Ignore them, and have as many flexible working and family-friendly policies as you can imagine and afford. This works best for people supported, and best for staff. Have employment contracts for as many different hour and day configurations as the people you support require; you can find staff who want to work them.

The range of contracted hours in United Response is matched very closely to what the people supported need and want to have. This is achieved through detailed review and communication with them and other stakeholders in their support about how they like and need their support to be.

Clearly also, the more you are able to match the hours that someone is available (and wants) to work to your offer of a contract of employment, the lower your turnover (and costs of recruitment) will be.

Performance management

Giving people regular feedback on their work, looking at how they are being supported, what they are learning and problem-solving together are vital for the welfare of both the staff and the organisation. This generic process of performance management includes elements sometimes called supervision, or one-to-ones, appraisal or performance review.

The United Response approach to performance management is known as 'Developing Excellence', and this is now explained in summary. In this approach, the terms 'supervision' and 'appraisal' have been removed, and the focus is much more on the manager as a coach than as a director and regulator of work. The 'how' is more important than the 'what', and the outcomes more important than the inputs. However, this does not mean that poor performance and ill-discipline are ignored and this aspect is dealt with in more detail in a later section of this chapter.

The process combines the use of:

- competency frameworks
- person-centred teamworking
- person-centred one-to-ones
- person-centred annual reviews
- Developing excellence portfolios (folders for all members of staff, which they use to keep their entire learning and development record)
- learning, development and training programmes.

The person-centred thinking tools used in person-centred one-to-ones in United Response are as follows.

To prepare:

- 'Good days and bad days' – every individual should identify what makes a good day or a bad day in terms of their job role, to help to identify individual strengths and development needs, as well as their role within the team.

- One-page profiles – these should be developed based on the previous tool and along with feedback from colleagues as part of person-centred team working. They should be reviewed periodically to ensure they remain a true reflection of how every individual perceives themselves, and how they are perceived (positively) by their colleagues.

At the meeting and the annual review:

- One-page profiles – these can be introduced initially to establish the best way for the meeting to be conducted, and to form the basis of agreed expectations for both the individual and line manager.

- Working and not working – to consider what is working and not working for the person, their manager, the whole team and, most importantly, the people the staff member supports. Input and ideas are gathered from the individual being supported, in the most appropriate way for them.

- Doughnuts – to review and agree tasks and identify what is inside or outside each person's Doughnut.

For the annual review meeting also, the Developing excellence portfolio evidence is used with the competency framework to assess development of competence. In addition, feedback is obtained from a range of other people on the individual's competence and performance. This is the 'many perspectives' principle of person-centred working, and may also include people supported (there are specially designed accessible forms for this purpose) and families, as well as colleagues and other managers or interfaces in the organisation. This is similar of course to the common 360-degree approach.

In Chapter 2 we introduced the person-centred supervision process. Here is a story of how a manager, Mark, used it with his colleague, Ann.

Mark, the head of learning and development, had recently had a complaint about the training Ann had done with one of the departments. The complaint was focused on Ann not listening to people on the training and becoming noticeably frustrated with one particular participant. The complaint had been addressed a few weeks previously, and when Mark had gone through the complaint process with Ann it was clear that she was very distressed about it. Although Ann acknowledged that the complaint was warranted, she had taken it really personally and was anxious about how people saw her.

Mark knew from Ann's one-page profile that good support would be to help her to work through her feelings. He also wanted to help her reflect on her behaviours without undermining her self-confidence. This is how he used the key elements of the person-centred supervision process.

Opening round – Mark appreciated Ann's desire to learn from the complaint even though it had been so difficult for her.

Ann gave Mark feedback about how supported she had felt, and that Mark had given her the information really clearly, without fudging anything, but had also given her time to process how she felt about it.

Negotiated agenda – this session was going to focus on learning and support because performance issues had been addressed in the way that the complaint had been managed previously.

Learning – Mark and Ann explored the context of the complaint and considered what might have contributed to her behaving as she had. It was evident that she had been under considerable stress at the time. Mark asked her to share a story about when she was performing at her best, and what contributed to this. Then Mark asked her to consider if she was aware of other stressful situations she had found herself in, and Ann acknowledged that this had happened before, although it hadn't resulted in a complaint, and the contributing factors had been similar.

Support – from this Ann was able to clarify what support she needed to spot the conditions that were likely to contribute to her feeling stressed, and she and Mark agreed how this would be respectfully communicated and what support Mark could provide.

Appreciations – at the end of the session Mark asked Ann what she had most appreciated about their time together. She said that it had been helpful to focus not just on the behaviours but also on the contributing factors, and she now felt more confident to manage her response during stressful situations.

Mark said that it had been important to him that they had been able to clarify what support he could offer without fear of undermining Ann's confidence.

In the context of staff supervision and appraisal, there is much debate about whether or not performance management should be related to pay and reward. Our preference is to have no direct link because, again, this is inconsistent with the focus on the outcomes for people supported in the health and social care environment. Many in other businesses, industries or sectors would argue that they are different, and so a direct reward for outputs is more appropriate. We are not convinced. If it is the overall success of the organisation, however, that is measured, then it may be appropriate that all staff should share in that, according to their level and contribution.

Learning and development

United Response is recognised internally and externally for its excellence in learning and development by the Investors in People Bronze Award, the National Centre for Diversity and the National Skills Academy for Social Care. The person-centred approach that flows through every system and process has been central to the organisation's being awarded and maintaining and improving its performance in the Investors in People award. One assessor said that she was:

particularly impressed with the behaviour and confidence of all the staff and the way they all strive towards one goal – ensuring that the people they support are at the heart of the organisation and govern the Way We Work. The staff team are confident in the use of person-centred thinking tools and described their work using the language of the tools fluently.

Staff quotes in this assessor's report included:

> The beauty of [United Response] is we actually do staff matching with the people we support to ensure we match values.

> Person-centred and building towards independence are our true values.

The result was that the assessor herself felt confident in using some of the person-centred thinking tools to report back on performance. She described how 'They (United Response) work with each person to develop a plan for what they want to do, based on both what is important FOR them and what is important TO them to achieve their wishes and goals.' Her feedback in relation to further areas to describe Strengths and areas of good practice and Areas for further development was received in the form of a 'Working and not working' list.

Another Investors in People assessor described the leadership and management development programme as one 'that would be the envy of many an organisation'.

An assessor for the National Skills Academy, in approving United Response for their Excellence Award, said:

> The organisation is very forward thinking in terms of learning and development and the value placed on this is clear to see and hear. All staff really understood learning, its impact upon themselves and its impact on people who use services. They were able to refer to both formal and informal learning opportunities and how much they value this and what United Response offers them. Learning, development, evaluation and improvement run through the whole organisation. Visiting United Response was an uplifting and inspiring experience. The whole organisation lives and breathes the social care values, and the inclusion of people who use their services is intrinsic to everything they do. They are an exemplar organisation, making a real difference to the quality of life for the people they serve, and they have much to be proud of.

Again, there are hard business benefits from this, because the holding of such awards is an essential 'ticket to the game' when tendering for business with local government or other funders. The area of learning and development being used to embed a culture and language throughout an organisation is another of those key differentiating factors for staff, as well as important to the people who buy the services, because it is obvious to them that it is an indicator of the quality of the product they will receive. Fundamentally, failing to develop people would be a clear indicator of not being person-centred.

In terms of creating a person-centred culture, it is clear that this has to be learning-led, by all staff in the organisation being trained in person-centred practices, so that it becomes, as mentioned earlier, the language of the organisation that everybody recognises, understands and uses.

Learning and development should be based on these key drivers:

- employees' needs
- competencies
- critical success factors
- value for money.

A full discussion of the operation of a learning and development function would be the subject of a further book, so here we will just highlight some of the key person-centred aspects of these drivers.

Employees' needs

Most learning and development professionals are likely to carry out some form of training needs analysis. The differences in a person-centred approach are the tools that are used and the people who are involved. Once again, one of the key aspects of the person-centred approach is to look at issues and decisions from a range of perspectives. In analysing training needs, therefore, we look at the widest range of stakeholders, including people supported, staff, business leadership, regulatory and legislative influences, and other key stakeholders. We include, of course, the sources of information on best practice in the industry. The product is a blended approach that supports a variety of learning styles. Individual learning styles are assessed and taken into account in the delivery of the learning and development.

So, for example, mandatory aspects of training required by regulators, such as the health and safety aspects of a support worker's role (part of the 'important for' content of the role), can be delivered via an e-learning process, with support for staff who may have difficulty with technology, and with additional information or learning delivered by face-to-face training or coaching from practice leaders and experts – who may either be professionals or people supported.

People who use services are involved in delivering training or development activities. They are 'experts by experience'. It is important that people who deliver the training are those who live the values and are skilled and knowledgeable in the use of person-centred thinking tools, while also being competent and engaging trainers. This reinforces the whole cultural approach from induction onwards. When external trainers are used, we expect them to reflect and use person-centred thinking tools – whatever the subject.

An example of this is training delivered by United Response outside the organisation to NHS professionals who needed to learn more about the best ways of working with people with learning disabilities. Here the training team consisted of two people supported and two staff members. All trainers had a one-page profile that they used with the other trainers to know how to support each other.

Again, a person-centred approach does not rule out using modern technological tools and techniques for learning and development, because these offer further opportunities for the activity to be learner-led, and to be carried out perhaps with different communication methods and so on. Clearly also, the use of learner support and administration technology such as learning management systems lowers the cost and sharpens the efficiency and effectiveness of the learning and development activities.

Competencies

A person-centred organisation needs to be very clear about what the values of the organisation mean in relation to the competencies that it wants to see in staff. There is debate about whether competencies add value commensurate with the time and effort it takes to design, agree, implement and maintain them. We have some sympathy with that viewpoint. In a person-centred context, anything that detracts from delivering what is important to and for the people supported is undesirable and should be minimised.

On the other hand, competencies provide a grounding for the people in the organisation that they can continually refer and redirect themselves to, so we see them as favourable and worth the investment. They must, however, clearly communicate what the values look like in relation to what is expected of staff competency. Additionally, they provide another opportunity for involvement and for checking that what is being expected of staff by the organisation aligns with what people who use the service want and expect.

So it goes without saying that getting staff, people supported and other stakeholders involved in defining competencies is crucial. The information derived from this needs to be combined with what is required for reasons of compliance and professional standards.

There are two levels at which this is done – the generic and the individual – through comprehensive data collection with a large number of stakeholders, a mass of data and information on what living the values of the organisation, and what is important to and important for people supported, means in relation to a set of generic core competencies. These will include both generic behavioural aspects – responding to the expressed 'important to' information received, and those related more to compliance nature – responding to the 'important for' aspects. So they would include perhaps something about communication skills and something about knowledge and awareness of regulatory requirements such as health and safety.

Therefore, a common generic set of competencies can be used across an organisation that reflects its values, but this will need to be supplemented at an individual level with information gained from one-page profiles, and staff-matching information about the people being supported, in order to identify specific skills, knowledge, interests and experience that will help support these people better.

In United Response, the competencies were designed by first identifying high-performing support workers by nomination from line managers, then conducting focus groups and interviews to establish what competencies they had which made them so good. At the same time, a group of people being supported were asked to identify what made a good or bad support worker for them. This information was then compared and aligned with the other inputs to finalise the competencies.

The key words mentioned earlier are that competencies should be something to which staff continually refer. This means that paying lip service to them, or using them for only one purpose, will quickly be spotted by your staff, and your laxity will be followed by them with absolute certainty.

So, if you fall into the camp that believes competencies are a good thing, then we recommend being wholehearted about it, and using them in recruitment and selection, learning and development, performance management, teamworking discussions and, where necessary, in dealing with poor performance and conduct.

Organisational critical success factors

In the UK, one of the key parts of the Investors in People award, and other national recognition systems such as Investors in Diversity and the National Skills Academy for Social Care Excellence Award, is that there is a visible link between the learning and development activities and the business strategy and aims. These awards also look at how the training undertaken contributes to those aims. One way of achieving this is to ensure that the link between a piece of learning and development activity and the critical success factors is specified in the training prospectus and plan. If this link cannot be specified, then you must ask why you are doing it. In a person-centred organisation, the critical success factors will of course reflect what is important to and for the people being supported and other stakeholders. A person-centred organisation also needs to be strongly outcomes focused (on the outcomes people want to achieve in their lives), and so have the investment made in learning and development of both financial and other resources stringently evaluated by external bodies on a frequent basis.

Value for money

In this book, we are largely discussing the health and social care world, where, it could be argued, money is in shorter supply than in commercial business. Indeed much of it is sourced from public funds or donations, and so it is imperative that it is used wisely, and can be shown to give value for money. So evaluation of the outcomes of learning and development activity becomes critical. The calculation of value for money in this area is notoriously difficult, but tools such as the Kirkpatrick™ method of evaluation can be adapted to use person-centred thinking tools and also to produce a notional return on investment calculation, based on reported success of participants in adding value to their work through the more effective delivery of outcomes for people supported.[88] So for example, you can use a 4 Plus 1 questions approach to the initial feedback or 'happy sheet' (evaluation form) from a training course. You can also use the same tool for follow-up with course attendees and managers. Alternatively you can use the 'Working and not working' tool, and ask managers to complete this with course attendees before the training and again in follow-up reports afterwards. To estimate a return on investment for a training session, you can ask attendees to report back on how well they felt the course objectives had been achieved, using a rating scale. You can do this immediately after the course, or at follow-up intervals, and also link the findings to how well outcomes for people supported have been improved as a result. In other words, you ask for a rating of the impact of the training on the people supported. The 'Important to and for' tool can be used to identify the most relevant outcomes for people supported that a piece of learning and development or training has an impact upon.

Disciplinary, capability and grievance handling

Ask most HR generalists what is the most time-consuming part of their job, and you will most likely get the answer that it is employee relations, and in particular the handling of grievances, disciplinary cases and capability issues. Many would include absence management in that list, and we deal with this separately in a later section.

Some observers would say that the area of disciplinary, grievance and capability management has become a minefield for managers and an industry for HR professionals and lawyers. In many ways, therefore, as a result of this, some organisations have defaulted to a defensive stance, almost as if they are at war with their staff. There are detailed and complex procedures to follow, and managers find it very difficult not to miss some part of the process.

In a person-centred context, conflict-based employee relations is an anachronism, and completely counter-intuitive to the values of the organisation. It is unrealistic perhaps to expect that nirvana can be achieved, and everyone will behave in a way that is always congruent with the values of the organisation. There are so many different people with their own peculiar frame of reference and beliefs that it would be impossible to manage every situation absolutely correctly. There is a different approach, however, using the person-centred thinking tools, and being less willing to become engrossed in formal procedures, without first trying to benefit from the relationships with staff that a person-centred approach can create. If you find yourself in a position where you feel you spend more of your managers' and HR team's time on unproductive conflict resolution rather than productive people development, then the following approach is worth thinking about. We believe it can be done, without falling foul of legislation or codes of practice.

Assume positive intent

This is a phrase first coined in the *Harvard Business Review* by Indra Nooyi (Chairman and CEO of Pepsi), which has received much attention and debate.[89] Some praise the concept as mind-changing, others as naive and dangerous. We believe that it is very relevant to person-centred thinking, and so recommend it here.

More often than not, people don't do what you want or expect them to do, not because they are bad people but because of some other reason that you don't know – yet. Don't waste your time on being angry or suspicious. Look for the reasons for bad behaviour or practice. Listen for the clues that tell you there is something else going on. Allow the time for people to explain what the problem is. Remember that the problem might be you, and maybe they don't know what you want, because you haven't told them, or explained it in a way that they understand.

Use the person-centred thinking tools

If you think you might have to get into a formal procedure, STOP, and try some of the person-centred thinking tools, for example:

- *Grievances* – if you haven't already got them, write down one-page profiles for you and the colleague concerned. Look at what they tell you about the way you both like to work. Try a discussion around 'Working and not working' from each perspective, to explore where the problem is.

- Exercise 2 in the Appendix of this chapter gives you an explanation of how the tools can be used for this.

- *Disciplinary situations* – explore a piece of 'bad behaviour' with people by discussing first what is not working. If they don't understand the problem, try discussing what is important to and important for the people supported or other stakeholders, and compare this with what is important to them. Finish by using 4 Plus 1 questions to review what happened and agree the next steps.

- Exercise 3 in the Appendix of this chapter gives you an explanation of how the tools can be used for this.

- *Capability* – again try a 'Working and not working' discussion to highlight the issue. Follow this with a 4 Plus 1 questions discussion to review what happened and agree next steps.

- Exercise 4 in the Appendix of this chapter gives you an explanation of how the tools can be used for this.

Of course, this approach is unlikely to work in isolation, and it must be built upon the firm foundations of regular review using the performance management processes we recommend elsewhere.

Absence management

All businesses know that absence is a problem. It is not uncommon, however, to find that they don't know the size of the problem or the impact and consequences of it. As a result, it sometimes does not receive the attention it deserves.

We have found that tackling absence simply as bad behaviour doesn't work. On the other hand, tackling absence in a person-centred way that focuses on what matters, and on individual cases from a well-being perspective, rather than an enforcement one, does get results.

Once again, the person-centred approach does not preclude the use of appropriate technology to assist the process. In United Response, for example, there is collaboration with a third-party occupational health provider on well-being and absence management using an information system that records and provides comprehensive monitoring information that enables the close management of absence and occupational health issues. As a result, long-term absence has been halved and overall absence reduced by around 25 per cent in the last three years by using person-centred practices and actively focusing on absence management. The main thing is to ensure that the cost and practicality of the use of the technology matches the expressed values of the organisation and what the staff feel is important to and for them.

The key features of a person-centred approach to absence management are as follows.

- *Understanding the problem* – this is about having very detailed and accurate information on where the issues actually are. It can be heavily influenced by what is important to and for an individual. For example, it may be important that members of staff ensure their children get to school on time or that an aged relative is safe and warm, and this may affect their ability to attend work. This is a very emotive area, and is often coloured by perceptions rather than the reality of the real levels and causes of absence. In addition, unless you have encouraged a culture of honesty in your staff, they will not tell you the real reasons for their absence. So what is really stress suddenly becomes a headache, or being managed badly becomes a bad back.

- *Continuous communication* – this starts when you are trying to introduce an absence management process, if you don't already have one, and continues forever. The vital part is that your staff know why it is important to manage absence, what your motives are for doing it, how their problems will be dealt with, and how it is going. So, in the United Response example, when a third-party monitoring process was introduced, the key message was that it was not just about cost. Although cost mattered, the real driver was to ensure that staff were at work often enough to provide consistent support for people. This was right, because the people supported had been asked and had said that the most important thing to them was having the same people supporting them, and getting to know them.

    Thus, the approach became one of being supportive and helping people to overcome their absence issues, rather than penalising them for poor attendance. This applied equally to non-medical issues, such as family problems and transport difficulties, as to medical problems. During implementation of the process and at regular intervals since, the operation of the process was reviewed with staff representatives and any problems or potential resistance to change explored and dealt with. This message was, and is, continually repeated, and supported by regular communications of statistics on absence and occupational health matters.

- *Strong well-being support* – given that the approach is overall a supportive one, it is essential that a comprehensive set of mechanisms to support well-being are in place. These might include an employee assistance helpline, free or subsidised health insurance, counselling, specific condition support such as physiotherapy, and general occupational health investigation and recommendation services. This is, of course, strongly showing that you are paying close attention to what is 'important for' each of your staff colleagues, in ensuring their health and safety.

- *Manager accountability* – one critical aspect is to make sure that the well-being and absence process is managed by the line management, and not by a remote set of people such as the HR department. We have seen many absence management processes that are run by HR, and in our view they don't work as well as having managers accountable for their own staff's well-being. Yes, HR and other specialists can support and train managers, but in the end it is local management action that gets the results.

  Exercise 5 in the Appendix of this chapter will help you with some ways of doing this.

Reward and recognition

This is a complex area, where specific market, industry, geographic, social and cultural influences have a significant impact on what is done in any given circumstances. All we can do here, therefore, is boil this down to some basic principles of what helps to build and sustain a person-centred organisation in this respect.

- *Pay* – for many people in the health and social care world, there is another reason for doing what they do apart from the monetary reward. This obviously differs in other businesses, but we would argue that there is often some other underlying reason that makes people get out of bed to go to work. That does not mean that you can take advantage of that motivation to hold pay down. The key in this area, if, like many, your business is faced with financial constraints on pay, is to be open about the situation that you are in, and communicate that regularly to your staff. It is much more likely that you will get a positive response (or at least a minimally negative one) if you have to restrain pay awards. The corollary, of course, is that if you have money available then you give your staff a fair share.

  Many would argue that it makes a difference if an organisation is unionised or not. In our view, the difference is slight, and the same principles of openness and integrity apply. In the UK in 2009–2012, many health and social care organisations were faced with having to bring about at best a standstill in earnings, and at worst some severe reductions in terms and conditions of employment. There is no doubt that having a good understanding of the business realities, and in particular of the needs of the people supported, helps staff understand if not be happy with such changes.

- *Benefits* – there is a huge industry now involved in 'helping' organisations choose the right benefits packages for their staff. The modern focus seems to be around the well-being of staff, and offerings in that area that encourage engagement with the organisation. It is interesting to observe how the style and labels of benefits provision seem to follow popular fashions and culture. It is very easy to be attracted by these fashionable offerings, and find that they don't actually make a difference.

Again for us some principles apply, based on some simple analysis using the person-centred thinking tools. This is that staff will appreciate things that match what is 'important to' them. So for some workers, cash now rather than a pension later may be more attractive. This obviously conflicts with a government direction to encourage saving for retirement and so makes the role of the employer quite complex in balancing individual needs with legislative requirements. Similarly, staff know what is value for money, and what is waste or not in line with the expressed values of the organisation. In other words, they know what is working and not working. So again this is an area for regular review and consultation with staff. Usually there is a finite budget for these things, and being open with staff about what that budget is and how they might like to spend it can work well.

In United Response, for example, a new pay and benefits package was introduced in 2005 after wide consultation with managers and staff on a range of options. This was reviewed regularly for effectiveness through the staff consultative mechanism, and as a result a number of changes have been made to remove or amend benefits in order to remain consistent with the current operating and financial environment.

- *Recognition* – again this is not the place for a lengthy discussion on the range of potential recognition and motivation/engagement techniques, but the person-centred thinking tools offer some help in this respect. We would encourage the use of one-page profiles to understand what works and what doesn't for individual staff in how they like to work with others. Again, a keen understanding by a manager of what is important to and for their staff will give many clues as to what style of recognition will be appreciated or embarrassing. You can also be opportunistic. So for example, when the cost of temporary agency usage in United Response needed to be reduced, the CEO set up a prize award for the best ideas to tackle this problem, and the winners were given national praise and recognition in the company magazine and through other knowledge-sharing mechanisms. The contributions of others were also recognised and shared widely in similar ways.

In IAS Owen Cooper introduced 'appreciation budgets' for all the managers. These were small, annual amounts of money for them to buy cards, bottles of wine, flowers or small gifts to show appreciation for staff who 'went the extra mile', and they were outstanding demonstrations of the organisation's values.

Everyone in HSA has an 'appreciation book' where each of the team has written what they appreciate about the person (see Figure 8.2). Jon says, 'If I am having a bad day, I get my appreciation book out to read. It makes me feel instantly better. When someone pays me a compliment or gives me great feedback, I record it in my appreciation book.'

An alternative approach, which couples the recognition approach to its obverse, the observation of poor conduct or behaviour, is to use the Praise and Trouble tool to identify those aspects that will attract positive or negative criticism. This can be done effectively by discussion with a staff team also. As far as practical, there should be no constraints on what recognition might look like. Giving managers a menu of possible tools and techniques can be helpful.

Finally, we should not underestimate the power of the simple thank you. Letting people know that you understand they have a choice about whether they do something for you or not (even if you are paying them!), and that you appreciate it when they choose to help you, is often an underused technique. This is no more than showing people that you are paying attention, and have noticed them – never a better spent 30 seconds or minute to give someone your absolute attention. One such method of recognition used in United Response was an invitation to members of staff to represent their area or service at divisional and national learning and reflection days and other forms of knowledge-sharing activity. Here they received direct thanks for their work from the top of the organisation, with the additional bonus that they knew their input would be widely shared and used to inform the ongoing strategy of the organisation.

Figure 8.2 The front cover of Jon's appreciation book

Equality and diversity

In recent years, equality and diversity has become an important topic, and the subject of much legislation, case law and other regulatory and enforcement activity. Again, in a person-centred organisation, there are some simple principles that don't ignore, but don't prioritise above each other, or above general good behaviour, any particular issue of race, gender, sexual orientation, religion or belief, age, or disability.

In a person-centred organisation, we are focused on people's ability and contribution, not on stereotypes and assumptions.

So we need to understand these things:

- *It's good for business* – we live in a hugely diverse market both for customers and for people to work for us. It is just good business to take advantage of all those potential contributions and opportunities.

- *Respect in the workplace* – it can be hugely complicated to understand all the cultural norms and practices of the vast range of people we now meet in our daily lives. In fact it is impossible. For us the key is simply to treat everyone with the same dignity and respect, and not to worry about any specific differentiating factor. It is about good behaviour, politeness and not being deliberately rude or offensive, rather than worrying about accidentally getting something 'wrong'. One-page profiles are a way for people to communicate clearly what good support looks like for them around any issues of diversity. Working and not working at an individual and team level are opportunities to build on what is working and address things that are not right.

- *Leadership* – it goes without saying, therefore, that an example must be set by the leaders of the organisation. This applies both in their daily behaviour and in their corporate actions. It is good leadership for the CEO or MD to lead the staff engagement activity in understanding and improving the diversity of the organisation.

Try Exercises 6 and 7 in the Appendix to this chapter to get some information on this for situations you are facing.

Staff consultation

Consultation with staff to influence local and corporate decision making and actions is very important, whether with the involvement of trade unions or not. Here again there are some things which help the process.

- *Leadership with humility* – individuals in a person-centred organisation are appreciated for what they do, not for any particular position they hold. This includes the leaders of the organisation. This is very much a first among equals approach, and not dissimilar to the position of a legal or political authority. Such an authority is allowed to work effectively by the consent of its constituents, and more importantly by their contribution. So it is vital for leaders to have the humility to accept that other people probably know how to do things better than they do, and should be allowed to say so and be listened to. Couple with this that leaders should continually remind their staff of when and where they influenced action, and how much that was appreciated.

- *Honesty and integrity* – easy to say but hard to do. In our experience, what works is to be absolutely honest with staff about the condition of the organisation; and equally to have the integrity to say that something is not acceptable and will not be done, rather than give false hope or mislead people.

- *Mobility* – getting closer to those parts of an organisation remote from Head Office, and allowing staff the opportunity to join in consultative activities if they are interested.

- *Communication* – ensuring that all staff have the opportunity to see or hear anything that is being discussed that affects their working lives and well-being.

Here is an example from United Response.

The Comprehensive Spending Review (CSR) on 20 October 2010 announced major public spending cuts, including a significant impact on social care – and the greatest austerity measures that most staff would have seen in their working life. It was essential to make sure that the organisation both remained sustainable now and into the future – crucially, without compromising the support provided – and continued to engage, involve and motivate staff through this difficult time. It was clear that they would, inevitably, be worried – but also that any attempt to gloss over the realities that were being faced would only make matters worse. The focus was on engaging with all staff via the internal consultative body (known as United Voice), as transparently as possible; on involving them in the thinking; and on harnessing their creativity in finding possible solutions. It was important to speak out against cuts that fell unfairly on the people supported – most importantly, of course, to try to make a difference and effect policy change, but also to demonstrate to staff that the organisation remained committed to its vision and values, and that they could still believe in their leadership teams.

Although the organisation is not unionised, the comprehensive internal consultative structure – United Voice – enables highly effective two-way communications and engagement of staff in the key decision-making processes of the organisation. There are frequent meetings at local and divisional level, supported by quarterly meetings at national level, where the Managing Director, HR Director and a divisional director meet with lead representatives of staff. These national meetings are also taken around the country to offer an opportunity for staff to attend somewhere local to their workplace and voice their opinions to senior management directly. This staff body is consulted upon and reviews all key decisions in the organisation, including HR, quality management policies and procedures, and reward and recognition processes.

Over the difficult economic times of the last few years, the staff representatives have been kept well informed of the financial status and strengths and weaknesses of the organisation. This has generated a very high level of trust in its leaders, and good understanding and support when difficult decisions have been needed.

At the same time, when the organisation has been able to be more generous to staff, many of whom are on lower salaries, this has been forthcoming, so building on that trust.

The key point is that throughout these consultations all parties to them are focused on the impact of any decision making on the people supported, and that is the benchmark against which decisions are taken.

The notes from national consultative meetings held five times a year are published to all staff, and the consultative infrastructure offers them the opportunity to comment on proposals and contribute ideas via managers or staff representatives. Senior managers are accountable for ensuring that staff can do this.

Policies and procedures

When you set about creating a person-centred organisation, it is highly likely that you will start off with policies and procedures that have been produced in a very conventional way, with due respect for compliance with legal and regulatory requirements. Becoming person-centred does not do away with the need for compliance with the law and regulations, naturally. What does happen, however, is that there is a growing disconnection or diversion between the emerging culture of the organisation and its written policies and procedures, operating manuals and staff handbooks, etc.

In an ideal world, you would prepare well, and re-write all your manuals before you started. In reality, that never works, for a number of reasons. First, it slows down the getting started while you do it. Second, when you start down the road of creating a person-centred culture, you don't necessarily know where you will end up. Why is this? Because the use of the thinking approach and the tools means that your actions must reflect what is important to and for the people you support, and other stakeholders. Third, until you are well down the process, the critical mass is not sufficient to carry through a willingness to take a more radical approach to policies and procedures. Last but not least, has anyone ever heard of a radical culture change pulled through by a new set of standards, policies and procedures, as opposed to a powerful vision, supported by new learning?

In a person-centred organisation there has to be alignment between the behaviours and attitudes you want to see in front-line staff and what is in the policies and procedures of the organisation. Without paying attention to this, there is a real risk that there will be different messages to staff about what should be done, and the desired way of doing it.

In United Response, staff and managers reflected that the progress that they had made in using person-centred practices was not mirrored in the existing policies and procedures. This then became one of the business priorities for the annual operating plan.

Ideally, it is better, therefore, to get started on the road, but remain aware that the culture you are creating is based on a focus on the people you support. As you progress, this will become increasingly at odds with policies and procedures that support a culture of generic rules and regulations, so the latter must be changed to align with the culture. Once the critical mass of believers in a person-centred approach is there, the resistance to changing the policies and procedures, and perhaps removing some of their 'security blanket', will be less.

The back office

Many cultural and operational change projects focus on the front-line delivery of services. Don't forget the back office staff, the support and administrative functions. Training staff in these areas is equally important, so that there is no clash of cultures. It is the same risk as suggested earlier of continuing with an outdated set of policies and procedures. If staff in the front line, who are trying their best to behave in a person-centred way towards the people they support, do not find themselves treated in a similar way by their support functions, a couple of things may happen. One is that they may lose trust in the belief of the organisation in a new culture. Another is that they just ignore whatever the support functions say, and go their own way. The latter may not be entirely undesirable if it drives change, but it may not be entirely helpful to have anarchy either.

So, in United Response, the support functions have received training in person-centred thinking tools. Workshops have been run with the HR team – for example, on subjects such as the best ways of engaging people supported in the administrative processes, and on the best ways of recruitment. These were largely led by people supported and their support workers, who acted in the role of consultants to the team using tools such as 'Working and not working' and the 4 Plus 1 questions to identify areas for improvement and actions to be taken. Most support staff also have one-page profiles and these are often displayed for people to see and understand. As a result, a number of staff in these areas have contributed to changes in procedures and ways of working.

Summary of tools and techniques

The following table summarises some of the issues addressed by HR and the conventional and person-centred practices that can help analyse, understand and deal with them.

The exercises in the Appendix to this chapter give more detail of how the person-centred tools can be used to meet specific needs. The person-centred tools can be used on their own or in combination with the more conventional tools.

What do we want to do?	What would be a conventional way of addressing this?	What person-centred practices can I use for this?	Exercise number
Resourcing	Interviews, assessment centres, aptitude testing, personality questionnaires	Matching tool	1
Disciplinary, capability, grievance and absence management	Formal procedures, investigations, hearings, appeals	One-page profiles Important to/for Working/not working 4 Plus 1 questions Doughnut Presence to Contribution	2–5
Performance management	Formal appraisal and supervision processes. Objective setting, targets, performance measures	Important to/for Working/not working Good days/bad days Person-centred supervision	See the Developing excellence process described earlier
Equality and diversity improvement	Formal policies and procedures, cultural training	Respect in the Workplace workshops	6
Equality and diversity impact assessment	Conventional impact assessments based on the protected characteristics	Important to/for Working/not working 4 Plus 1 questions	7

Conclusion

Martha Forrest was a leader in the inclusion movement, and her rallying cry was 'Tis people, tis people, tis people.' HRM creates the framework and practices to bring the best out of people, clarify decision making, support people well and get the best match between staff and the people they support or the roles they have in the organisation.

In the next chapter we chunk down from HR practices at an organisational level to what person-centred practices look like at a team level.

Exercises

Exercise 1: The matching staff process

Purpose: Giving a structure to look at what skills, knowledge and people characteristics make good matches.

Audience: Any staff.

Typical uses:

- Selecting staff for particular roles.

- Choosing project team members.

- In health and social care, to provide information for support plans.

How to do it:

Create a picture of the requirements using the approach below, or alternatively in a tabular form; then check how prospective workers match up to these criteria. If you are using this for individuals you are supporting, take the information from talking to the person supported and using one-page profiles, or person-centred plans.

Exercise 2: Handling employee relations issues (1)

Purpose: To explore solutions to employee relations issues before resorting to formal processes.

Audience: For use in one-to-ones with staff.

Typical uses: In potential or actual grievance situations.

How to do it:

Many of the person-centred thinking tools can be adapted for different situations, but here are some examples. We are confident you can find other tools and ways of using them to match your own characteristics and the people you are working with.

In grievance situations:

- One-page profiles can be used to explore what the parties in a relationship need from each other in order to make things work effectively. They can also identify where someone may not be receiving the support they need to help them be successful in their efforts.

- 'Important to/for' – as part of the one-page profile or separately, this tool can be used for discussion of what differences there might be between people in what they feel is important, or whether there is something that a person feels is important that they are not getting.

- 'Working/not working from different perspectives' can be used for a person to raise a concern about something that they feel they are not getting or is not happening correctly for them, or looking at the same issue from the staff's perspective, the manager's perspective and, if appropriate, the supported person's perspective.

- 4 Plus 1 questions can be used to review an event or series of events to explore where things have gone well or not so well, and to agree what to do about it.

Exercise 3: Handling employee relations issues (2)

Purpose: To explore solutions to employee relations issues before resorting to formal processes.

Audience: For use in one-to-ones with staff.

Typical uses: In potential or actual disciplinary situations.

How to do it:

Many of the person-centred thinking tools can be adapted for different situations, but here are some examples. We are confident you can find other tools and ways of using them to match your own characteristics and the people you are working with.

In disciplinary situations:

- 'Important to/for' – a manager can use this tool to explain to someone why their conduct in a situation has caused a problem that really matters to someone else or to the organisation.

- 'Working/not working from different perspectives' – can be used for a discussion of what parts of a job someone is doing well and not so well, and to highlight and explore why something is not working.

- 4 Plus 1 questions can be used to review conduct that has not been wholly acceptable, and to explore what can be done differently.

- Presence to Contribution – a variation of this tool can be used to explain to a staff member where their conduct is not fully meeting expectations, and what a fuller contribution might look like.

Exercise 4: Handling employee relations issues (3)

Purpose: To explore solutions to employee relations issues before resorting to formal processes.

Audience: For use in one-to-ones with staff.

Typical uses: In potential or actual capability management situations.

How to do it:

Many of the person-centred tools can be adapted for different situations, but here are some examples. We are confident you can find other tools and ways of using them to match your own characteristics and the people you are working with.

In capability situations:

- 'Working/not working' can be used to explain why someone is not doing a job to satisfaction.
- 4 Plus 1 questions – to review progress with a staff member.
- Presence to Contribution – to lay out what acting with full capability might look like, and where a person is on the spectrum.
- Learning logs – to agree and record progress on improvements in capability.
- The Doughnut – to discuss and agree where the expectation of performance of a role lie.

Exercise 5: Handling employee relations issues (4)

Purpose: To explore solutions to employee relations issues before resorting to formal processes.

Audience: For use in one-to-ones with staff.

Typical uses: In potential or actual absence management situations.

How to do it:

Many of the person-centred tools can be adapted for different situations, but here are some examples. We are confident you can find other tools and ways of using them to match your own characteristics and the people you are working with.

In absence management situations:

- 'Important to/for' – to explain why regular attendance matters, and the consequences of poor attendance.
- 'Working/not working' – to explore with someone where the underlying issues with attendance might be.

- 4 Plus 1 questions – to review progress in improving attendance or in rehabilitating from illness.
- 'Good days and bad days' – where someone has an ongoing underlying health issue, to discuss how that might present itself and how it can be managed.

Exercise 6: Respect in the Workplace workshop

Purpose: To establish an agreed code of conduct for behaviour towards each other.

Audience: Any groups of staff or between individuals.

Typical uses:

- Clarifying behaviours towards each other.
- Testing out reactions from potential team members during recruitment.

How to do it:

This workshop is a variation on developing a one-page profile, which invites people to think about, write down, and share with others, the answers to three questions. These questions are: What do people like and admire about me? What is important to me (through thinking about 'Good days and bad days')? and What do others need to know or do in order to support me or work with me? These same questions underlie the process for Respect in the Workplace. The output is essentially a team charter (or a type of one-page team profile), which is devised using information from individuals being asked to make the following statements, which are discussed and clarified in the workshop and recorded for the team as a whole. The individual preparation is:

List four Respect in the Workplace things you do towards others (how I support others)

1.

2.

3.

4.

List four Respect in the Workplace things you would like to see from colleagues (how I would like others to support me)

1.

2.

3.

4.

List four Respect in the Workplace things you would like to see from the organisation towards you and your colleagues (how we would like the organisation to support us)

1.

2.

3.

4.

Exercise 7: Equality impact assessment

Purpose: To establish whether an activity, policy or change has an unexpected impact on particular groups or individuals.

Audience: Any.

Typical uses:

- Testing the impact of an office move.

- Checking how a new policy affects people.

How to do it:

The impact assessment tool

This tool provides a quick and simple way to carry out the assessment incorporating some of the person-centred thinking approaches.

By considering the activity/practice/policy/event in hand, and its aims and objectives, it is possible to assess the following:

What's working

Here we identify positive impacts so that we can capitalise on them and ensure they contribute the greatest benefit to the organisation and its stakeholders.

What's not working

Things identified here can be grouped as follows:

Low risk – not discriminatory by current legislation. However, it might not be seen as in line with good practice.

Medium risk – not discriminatory by current legislation. However, it is not in line with the policy or vision, mission and values.

High risk – is discriminatory by current legislation (i.e. it is unlawful), and therefore also contravenes policy or vision, mission and values.

Once these have been identified, we can go on to identify actions (perhaps using the 4 Plus 1 questions tool) to minimise or reduce the impact on equality. Ensure an identified person and completion date are attached to each action. There is space at the end of the tool to record all this.

The impact assessment tool		
Activity/practice/policy/event, etc.		
Aims and objectives		
Equality area	What's working	What's not working
Age		
Gender (including transgendered people)		
Race		
Faith/belief		
Disability		
Sexual orientation		
Low income		
Carers		
Etc.		
Action required to remove or minimise impact (Use 4 Plus 1 questions to help identify these)		
By whom:	By when:	
Date assessment completed:	By whom:	

Chapter 9

Person-Centred Teamworking

Helen Sanderson, Mary Beth Lepkowsky and Stephen Stirk

Real teamwork is characterized by shared responsibility, shared decision-making, and differentiated actions.

Jeanne M. Plas[90]

Introduction

Henry Ford famously described teamworking as 'working together even when apart'. Teams are the engines that drive organisations, yet you will not find the term 'person-centred team' in the business literature. The closest fit is a 'high-performing team'. High-performing teams are 'deeply committed to one another's personal growth and success'. These are characterised by:

- a higher degree of commitment to performance and to one another
- an attitude that if one fails all fail
- shared leadership.

In this chapter we will share how you can use person-centred practices to become a higher performing, person-centred team. Any team in the organisation can become a person-centred team – HR teams, finance teams, directors' teams and boards, as well as teams that are providing direct support to people, and use the approaches suggested in this chapter.

We introduce the person-centred team development model, and ways of using person-centred practices to develop your team and team leadership. We present some exercises for you to try out, in the form of recommended tasks under each heading of our model, rather than example exercises at the end of the chapter.

What do we mean by person-centred teamworking?

What do we mean by a person-centred team? How would you recognise one? Becoming a person-centred team involves recognising that, above all else, people are central to any team activity or success. Person-centred teams:

- have a shared sense of purpose

- know what is important to their individual team members, and how to support each other

- allocate roles and tasks based on members' strengths and interests

- regularly reflect on and share what they are learning with the aim of continuous improvement

- maintain a 'living record' of what the team is, its purpose, how people work together, a list of performance goals and corresponding action steps – a person-centred team plan.

Working in a person-centred way with staff can make a significant impact on how long team members stay with an organisation. Retaining the right staff is a huge challenge across the UK and the authors of *First, Break All the Rules* describe research that shows how the first-line manager is key to whether staff stay or not.[91] The impact of the manager's behaviour is more important than other employee-focused initiatives:

> If she (your manager) sets clear expectations, knows you, trusts you, and invests in you, then you can forgive the company its lack of profit sharing programme. It is better to work for a great manager in an old fashioned company than for a terrible manager in a company offering an enlightened, employee-focused culture.[92]

A staff member's relationship with her manager will – in the main – determine how long she stays and how productive she is while she is there. In *First, Break All the Rules* there are 12 questions that relate to great management; the first six of these are specifically linked to retaining staff and reflect 'the core elements needed to attract, focus, and keep the most talented employees'.

Team members should be able to answer 'yes' to each of these questions. Here we introduce the questions and share the person-centred thinking tools and practices that you can use to make that more likely.

Question	How person-centred practices can help
Do I know what is expected of me at work?	Use the Doughnut to clarify roles and expectations. Having a clear, recorded purpose and values.
Do I have the materials and equipment I need to do my work right?	Train and coach people in the use of person-centred thinking tools and practices. Use 'Working/not working' or 4 Plus 1 questions with team members individually or as a team to learn whether they have everything they need to do their work right.
At work, do I have the opportunity to do what I do best every day?	Ensure that as far as possible staff are matched according to their strengths and interests using the Matching person-centred thinking tool and with reference to their one-page profile. Use 'Working/not working' or 4 Plus 1 questions with team members individually to reflect on whether they have the opportunity to do what they do best in their work role. Address this in person-centred supervision/one-to-ones and annual appraisals.

In the last seven days have I received recognition or praise for good work?	Use the achievement exercise to enable people to reflect on what they have done well. Use opening rounds in meetings as a way to hear from people about what is going well, and perhaps give further feedback on this outside the meeting. Use the person-centred supervision/one-to-one process to give positive feedback and appreciation at the beginning of each session. Use Praise and Trouble with the team to learn how you are doing in giving feedback to the team overall, and act on what you learn.
Does my supervisor, or someone at work, seem to care about me as a person?	Developing one-page profiles and acting on them is a great way to know what matters to people and creates opportunities to show that you care about the person. Keeping listening to people shows that you care about people and what they think, and want to get your support of them right – for example, using 'Working and not working' individually in supervision/one-to-ones.
At work, do my opinions seem to count?	This requires that people are clear about the decisions that they are involved in, through having a team communication plan, and that there are opportunities to listen to one another and that things change because of this. Positive and Productive Meetings are structured to ensure that people's views are heard – through rounds and timed talk, for example. Person-centred thinking tools such as 4 Plus 1 questions and 'Working/not working from different perspectives' are ways for people to share their views and opinions, and both tools lead to action plans. Using Working Together for Change with staff teams is a way to ensure that their views count beyond just how the team works, and to inform organisational development.
Is there someone at work who encourages my development?	Person-centred supervision/one-to-ones and appraisals are the way that this will happen on a regular basis. A good one-page profile will form the basis of discussions about how to develop the person's strengths and areas of interest. Matching opportunities for development in the team with team member's interests and strengths is another way to use the Matching tool.
Does the mission/purpose of my company make me feel like my work is important?	Having a clear, shared team purpose that aligns with the organisation's overall mission is a way to have discussions that link personal values with the team's purpose. In health and social care organisations, everything the organisation does should reflect the importance of providing the best possible support to people (see Chapter 6 for more on this).

cont.

Question	How person-centred practices can help
Are my co-workers committed to doing quality work?	This is where the 'accountability' values in person-centred organisations are so important. Sometimes people don't produce quality work because they do not know what is expected of them – so the team purpose statement and the Doughnut are crucial here. Getting feedback on performance is a key part of the person-centred supervision/one-to-one process.
Do I have a best friend at work?	Encouraging the sharing of personal information in one-page profiles (hobbies/interests) can support people getting to know each other and support friendships developing.
In the last six months, have I talked with someone about my progress?	This reflects the importance of both the frequency and content of person-centred supervisions/one-to-ones and appraisals.
At work, have I had opportunities to learn and grow?	Learning is one of the key areas in the person-centred supervision process. Using the 4 Plus 1 questions helps people to reflect on what they are learning in their work. Appraisals are opportunities to set goals about the areas that the person wants to learn and grow in. Managers can use the Matching tool to get the best fit between opportunities for development and the best match for this within the team.

How are you doing?

In Chapter 7 you will have looked at how you are doing as a leader, so here we will focus on how you are doing as a team manager. You can use the 12 questions and think about whether all your team would be able to answer 'yes' to each of them, or ask them directly. One team leader did that – she created a questionnaire from the 12 questions and gave it to every team member, asking them to complete it for her anonymously. At the next team meeting she shared back with the team how many people had been able to answer 'yes' to which questions. She shared what this told her, what her strengths as a manager were, and also the areas that she could improve in. She shared with the team the very specific actions she was going to take to improve, and that she would report back every two months in team meetings on her progress, and ask for feedback.

Here is a way to self-assess how you are doing as a person-centred team leader – in the way you lead, manage and coach your team.

The following table is a way to rate how good your person-centred teamwork may be adapted from both the Progress for Providers self-assessment tools. You can use it to rate your own performance using a scale of 1–5, where 1 is very poor, 2 is poor, 3 is fair, 4 is good and 5 is excellent, to give a rough first assessment of your progress as an organisation.

Measure	Rating (1–5)
The team know what their team purpose is and what they are trying to achieve together, and all team members know their purpose in relation to the people they support, their team and the rest of the organisation.	
The team purpose is recorded – for example, in a purpose poster or team purpose statement.	
The team's purpose informs the work of the team, and there is evidence of this in practice.	
The team principles and ways of working are clearly documented (for example, ground rules, team charter, person-centred team plan, team procedure file, etc.).	
The team regularly evaluates how they are doing against these agreed ways of working (for example, by using what is 'Working and not working from different perspectives').	
Managers ensure that each team member reflects on their own practice and is accountable for this.	
The team regularly use person-centred thinking tools in the team to listen to each others' views and experience (for example, 4 Plus 1 questions).	
There is a mechanism for recording and sharing best practice across the organisation.	
As a team we know and act on what 'good support' means to each person. This information is recorded – for example, in a person-centred team plan.	
Decisions about who works with whom are based on whom the person supported wants to support them. Where the team leader makes this decision, it is based on which staff get on the best with different individuals, taking into account what people and individual staff members have in common (for example, a shared love of country music) as well as personality characteristics (for example, gregarious people and quieter people), necessary skills and experience.	
Rotas are developed around people using the service based on the support they want, the activities they want to do and whom they want to support them.	
Our team has regular, productive team meetings that are opportunities to hear everyone's views, and everyone contributes. Team meetings include sharing what is going well and problem solving difficulties (for example, practising using person-centred thinking tools to solve problems).	
We review team members' performance on their ability to provide support in the way that someone wants.	

Developing person-centred teams

Now that you know what your strengths are as a team leader, we share ways that you can work with your team to develop as a person-centred team. In this section we introduce a model of person-centred teamworking, and our suggestions as to how you can put it to work. Our suggested approach to developing teams is to think about the team purpose; the people in the team; what performance means in the team; the process of developing the team; and progress in using these approaches in all areas of the team's work. This is shown in more detail below.

Purpose

Why are we here?

Why am I a part of this team?

People

Who are you?

How do we support one another?

Performance

What do we do to fulfill our purpose?

What programmes, products and services do we make available to others to fulfill our purpose?

What does it look like when it is done well?

Process

Who is going to do what in the team? How will we focus on being person-centred in all we do?

Progress

How are we doing? What else can we try?

In this chapter we will look at each one of these in detail, and consider the coaching role of a person-centred team leader. The process described in this chapter is based on the team performance model of Drexler, Sibbet and Forrester, that has been adapted through six years of research, using the process in the context of person-centred working in human services.[93, 94]

Purpose

Stephen Covey tells a story about staying in a hotel and being impressed by the exceptional service he received from the staff.[95] He was so impressed that he sought out the manager to ask how he had managed to produce such service. The manager explained that every team within the hotel had spent time developing their own purpose statement, connected to the overall mission of the hotel, but developed for their specific team and expressed in their language.

You would see this in a person-centred team. Person-centred teams have a clear, compelling and shared sense of purpose. This is closely aligned to the purpose or mission of the organisation. In social care, the goals of the team will flow from what is important to the person the team supports within the context of the organisation's mission, vision and values.

Different teams will have different emphases, depending on whom the team is there to support. For example, a supported living team would think about its purpose in relation to the three people they support: an inclusion team may see its primary purpose as enabling staff to work in ways that build community, and therefore the people supported are staff. Similarly, the people whom the HR team supports could be all the staff and managers in the organisation.

To think about the core purpose of supporting people to live the lives they want, and also to fulfill an organisation's expectations, it can be helpful to think about purpose at different levels, for example:

- What is our purpose in relation to the people we support, or who we provide products and services for?

- What is our purpose in relation to each other in the team?

- What is our purpose in relation to the organisation?

- What is our purpose in relation to the community and the external world?

This information – the team's purpose – can be used in team meetings, one-to-ones and in daily decision making. For example, in team meetings the purpose can be used to support decision making, by asking 'Does this decision take us closer or further away from our purpose?'

In United Response many teams have been working to achieve this. It has happened at established team level, and where groups or teams come together to achieve a particular purpose. One example is the coaches group (a group of managers and other staff), established to support embedding person-centred practices in that division. Julia (the area manager) described how they met to create their purpose poster:

> On that first day the coaches were inspired and fired up to take on the world and could really see how they could make a difference to people's lives. There was a lot of passion put into the original purpose poster. The poster represented the coaches as the rocket supporting people to reach for the sky and out to different worlds to reach their dreams. Feelings ran high as this was going to be

real and not just lip service and that we were really going to move things on. There was a conviction that this was it. Over time, in subsequent meetings, there seemed to [be a] lack of that same air of determination. Membership fluctuated and enthusiasm really seemed to wane. There was an atmosphere of confusion as to what needed to happen.

We then acquired some new members of the coaches team and at a meeting we desperately tried to convey the message of the original poster to them. We struggled. The original passion sounded hollow and unconvincing, the vision was confused and we lacked direction. It was time to start from scratch. We learned that a good purpose poster needed to communicate clearly to everyone, not just the people in the room on the day. It needed to be clear enough so that there was never any confusion about what we were here to do.

Together we looked again at our vision and purpose. Rather than rushing to an image this time, we worked out on a flip chart what we saw our purpose as, and when this was clear and shared, then looked at how to represent this visually, in a way that powerfully communicated its meaning.

Our vision was not a jumbled Rubik's cube but a way of fitting parts of a jigsaw together. This included a communication piece, a listening piece, and a 'making the tools a habit' piece, etc. in order to support people to get better lives. Relief was tangible in the team of coaches and there was a plan in place to work through what we needed to achieve. Since that meeting, there have been ups and downs – but there has always been that shared sense of purpose and clarity.

In summary then, once there is clarity of purpose, vision, mission and values, the key is to ensure that these are acted on, rather than remaining on a poster or fine statement.

The operations support and development team in United Response devised the purpose of the team in relation to including the people supported in the organisation by working with some people supported and looking at how in each area the activities of the department had an impact on them. This was then translated into a detailed action plan to improve ways of working.

Here are some tasks to consider in clarifying and communicating the purpose of a team, and different ways that teams have achieved this.

Team tasks for this stage

- Reflect on vision, mission and values of the organisation and what this means for the team's purpose.
- Develop a clear shared and recorded purpose.
- Reflect on the implications of the purpose on the team's day-to-day work.

Ways that teams have approached this

- Devising their own team mission statement informed by the organisation's values, mission and vision.

- Setting aside time in each team meeting to do exercises that relate to values and purpose – for example, doing a round in a team meeting to answer the question, 'What am I proud of this week that reflects the purpose of our team?'

- Graphically capturing the team's purpose as a poster to display in the office.

People

This section is about building trust within the team. There are two questions to consider – 'Who are you?' and 'How can we work together?' Answering the first question requires that team members consider what they like and admire about each other, what is important to them, and what support they want.

The second question, 'How can we work together?' focuses on building trust within the team because answering the question, 'Who are you?' also means answering the hidden question, 'What will you expect of me?' Without trust, the flow of information on the task and goals is threatened and information may be withheld and distorted. The amount of trust will vary across team members and over time. Research on trust and familiarity between team members demonstrates that little trust is associated with lower levels of productivity.

Supporting the team to develop their own one-page profiles is a way to begin this. Teams can also create a clear list of principles or agreements about how they work together and support each other (see the section on trust in Chapter 7, pp.171–175).

Some of the fundamental principles of person-centred thinking and planning are that people are involved in all decisions about their life, that they build their existing skills and interests, and that they get the support they want and need.

Developing person-centred teams extends those principles to staff. This means that managers and team leaders need to:

- discover existing skills and interests of staff and see how these can be used to deliver the team's purpose

- find out what support staff need and discover the best way of providing it.

As with person-centred planning, the process of developing person-centred teams begins with getting to know people, their skills, interests and support needs, and matching these as closely as possible to what the people using the services require. In person-centred teams, the support staff's strengths and interests are used to meet what is important to the person supported. In other teams this principle still applies – how can we use the strengths and interests of team members to better deliver our team's purpose? The Matching tool is obviously important here.

In the operations support and development team in United Response, all team members are asked to write a one-page profile when joining the team, and to share this with their fellow team members. These are very useful tools for getting to know new people, and also for referencing when, perhaps, something happens that is not easy to understand, but can be clarified by looking at what is important to the individuals concerned, or the way they like to be supported.

Here are some tasks to consider in enabling a team to know each team member and clarifying how to support each other.

Some teams in United Response develop a 'Respect in the Workplace' charter to describe how they work together (see Chapter 8 for more information).

Here is an example that one team in United Response developed:

Respect in the Workplace Charter

I show respect to my colleagues by:

- listening, acknowledging and speaking politely to my colleagues
- respecting everyone's ethnic background
- respecting other's views
- recognising each others' hard work
- understand each others' needs
- being patient.

I would like respect from my colleagues by:

- discussions taking place in an appropriate environment when there is a difference of opinion
- their telling me when they are upset or unhappy about something I have done
- their completing their tasks as I complete mine.

I would like respect from United Response by:

- having praise and acknowledgement from Head Office when we do a good job
- their listening to us before making corporate decisions
- senior managers visiting the service more often.

Team tasks for this stage

- Identify individual team members' talents and interests and see if there are ways to use these to support each other or the organisation.

- Know what is important to each team member and what support each person needs.

Ways that teams have approached this

- Using formal team assessments – for example, Belbin's team roles,[96] or the Myers-Briggs Type Indicator.

- Developing individual one-page profiles.

- Using 'Good days and bad days' and asking what the team can do to help each other have more good days.

- Developing Respect in the Workplace charters.

Performance

The 'Purpose' and 'People' sections help to create a culture of trust and appreciation. Performance helps us focus on accountability. Where the team purpose is around people supported having choice and control in their lives, for example, team members can be resistant to defining what success in that would look like and what their standards of performance should be. This can seem too impersonal and too 'businesslike'. We think defining performance helps a team focus on getting results for and with people that can lead to significant change in providing support in the most effective and efficient way, particularly when it is directly based on and linked to the expressed desired outcomes of the people supported.

Team members need to know why they are doing what they are doing (Purpose), what support they get to do this, how they support others (People) and exactly what is expected of their performance.

Broadly, the term 'performance' refers to the services that a team makes available to others. To deliver high-quality services, team members must have a clear and thorough understanding of the work of the team, and how well it is expected to do the work, or the 'performance' standards.

Performance (what we do) is different from the next stage, Process (how we do it). We first need to understand our performance by clarifying what we need to do to fulfill our purpose and how well we will do it. In a person-centred team the focus on performance begins with understanding what you bring to those who are supported by the team. What difference do people you support want you to make in their lives? This information will come from listening to people well, and is likely to be recorded in their one-page profiles or person-centred descriptions, their outcomes for the next year, and learning what is working and not working for people through person-centred reviews.

The challenge for a person-centred team in a health and social care environment is to strike the right balance between the drive to improve the quality of life for the people being supported, and the requirement to comply with a range of corporate obligations and strategies. It is not easy to live in a culture that wants to be person-centred yet has to comply with certain rules and expectations, both internally and from regulators. Therefore performance standards come from both the people a team serves, and what is 'important for' the team and organisation to comply with expectations of funders and regulators.

Tony managed a team providing services in the North East. He asked his team members to develop their own one-page profiles, before working with the three individuals that the team supported to enable them to develop one-page profiles. When team members shared them back with him, Tony saw such a variation of detail and breadth of information. Some people had just put single words under what was important to them. Other people had used very general statements that would apply to anyone and did not tell you anything personal or individual – for example 'sleep'! He talked to his manager, Lynn, about this, and together they decided to create some agreements of what a one-page profile should include. Another way of describing this is that they needed to agree the performance standards for a one-page profile in the organisation. Tony and Lynn searched the Internet for other organisations that had done the same, and found three other examples that they used to inform their own. They worked with a group of staff to co-develop a clear set of expectations about what one-page profiles should look like – for example, in relation to the expected level of detail in the statements. Tony was then able to support and coach his staff to achieve the expected standard in creating one-page profiles that the team could use to learn more about each other and know how to support each other well.

Here are some tasks to consider in thinking about clarifying what is meant by performance with a team.

Team tasks for this stage

- Go back to the purpose statement and identify as specifically as you can how you will know you have been successful. What does this mean for the performance of the team?

Ways that teams have approached this

- Writing down a description of what success looks like, the person-centred practices you can use to achieve that success, and how you will measure your success – such as the Positive Futures example in Chapter 3.

- Other organisations have developed comprehensive IT systems that record and monitor daily activities and how they contribute to the achievement of goals and outcomes.

Process

This section covers the processes used by a team to achieve its purpose and performance expectations and goals. This includes agreeing who does what, when and how, how the team communicates and makes decisions, and what this means for team meetings and one-to-ones.

In health and social care this means taking the outcome that the person who is supported wants to achieve and asking, 'Who needs to do what, where, when?' to make the plan happen. It also returns to what was learnt from People about team members, so the interests and talents of team members can be used to support the individuals who receive services. The person-centred thinking Matching tool is important here, and we talked about this in the last chapter. Person-centred active support provides specific procedures for implementing person-centred plans.[97]

Deriving individual activities and objectives for staff

The way these might be determined in traditional business terms might be to derive individual goals from a cascade of objectives, for example:

- Corporate vision/mission to...
- Divisional/business unit strategy to...
- Divisional/business unit goals and targets to...
- Departmental/site objectives and targets/key performance indicators to...
- Team objectives/targets/measures to...
- Individual objectives/targets/measures...

A person-centred team that provides direct support to people would have the following instead:

- How the person wants to live now and in the future; our team purpose is to...
- What are the person's specific outcomes for the next year? These become our team goals to support them to achieve.
- How will we know we are successful (success statements and performance standards)?
- What is each team member's individual contribution to this – who needs to do what, when and where? And what does this mean for our processes within the team (how we meet together, how we organise our schedules and rotas, how we make decisions together)?

Clarifying authority

The question also needs to address issues of the team's individual and collective power in taking decisions and making changes. Staff must be clear about what they can change and what they cannot change. The emphasis must be on giving power to the lowest level possible within the organisation – the direct support staff – wherever possible.

Giving away power or sharing power is managed by clearly defining job boundaries – and in the process of agreeing how decisions are made.

Teams can use the Doughnut to clarify what they need to do to deliver what is important to the people they support, in the exact way that they want to be supported, and how they work with those people to achieve their goals. This information can be developed into a decision-making agreement, which clarifies the power of decision making that the person, staff and managers have.

Decision making often happens in meetings, and the process of meetings is a key one in person-centred teams. How team meetings look, feel and sound tells you a lot about the culture of a team, and how person-centred it is.

Positive and Productive Meetings

In a 2010 *Harvard Business Review* article managers were reported as spending 50 per cent or more of their time in meetings, and in another study consulting firm Bain & Company claimed that two-thirds of meetings end before participants can make important decisions. Not surprisingly, a vast majority of employees and executives are dissatisfied with the efficiency and effectiveness of their organisations' meetings.[98]

Positive and Productive Meetings are a way to embed person-centred principles into meetings. It can be shocking to discover how many hours people spend in meetings each week and how little value they add. Every team has different struggles, but certain themes consistently emerge:

- People don't feel listened to.

- Agendas are too full.

- Certain individuals dominate discussions.

- Meetings are boring.

- At the end of meetings people are unclear about what was agreed and what they need to do because it was not recorded properly.

- The Chair does everything.

It is vital to ensure that meetings reflect person-centred values and are a productive use of time. Positive and Productive Meetings are based on three simple guiding principles. Teams that want to work together positively and productively must:

- have a clear purpose and a clear outcome for each meeting

- have a process and an environment where people are listened to and think for themselves

- work to people's strengths and share responsibility for different roles in meetings.

Positive and Productive Meetings uses questions to focus teams, and these are linked to a menu of tools and strategies, including person-centred thinking tools.

In Chapter 2 there is a graphic of the Positive and Productive Meetings process, and here are two examples of how these meetings are different from traditional meetings – the layout of the agenda and the use of meeting maps.

Agendas look different when people use Positive and Productive Meetings. Each one clearly states the questions or issues to be discussed; who is bringing each one to the meeting; what the outcome of that agenda item will be; how long is allocated for it, whether it is for discussion or information and, if the former, how people need to prepare.

Another feature of Positive and Productive Meetings is a meeting map, shared at the beginning of a meeting. It makes it clear what the purpose of the meeting is, the agenda, times, roles and rules. Figure 9.1 shows one used at a Trustees' meeting (ground rules were agreed and shared separately in this example).

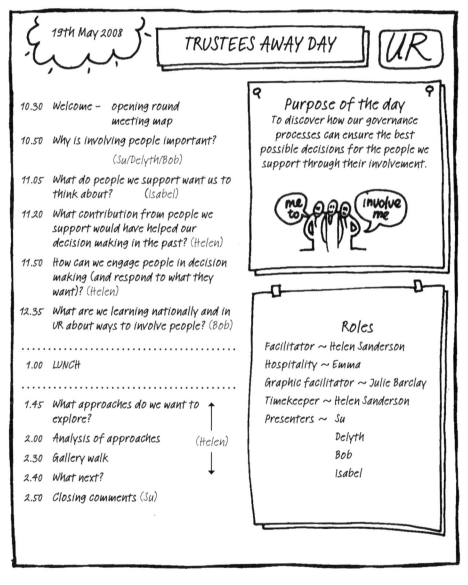

Figure 9.1 United Response trustees' meeting map

Person-centred one-to-ones (supervision)

Person-centred one-to-ones (supervision) use the same principles as Positive and Productive Meetings. Person-centred supervision starts with a shared appreciation of each other and uses this to establish a respectful environment. The process focuses on clarity in relation to role, support and learning. It enhances how teams function and how organisations work. Individuals come away from one-to-ones feeling understood, supported and motivated with a clear direction for action. In one organisation, all staff members are supported to develop a one-page profile as part of their induction training. In their annual appraisal, they use the one-page profile to inform what is working and not working from the staff member's perspective and the manager's perspective, and to develop actions from this. One-to-ones are also used as an opportunity to keep one-page profiles updated and to support people in developing their skills in using person-centred thinking by using the processes described in Chapter 6 around making person-centred thinking a habit.

Here are some tasks to consider in thinking about the processes used within a team.

Team tasks for this stage

- Know who is responsible for what.
- For each responsibility, know what is core and must be done, and where people can use their creativity.
- Agree on a meeting process that reflects people's values and ensures productive meetings where everyone contributes.
- Decide on a supervision process that enables people to get good feedback, celebrate success and problem solve.
- Know what is important to each team member and what support each person needs.

Ways that teams have approached this

- Using the Doughnut.
- Using 'Working and not working' around team meetings and one-to-ones – then building on what is working and changing what is not working.

Progress

'How are we doing?' needs to be asked on a continual basis through a cycle of learning. This learning happens on an individual basis – with team leaders giving team members feedback about individual job performance – and at a team level. Performance improves in relation to the quantity of feedback received: the absence of feedback is accompanied by high hostility and low confidence, whereas a high level of feedback, good or bad, fosters high confidence levels and friendly attitudes. Setting goals, roles and responsibilities and then forgetting about them only produces frustration and inefficiency.

In a health and social care context, in addition to reviewing existing goals and processes, a team must use other methods to discover more about the people whom it supports, specifically by using different ways of thinking about those people's lives. For example, the person-centred thinking tool, Presence to Contribution, can help a team think about opportunities for community connections and contribution.

Other teams in the organisation that are not engaged perhaps in direct support need to get an equally full picture of how they are doing. This can be done by:

- asking the people they report to

- asking other staff they provide help to

- asking colleagues in their team

- at an individual level, having a buddy who can give honest and straightforward feedback (a good technique).

In some manufacturing environments, visual performance indicators are used – for example, on flow rates, production per hour, or error rates. You would also find this in call centre-type operations where it is common to see televisual displays of incoming calls matched with handling rates, and sometimes with available staffing. Having a visual way to see and act on information about how you are doing can be useful to a range of teams.

> The leadership team of a national provider is working to implement person-centred practices throughout the organisation. The team is using a quarterly 'dashboard' to provide a quick, visual way at the beginning of the meeting to review progress.
> The team members agreed their success indicators at the beginning of the year, and then for each indicator decided what they were aiming for and how they would measure it. They have eight key indicators. These include:
>
> 1. The number of people they support who have a person-centred review with a specific and measurable action plan.
> 2. The number of people they support who have a decision-making agreement with actions that increase the depth, range or number of decisions the person makes.
> 3. The number of people with active circles of support (defined as circles that meet at least every quarter and involve people other than paid staff).
>
> Each quarter their dashboard shows with an arrow whether this number has gone up, down, or stayed the same over the last quarter. And then the discussion about it begins!

Here are some tasks to consider in thinking about the progress within a team.

Team tasks for this stage

- Have a clear process for reviewing progress against goals and performance standards.
- Establish ways of reflecting and learning together.
- Identify ways to continually improve, and build these into normal ways of working.

Things that teams have used to meet them

- 4 Plus 1 questions.
- Learning logs.
- 'Working and not working.'
- Person-centred reviews.
- Visual performance indicators.

Describing the team and how it works: a person-centred team plan

A person-centred team plan is a record of what has been learnt and decided as teams think about their purpose, people, performance, process and progress. Here are three ways that person-centred team plans get started:

1. A person-centred team plan can begin as a one-page summary of the team. This can be done, for example, in the form of a team charter derived through the Respect in the Workplace process, or as a one-page team profile like the one from Positive Futures (see Figure 9.2).

2. Another way to get started is by all team members doing their own one-page profile, and the team thinking about and recording their purpose.

3. Other team plans begin by creating a graphic 'team foundation' poster together, that describes the team's purpose, what is important to the team, and what support members need.

Whichever way the team plan starts, it is important then to look at what is working and not working about and for the team, from everyone's perspective. From this it will be clear what is going well, that can be celebrated, and where the team needs to focus its energy.

What is not working for the team may suggest a person-centred thinking tool that can help. For example:

- If what is not working is lack of clarity about roles, then a Doughnut would be a helpful next step.
- If what is not working is confusion about decision making, then a decision-making agreement may be required, and can then be added to the team plan.

Our purpose

To ensure that person-centred practices permeate all aspects of the organisation.

Great things about us

- Agnes is passionate, enthusiastic and committed.
- Nicola is honest, committed and friendly.
- Paul is dedicated with knowledge and a vision.
- Pauline is creative, supportive and committed.
- Lorna is honest, good fun and enthusiastic.
- Peter is creative, open and a good team worker.
- Lesley-Ann is approachable, enthusiastic and has integrity.
- Louise has a calm approach, always follows through and is able to see multiple perspectives.
- John is open, honest and committed.
- Martin is fair, funny and a good listener.
- Tim is a good listener, supportive and committed.
- Helen is supportive, always positive and good listener.

What is important to us

- That we have a clear plan, regularly reviewed, that achieves positive outcomes for the people we support.
- We are open and honest, considering individual perspectives.
- That there is effective communication both within the team and in the wider organisation, which includes 'top down' and 'bottom up'.
- We are punctual and do what we say we will. We 'walk the walk'.
- We work in a person-centred way with each other, including humour in what we do.
- We set SMARTA actions (Specific, Measurable, Achievable, Realistic, Timebound and Agreed) which take into account resource implications.

How others can support us

The Board

- Understand and demonstrate the person-centred ethos of the organisation.
- Use the tools - and see the values of their use in their person-centred thinking role.

Managers

- Share the vision.
- Recognise that they have a key leadership role to the success of person-centredness permeating the organisation and changing people's lives.
- Champion the use of person-centred practice in all aspects of their work using the person-centred thinking tools and supporting staff to use them and through their language and ethos.
- Communicate to the leadership team success, challenges and issues within services.
- Share what we are learning about person-centred practices.

How we can support each other

We support each other to think well together:

- We don't put people on the spot to make quick decisions.
- We have time on the agenda to think and use timed talk to give time for this.
- We support each other and use the skills in the group.
- We send out the agenda and papers for meetings two weeks in advance.
- We treat each other with respect and make meeting and working together enjoyable.
- We manage our time well - using a time keeper in our meetings, work within agreed timescales.
- We share responsibilities and share the workload.
- The agenda specifies how people can prepare for the meeting.

Coaches

- Share the vision.
- Champion the use of person-centred practice in all aspects of their work using the tools and supporting staff to use them and through their language and ethos.

Everyone

- Share the vision.
- To be changing people's lives through using tools, language and ethos.
- Demonstrate person-centredness in every aspect of their role.

Voices for choices and people we support

- Tell us how they experience the impact of person-centred practices in their lives.

Figure 9.2 One-page team profile

In this way a team plan can grow over time, by using person-centred thinking tools that reflect the team's priorities for change.

Eventually, a team plan could grow to reflect the following structure:

Team purpose

To give people:

- a shared understanding of the purpose of the team within the context of the organisation's mission statement
- clarity over the principles of how the purpose is delivered.

What do we like and admire about each other (or use one-page profile)?

- Describes the qualities and strengths that individuals bring to the team and are valued by team members.

What is important to the team about how we work together?

- Some ground rules for how people relate to each other.
- Clarity about the core responsibilities within our roles and where we can use creativity and judgement.
- Shared understanding that within core responsibilities individuals have room for creativity and judgement in implementation.
- Clarity about how decisions are made and communicated.
- Ensuring that team members are clear about what is expected of them within the context of the service's aims, objectives, policies and procedures.
- Clarity about responsibilities and accountabilities across team boundaries and how this is communicated between individuals, teams and organisations.

What is important to individual team members to enable us to work as effectively as possible (or use one-page profile)?

- Understanding what matters to individual team members (for example, about environments, structures and interactions).
- Those things that might put people off working effectively with someone.

What support we need as a team from others

- Identifying what is required from other people to enable the team to work as effectively as possible.
- How we interface with other teams and our expectations of support from them.
- How we recognise and reward success, creativity and innovation.

- What support we need as individuals.
- Identifying what individual team members require from others to work to their full potential.

Team actions

This may be a strategic plan for the team, or simply team members' current actions based on what is working and not working for them.

Creating team plans can make a big difference to teams.

I found the process of putting together our team plan extremely useful. It allowed us, as a management team, to spend time away from the office, giving us the opportunity to fully explore areas for development and identify a way forward that would suit each person as an individual. Every member of the team was encouraged to participate fully and personal views and opinions were listened to and acted upon if necessary. The process, as well as the final team plan, has enabled me to feel more comfortable in my role within the management team and more able to challenge any issues that may arise; having clear guidelines to work and refer to and a better understanding of the team as a whole has made me feel a more valued member of the team. Seeing the final plan gave me great satisfaction and an indicator of how much work the management team has done to put this plan together. (Diane, Administration Manager, Sure Start)

Some key skills for person-centred team leaders – coaching

To develop a person-centred team from Purpose to Progress, the team leader needs a range of skills, of which one of the most important in person-centred teams is the ability to coach:

Coaching provides the structured support and feedback needed to feel more competent and confident when applying newly learned person-centred practices. The coaching process is a vehicle to listen, understand and move the action forward.[99]

Person-centred thinking skills are central to developing person-centred organisations and teams. Therefore, within the team leaders' coaching role, there will be a focus on enabling team members to use person-centred thinking and support tools as a habit. There are many excellent books on coaching and we are not seeking to replicate that information here, but to share some ways that you can support team members to develop their competence in using person-centred thinking tools and practices on a day-to-day basis. Here is a summary of some of the approaches you could use:

1. Modelling person-centred thinking and support skills in a variety of situations ('I am using this person-centred thinking tool to...').
2. Informally teaching the skills ('Let me show you how we can use this person-centred thinking tool to...').

3. Enabling people to see opportunities to use the tools ('Would any of the person-centred thinking tools help in this situation?').

4. Providing feedback on the use of the skills ('What do you think worked and did not work about using that person-centred thinking tool?').

5. Reinforcing the use of the skills, and helping the use become a habit ('It was great that way that you…').

6. Sharing the learning about accomplishments and challenges within the organisation – up, down and across ('One way that I have seen that done elsewhere is…').

When and how to coach people in using person-centred thinking

A good place to start is where you can have easy success and use natural opportunities in your work. Michael Smull talks about using 'teaching moments'. A teaching moment is when:

- the skill is a natural fit for the issue at hand

- demonstrating or using the skill takes no more time than people have at that moment

- the skill feels immediately useful to those participating.

A team leader, whether leading a finance team, direct support team or the senior managers, has a clear role in leading, managing and coaching. A person-centred team will habitually use person-centred thinking skills to achieve its purpose, with people it supports, with each other, and in how the members relate to the rest of the organisation and the community. Therefore, coaching the team members to develop their skills in using person-centred thinking skills is a key role for team leaders. A team leader's coaching role is about a lot more than enabling the team to use person-centred thinking skills as a habit within its work.

One of the key principles is to start with where people are now, and think about how motivated they are to develop their skills in person-centred thinking and support. To find out where they are now you might need to observe how they are using the skills already, or to ask them to rate their skills themselves.

Team leaders will then need to adapt their style or approach according to the people they are coaching and the circumstances. In this respect, the ideas put forward by Landsberg[100] in adopting different styles according to the motivation and ability of an individual can be helpful. Alternatively, the highly developed situational leadership approach of Blanchard and Patricia and Drea Zigarmi,[101] and Hersey[102] offer numerous additional suggestions.

A key part of coaching is giving feedback. The Praise and Trouble exercise can also help to identify the areas you may need to pay attention to. Therefore make sure that you spend more time giving praise and feedback on what you see people doing well, as well as on behaviours that you want to change. A simple approach is to 'catch people doing something RIGHT', again mentioned earlier.

Conclusion

Person-centred practices enable teams to deliver, at their best, in ways that work for everyone. In a person-centred organisation each team will look different and work differently according to its purpose, and the individuals within the team; yet each will share the values of the organisation and will be contributing to delivering outcomes for people.

Chapter 10

Enabling Risk

Shonagh Methven

People's autonomy used to be compromised by institution walls, now it's too often our risk management practices.

John O'Brien[103]

Introduction

We all take risks in our lives, from getting a new job, to trying a new hobby, going on holiday or just crossing the road. Yet – understandably – cultures have developed over the years focused on keeping some people, who may have some need for additional support, safe, to the exclusion of all other life chances – wrapping people in cotton wool and restricting their experiences and development. How can you keep that important focus on safety – but also ensure that people have the opportunities to try new things and yes, to take risks, as others take for granted?

Although this chapter of the book is concerned with a person-centred approach in the social care context, this approach can benefit any organisation, ensuring that 'risk management' starts from the point of what makes sense to a person; and recognising that people will be more willing to fall in line with systems and processes that reflect something that is important to them, and which is not counter-intuitive.

What does 'risk' mean in a person-centred organisation?

Let's start with the legislation and definitions around risk. Health and safety risk management is by definition concerned with people. In this context, the recognition and management of risk aims to protect the health, safety and welfare of those who might be harmed. The legal framework within the UK is the Health and Safety at Work etc Act 1974 (HSWA).[104] This enabling piece of legislation laid down the requirement for employers to act to reduce risks to their employees and to anyone else affected by their work. The means of complying with this responsibility was later expanded in the Management of Health and Safety at Work Regulations 1999 (MHSWR)[105] through the requirement for a suitable and sufficient risk management system to recognise and assess the potential for harm; to control the identified risks; to communicate the information on risk and its controls to people who need to know; and to review the information regularly to ensure it remains appropriate and effective.

The definition of risk contained in MHSWR is clear. A risk is the likelihood that a hazard will cause a specified harm to someone or something. The assessment of risk also takes into account the extent and severity of harm that could occur.

Organisations must manage many types of risk: strategic; legal; structural; financial. This chapter addresses risks to people. In the social care context, these are people in receipt of services, their paid supporters, and anyone else who may be affected by the work, such as families, friends, contractors and members of the public.

So given all that, what does it mean for a person-centred organisation? A person-centred approach to risk undoubtedly improves on the basic system of risk management contained in MHSWR. Instead of using the abstract term 'risk' as a starting point, it instead identifies what matters to people, and their wishes at the beginning of the process, so that everyone involved has a shared understanding of the purpose of a 'risk assessment'. The process recognises that the identification and management of risks in relation to people is best guesswork, rather than a precise scientific calculation, and establishes the wishes of the people concerned as a starting point for the process. This in turn supports The Mental Capacity Act 2005 Deprivation of Liberty safeguards introduced in April 2009, which are 'designed…to prevent arbitrary decisions that deprive vulnerable people of their liberty'.[106]

Traditional risk management failed to recognise that support for a person should address different needs, those that are important to the person as well as those that are important for the person.[107] Support that provides those things that are important for the person includes ensuring that medication administration is carried out correctly, or that suitable manual handling procedures are devised and used by staff. These things are important and it is crucial for the person supported that staff get them right, but they don't support the person's hopes and dreams. How dull would a life be if the most fervent wish of an individual was to receive the correct dose of medication each day? An organisation must be able to demonstrate that it has adequate and appropriate systems that ensure the safety of the people supported in day-to-day tasks.

Below is an example of how United Response has worked to develop a person-centred approach to risk – from risk management to a risk enablement culture.

From	To
Health and safety risk management seen as something separate from person-centred support (operational) planning	Risk enablement integrated into support (operational) planning.
Risk assessments that only reflect things that are important for people, such as medication procedure, hoist servicing	Generic risk assessment of things that are important for people documented with evidence of effective communication and regular review.
	Focused and personalised risk assessments that support a person's hopes and dreams; those things that are important *to* them, again documented with evidence of effective communication and regular review.

cont.

From	To
Up to 20 risk assessments per person	Maximum of three risk assessments in relation to support for a person; risks from the environment; from others, and those posed by themselves.
Staff swamped with information	Assessments limited to vital information so that managers can test staff knowledge and competence.
Risk assessments that record all possible risks regardless of their likelihood	Robust risk assessment reflecting real and likely risk as described in HSE *Principles of Sensible Risk Management*.[108]
Risk assessments written mainly by managers with some staff involvement	Risk management involves the person themselves and their circle of support, including family and paid supporters.
Safety information recorded in more than one place, and sometimes in more than one risk assessment	Things recorded once so staff know where to find them, and so that managers can use the right information to test staff knowledge and competence.
Risk assessments that only describe negative attributes and characteristics	Risk assessments and one-page profiles that recognise positive attributes and characteristics.
Multiple staff-related risk assessments	In United Response, only assessments re. fire, stress and lone working are required in all work locations; other assessments are required only if the safety information is not recorded elsewhere, for example, manual handling information and competence can be demonstrated through training records, a regular checks folder and assessments about the person supported.
Support for staff implicit, but not always carried through	Explicit statement of support for staff when taking managed and positive risks even when the desired outcome is not achieved.

How are you doing?

The following table is a way to rate what you are doing at the moment in working together and engaging everyone in risk enablement, adapted from both the Progress for Providers self-assessment tools. You can use this table to rate your own performance using a scale of 1–5, where 1 is very poor, 2 is poor, 3 is fair, 4 is good and 5 is excellent, to give a rough first assessment of your progress as an organisation.

The table is written within a health and social care context, but can be adapted by inserting other job titles and roles. So, for example, where the text mentions people supported and their families, this can be substituted with customers, clients or other important stakeholders to suit your own needs as appropriate.

Category	Measure	Rating (1–5)
A person-centred approach	We ensure that risks are thought through in a person-centred way that reflects what is important to and for the person, and decisions are clearly recorded.	
An inclusive approach	We developed our approach to risk in conjunction with the people we support, their families and other stakeholders and believe we have an approach to risk that is based on listening to what is important to people.	
Managing positive risk taking	We have supported some people to make decisions that we (and their circle of support) didn't agree with and manage the risks and tension in this.	
Enabling staff	This approach is embedded across the organisation and all staff are clear about their responsibilities in this respect.	
Support for managing positive risk taking	Positive risk taking is rewarded and we accept that this will not always be successful.	
Learning	We have a no blame culture and learn from successes and mistakes as an organisation.	

Making risk enablement person-centred – what can you do next?

Moving from risk management to a culture where risk is encouraged and enabled could be one of the things that makes the most difference to the lives of the people you support, as John O'Brien's quote at the beginning of this chapter suggests.

To move in that direction, you may consider how to engage with staff to create this cultural change; how to deliver consistent support; how to fully involve the people themselves and other key people in decision making and communicating this approach to staff. First of all, we will look at how person-centred thinking and practice could be helpful in creating a positive, enabling approach to risk.

The following table summarises how some of the person-centred thinking tools and practices can help you move forward from your point of assessment. The later sections then add more detail to the actions that you could take.

Person-centred thinking tools and practices	How each tool or practice can inform, communicate or develop your approach to risk enablement
'Important to/for'	Identifies the areas of risk enablement for staff to focus on and enables staff to differentiate between things that are important to an individual and things that are important for an individual (managing risk in relation to tasks the paid supporter is paid to carry out).
History	Informs the risk enablement process by detailing what has gone before and the outcomes of that although information is scrutinised to identify that which is inaccurate or no longer applicable.
4 Plus 1 questions	Ensures that we are learning from what has been tried before.
'Working/not working from different perspectives'	To identify what is currently working and not working from the person's perpective and from others'. This will clarify where important outcomes for people that are not being met because of a risk-averse approach by paid supporters or others. This is also useful in identifying whether recognised risks in a person's life are sufficiently controlled.
Working Together for Change	Will give information from people supported, paid supporters and other stakeholders to work together to assess how the organisation is doing with enabling risk overall, and identify where changes in culture and practice need to be made.
The Doughnut	To allocate responsibilities for risk enablement. To identify where a decision on risk is not the responsibility of paid staff.

Social care providers must have in place systems that adequately control risk in relation to the fundamental things in the day-to-day lives of the people they support; things that are important for them, such as freedom from the risk of fire or of equipment failing. However, such systems are not solely the content of person-centred risk assessments. Risk assessments should focus on expanding the choice and control people have in their life, and enabling people to try new things and develop their skills and competences.

It was recognised in United Response that, if all the people in receipt of the services provided were to achieve the control over their own lives envisioned in *Valuing People*, the approach to the identification, assessment and management of risk had to change.[109] In Chapter 6, we shared the story of how the organisation changed its approach to risk. The approach was to start with a recognition that in real life things can and do go wrong from time to time. After many years of crossing a road, one day an individual could be hit by a car. Falling in love can end in divorce. Climbing a mountain can result in a fall. These consequences don't result in people never again crossing a road, falling in love or climbing a mountain. They are acknowledged as learning points in life. It was accepted that there will always exist an element of risk in all people's lives and that it is acceptable to take reasonable risks in order to achieve positive outcomes. For people in receipt of support to achieve a life like that of everyone else, risks must be identified, taken and managed. In this way, people can be supported to be more independent and, as a result, have more freedom and choice in how they live their lives.

The United Response system includes the standard information, instruction and training of staff, the maintenance of required checks and servicing information in relation to equipment, from bedrails and hoists to vehicles; mechanised control systems regulating water and radiator temperature; suitable fixtures and fittings including the use of fire-resistant materials and window limiters; and, crucially, fire prevention and protection measures that you would expect to find in any system.

The person-centred approach, however, seeks to de-objectify the people in receipt of services, to support them to rise above the second tier of Maslow's 'Hierarchy of Needs' and to get what is important to them in life.[110] Examples could be finding a job, making new friends or a loving relationship, moving to a home of their own and exercising the right to live as they wish. Making those things happen will usually involve taking additional risks. This presents a huge challenge to service providers because each of those aspirations has the potential to go wrong.

United Response decided to take a radical approach in relation to health and safety risk enablement and to use it as one of the drivers of change. A person-centred approach to support had been in place for a number of years, but health and safety was seen as something separate to the support planning process, its importance sometimes outweighing what were perceived as softer outcomes for people, such as inclusion in domestic or community activities. Although it was recognised that people should, and often could, be involved in making their own cup of tea, the risk of scalding from the kettle was often perceived to be present just because they were in receipt of support. The person-centred approach required staff to consider how something could happen, rather than whether it should. The process of boiling the water could be achieved through a small device inserted into a cup of cold water; a kettle tipper could stop hot water being spilled from the kettle. The process was changed from one that banned normal activity, because it posed some risk, to one where the risks would be managed to enable the activity to take place.

Moving from a position of power over people to empowerment of the people supported caused some staff to move out of their comfort zone. They were still afraid of the consequences for themselves should something go wrong.

There is more detail of the implementation of this approach later.

Creating a positive culture that enables risk taking

We highlighted the cultural importance of risk orientation and enablement in Chapter 6, but it is worth going into some detail here.

A person-centred risk approach can support a move to a better, community-based life for people with learning difficulties, but a change in the culture surrounding risk management is also required to encourage staff to enable people to try new things and develop new skills. An organisation has to foster a culture of positive risk taking in contrast to the risk-averse culture that too often predominates in the health and social care sector. A culture of risk assessing almost every aspect of an individual's life has developed over the years – a practice that is both unnecessary and time-consuming for staff teams who have to undertake assessments, and potentially restrictive and patronising for the people supported.

In order for risk management to be effective and to empower individuals, a partnership has to be forged between the people being supported, their family or unpaid circle of supporters, staff paid by the support provider and any other relevant stakeholders.

Working together– the key to unlock confidence

The involvement of employees in the management of health and safety risk in the UK is enshrined in law. The Health and Safety at Work etc Act 1974 (HSWA) was based on the findings in the Robens Report that were 'designed to create a framework within which employers and work-people jointly can achieve a more self-regulating system for securing safety and health at work', suggesting that those who create the risks should have the responsibility for managing them.[111]

The joint working model envisaged in the Robens Report is reflected in the social care sector through the partnership between the people being supported, their unpaid circle of supporters and staff paid by the support provider to manage an identified risk. In the same way, people delivering a service or working on the front line in industry have a day-to-day knowledge of the work processes and the risks involved, and can often suggest safer systems of work.

However, an organisation's culture can have as big an influence on safety outcomes as the safety management system. The Confederation of British Industry describes the culture of an organisation as 'the mix of shared *values, attitudes* and *patterns of behaviour* that give the organisation its particular character'.[112] Safety culture will reflect the overall organisational culture and priorities as modelled by leaders, whether these are characterised by a bias for output over safety, a tendency to focus on short-term reactive solutions, or a preference towards taking a long-term, considered and proactive approach.

You have seen in the example of United Response that the organisation found that the culture and style of management are crucial in encouraging open debate about risk and the best means of managing it. Success comes from good leadership, real employee involvement and good communications.

In contrast, an organisation that seeks to exclude employees, and to impose compliance without sufficient understanding or justification, seems doomed to fail if its own employees are not engaged. Similarly, an organisation that looks to apportion blame or scapegoat an individual after an incident will lose trust and goodwill in relation to all spheres of the business including safety.

Consistency of behaviour

The post-incident investigation enables an organisation to identify underlying causes, but only if there is sufficient trust and honesty between employer and employees to uncover what really happened. Many investigations identify individual error as the cause of an accident, but the underlying causes of individual error must be identified: did the person not know what to do?; did they not understand what to do?; had they acted in the unsafe manner on previous occasions and never been hurt, and, importantly, never faced consequences for their actions?

Nearly 50 years ago, Heinrich developed an accident prevention model called the Heinrich triangle, which states that one major incident will be preceded by 29 minor incidents and 300 unsafe behaviours.[113] Thus an employer has over 300 opportunities to identify and rectify unsafe behaviours. But the behaviours will only stop if the culture that employees experience is one where such behaviour is not tolerated, and where the prohibition of the behaviour is explained and understood by them. Safe ways of working must make sense to people either because they understand the risks to their own safety, and even continued employment, should they deviate from them, or because they recognise that *that's the way we do it here.*

For more detail on these leadership and behavioural aspects of risk management and culture, please see Chapter 7.

Involving people who use services and other stakeholders

In providing support staff, employers are legally required to take adequate steps to ensure the safety of staff and people, for whom they provide support as set down in health and safety legislation. Unfortunately, health and safety risk management is often used to stop activity rather than enable it. Fear of something going wrong, and blame being apportioned, can afford health and safety concerns the power to ban normal activities. Organisations and individuals within them can seek to protect themselves from imagined future blame, prosecution and fines, at a cost to the freedom of the people they are paid to support. Decisions presented as *protecting* an individual from possible harm, which consequently limits the scope of their life, can really be aimed at protecting the reputation and finances of the organisation.

MHSWR requires employers to ensure they get competent assistance in managing risk. Competence is defined as sufficient experience and knowledge with which to make a decision.[114] It can be argued that people receiving support and those closest to them bring a distinctive brand of knowledge to bear on the assessment of risk. Indeed the Commission for Social Care Inspection (CSCI), now the Care Quality Commission (CQC), refers to people in receipt of social care services as 'experts by experience'.[115]

A properly trained and well-managed support worker can bring a wealth of experience to the process. Recognising and managing risk to support a person to get something new or achieve in life brings the process into staff members' areas of expertise. It demonstrates that their knowledge and experience mean that they are among the best people to recognise risk and identify suitable and appropriate control measures, in partnership with the person and other people in their lives.

However, the possibility that what the person wants and what others want may not be the same thing cannot be ignored. Sometimes those in the circle of support, whether relatives or paid supporters, will not wish to expose the person supported to the risk of harm, or failure, or hurt, although this is inherent in the nature of positive risk taking and management, and indeed is inherent in life.

This caution does not inevitably spring from a wish to protect themselves or to 'cover their backs' and can arise from a desire to protect an individual. Perhaps this is a failure to see beyond the vulnerabilities of the people they love or provide paid support to, and to see their capabilities and desires. The challenge for providers is to enable their staff to recognise that support workers are in a person's life to provide support, advice and guidance, but not to take control. This will become ever more important as the personalisation agenda grows and places an additional onus on support providers and front-line staff to work with people to take positive risks in their lives. The role of paid staff becomes more important when people do not have natural circles of support in place – perhaps because they have lost touch with their families, for example. It is vital that these people are given the same opportunities to fulfill their dreams as those who have an unpaid support network in place.

Implementing and communicating the risk management policy in United Response

The starting point for communicating the change in the approach to risk management within United Response was the 'Statement of Intent' on the first page of the risk management policy. It placed the people supported firmly at the centre of the process. It made it clear that staff are involved in people's lives to help them achieve what they want in life. It looks like this.

STATEMENT OF INTENT

The people supported by United Response tell us that they want to be involved in the community, access opportunities, and to achieve their goals like everyone else in society.

With an ordinary life comes risk, and sometimes accidents may happen. The people we support, as with most people, will not always choose to live in a totally healthy and safe way. We will support people to manage the risks involved in exercising control over their own lives, through offering advice and guidance.

The Commission for Social Care Inspection (CSCI) states that 'The approach that UR is taking in relation to risk management is in line with the current Commission approach to person centred outcomes and a proportional approach to life skills and independence.' CSCI was replaced by the Care Quality Commission on 1 April 2009.

In managing risk, we will take sensible precautions to reduce the risk of harm to staff, the people we support and anyone else who may be affected by our work. Those precautions will effectively balance what is important *to* the people we support with what is important *for* the people we support. Risk assessments will not be used to curtail or ban activity.

The Health and Safety Executive states that sensible risk management is not about 'generating useless paperwork mountains'. Risk assessments should address real risk, in other words, risk which actually exists. Written assessments should contain information essential for maintaining safety.

As part of our commitment to enabling people we support to take planned risks, United Response as an employer will always support staff who have used sound judgement and taken sensible precautions, even if these have not been sufficient to avert an accident or incident.

Support from the Commission for Social Care Inspection (now the Care Quality Commission) for the proportionate approach in balancing risk with attaining life skills and independence lent weight to the change. Its inclusion in the risk management policy statement provided staff who needed it with encouragement to move to a more empowering risk management strategy rather than a risk-averse approach. The clear statement of support meant that managers and staff could also demonstrate to an inspector that United Response's approach was in line with that of the Inspectorate. The Care Quality Commission is building on the person-centred approach to regulation practised by the Commission for Social Care Inspectorate by using performance indicators that measure the outcomes for people. Outcome 1 is *Respecting and involving service users*, which includes the requirement to 'provide appropriate opportunities, encouragement and support to service users in relation to promoting their autonomy, independence and community involvement'.[116]

The final plank to encourage staff to make the change to a more empowering risk management strategy was an explicit statement of support for them, acknowledging that sometimes unforeseen events can cause harm. Staff are assured that, as long as their decisions have been reasonable and their judgement sound, management will always support them should an accident occur. The emphasis on reasonableness and use of judgement is important: staff are expected to show that they have properly thought through what might happen and acted responsibly in line with this; but it does encourage a strong focus on positive risk taking to open up the choices and experiences available to people.

The full policy also includes the Health and Safety Executive's (HSE) *Principles of Sensible Risk Management*, which defines sensible risk management as enabling innovation and learning, not stifling them, and focusing on reducing real risks – both those that arise more often and those with serious consequences.[117] The *Principles* also state that sensible risk management is not about creating a totally risk-free society or generating useless paperwork mountains, but equally it is not about reducing protection of people from risks that cause real harm and suffering.

The UK health and safety legislative framework is not a barrier to positive risk taking. Indeed there is support for innovation and a ban on infringement of liberty. A person-centred approach manages and reduces risk, in line with legislative requirements, while meeting the needs of people in receipt of support.

The monitoring and audit process had revealed that some people supported by United Response were described mainly through the risks they were perceived to pose and that this information was communicated in a large number of risk assessments. New staff had been inducted by being asked to read about the dangers posed by people, rather than by seeing, hearing or reading anything positive about who the people really were, and what was important to them.

This objectification of people, depicting them as dangerous – again, sometimes just because they are in receipt of services – is a huge barrier to achieving a support service that is truly person-centred. As long as people with learning disabilities are characterised as displaying challenging behaviour, rather than having different moods, as we all do, then they will continue to be seen as a problem to be managed, rather than as individuals with rights and responsibilities.

One-page profiles had been introduced by United Response to enable the people themselves and their supporters to gather key information.[118] One-page profiles describe individuals and include their positive reputation as well as helping staff and others to support them in the way they prefer, thus reducing the risk of disagreement and situations that prevent the people from being, and being seen as, valuable members of society.

We saw that having one-page profiles alongside up to 20 risk assessments describing a person's negative traits was incongruous. Risk assessments were never supposed to limit choice and freedom; they were designed to enable people to live the lives they wanted as safely as possible. Ironically the danger of having so many risk assessments for each person supported was that genuine risks and information people needed to be aware of to ensure the prevention of harm could be lost, and buried among numerous risk assessments relating to risks that were unlikely and improbable.

Therefore the decision was made to change the risk management paperwork to support the organisational person-centred approach. Written risk assessments were limited to a maximum of three assessments per person and revised risk assessment templates were introduced, requiring the assessment of risks, if any, posed by the environment, by other people and by the supported people themselves.

The intention was not to replace 20 assessments with ones that were 20 pages long. Guidance for staff required that they limit the information to that which was crucial to protect the health, safety and welfare of the person, staff and anyone else who might be affected. Reducing the paperwork underlined the message that supporting people safely is the key task of a support worker; it meant more time freed up to be with and think about a person, rather than using that time to write, review, read and sign many ineffective risk assessments.

A revised risk assessment template was devised, and is shown in the Appendix to this chapter.

The risk assessment template started by asking the question, 'How does this assessment reflect what's important *to* the person?' The intention was to ensure that staff started from the point of view of the person. What had the person to gain from the risk being considered? Was there really a risk at all? If so, what did the person concerned gain by the implementation of the control measures?

The assessment listing risks and controls in relation to the internal and external environment was aimed at preventing lots of assessments listing why people couldn't enter their own kitchen, boil a kettle, or use an accessible bus with their wheelchair, often only because they never had in the past. The single assessment ensures staff identify real risks and list control measures to enable people to take part in community and domestic life with suitable and sufficient support.

It moves the assessment of risks – for example, in relation to accessing the community – from just looking at the mechanics of physically getting to a shopping centre to an analysis of the barriers that can hinder a person from being seen as a valued member of society. The assessment would then list measures that staff should take to make that societal acceptance more likely. For example, if people supported are likely to panic in a crowd, then staff can support them to shop when stores are less busy so that the risk of distress is reduced and the trip has a greater chance of success.

Another example would be an analysis of barriers that stop people with learning disabilities from exercising their rights as citizens in the political process. This would again go beyond issues of physical access to a public meeting or the voting booth, and would include measures to ensure people have access to appropriate information and to candidates so they can make an informed decision when casting their vote.

The assessment addressing risks from other people and suitable control measures includes consideration of safeguarding issues. It also enables an examination of what construes suitable support from staff and others, and makes explicit the responsibility that they share in incidents of challenging behaviour. In this way such behaviour is not seen purely as a result of people's disability, but as a result of the interaction between them and others in their life.

The third assessment lists risks posed by people to themselves or other people. This enables staff to look at why people may exhibit self-destructive behaviour, and lists controls and strategies to support people to reduce the likelihood of such behaviour and to help them if it occurs.

The person-centred approach does not ignore the challenges faced by people in communicating what they want or how they feel to the people who support them, or the challenge to staff in balancing independence with risk management. It merely roots the process in the life of the individual rather than in the abstract idea of risk.

Here are two stories to illustrate the approach.

JOHN'S STORY

John is 34 years old and has always been a very resourceful and determined young man. He is deaf, does not speak and has learning difficulties and autistic tendencies. His robust nature has always presented a challenge to staff and for some there has been – and still is to some extent – a fear of being physically challenged.

In the past, lack of confidence among staff has had an impact on the type of support available to John. The normal approach was 'we had better not do that' or 'what if'. This meant that John would only go shopping to small shops, or if visiting a McDonald's the drive-through option would be chosen to avoid any perceived difficulty, which denied him the option of eating inside and choosing from the photos of food available.

He was never supported to use public transport, and his choice of holiday would be limited to a remote location with as few members of the public around as possible. He would often show in a physical manner his frustration at not being able to go into shops when his car was parked outside. His challenges to staff reinforced their fear both of him physically and of the potential that he might cause damage in a shop or injury to other people. It was not until staff recognised that his frustration at not being able to get out of the car was a cause of the physical challenging behaviour, and that supporting him to use public spaces rather than restricting his movements would reduce the risk of harm rather than increase it, that things began to improve and change.

A new staff team brought a changed attitude; they decided to focus on the positives in working with John and not the negatives, as simple as that. The team decided that there had been far too much emphasis on what might go wrong rather than 'let's take the risk and really put in the support'.

Along with John and his family, the team developed a person-centred plan that was put on the wall so every member of staff could see and learn from it. The plan was to start with small steps by visiting shops at quiet times, ensuring that support was provided by the team members who knew John best, and then to share learning with other members of the team. In this way the confidence of the team and John's confidence in them increased. Knowledge held by family members about what had worked well in the past was added and, as time passed, John accessed more of the community and met new people.

He now does his shopping in all the major supermarkets, visits major tourist attractions such as the London Eye and has holidayed abroad for the last four years. After filling his car with fuel, he goes into the kiosk to pay the cashier. He goes swimming, takes long walks, climbs mountains, goes cycling and to the gym, and regularly eats in restaurants.

Risk is assessed properly but it doesn't inhibit his participation in life. By learning as they go and empowering colleagues, the team members were able to offer John the support he wanted and this has resulted in a life where he is visible in the community and where staff feel more confident that he will enjoy his time, rather than fearing the worst.

John now demonstrably expects a high standard of support, and the challenge is to maintain this progress. His home is full of hundreds of photographs of him in the community enjoying life. He trusts the team members and they can feel that. That is a wonderful feeling and one that they work hard to maintain.

EMILY'S STORY

Staff started to get to know Emily by meeting up with her and her mum at home and in the office. Meetings had to be with her mum present at first because Emily was very nervous and she felt more confident with her mum around until she and the staff got to know each other.

Emily's mum was very supportive of Emily and wanted her to find a job she would be happy in, but she did have concerns as to whether Emily would manage it because of her disability and lack of confidence levels. As Emily's confidence in the support team grew, she began to go out with staff and without her mum, and to discuss jobs she would like to do and look around places that she might like to work. She decided she would like the idea of working in a pub, and if possible somewhere not too far from home. Jointly staff and Emily started off by looking at a pub a few doors down from where Emily lived because she had visited it with her sister. Although the landlady was very positive and friendly, she could not offer Emily any work. She did suggest a pub from the same brewery that was not too far away.

With support, Emily secured a job at the second pub seating customers in the restaurant area, setting and clearing the tables, and serving drinks at the table. Although she was nervous, she undertook every task with great determination. After a short trial and one-to-one job coach support, the pub offered Emily a permanent paid position as a front of house assistant.

Then she began travel training. For several weeks a member of the staff team would meet her at home and travel on the bus with her to work. This was repeated until she was comfortable with doing this alone. Emily's mum was very impressed because she thought Emily would struggle and she was prepared to take her in the car; there was no need for this because Emily picked it up brilliantly.

The employers and colleagues at the pub are incredibly supportive of Emily. They are always there for guidance and support if needs be, and encourage her to develop her skills at all times. The customers also think it is great that Emily is working there and say that they receive top-quality service with a smile when she is on duty. Emily has already built strong friendships with her colleagues and it is hoped that these will continue to grow. Along with a lot of hard work, Emily enjoys chatting and laughing with colleagues and customers alike.

Her confidence has grown immensely since she started paid work. She has a lot of pride in herself; especially when she sees herself in her uniform ready for work. She has learnt many skills in her job that she can transfer to other areas of her life, from helping her mum out in the kitchen to being confident chatting to people she may have met for the first time.

Conclusion

For some staff, health and safety can be seen as something outside their area of competence; something to be feared or avoided and only to be undertaken by experts. And it's important to remember it's a continuously evolving process; at United Response there is a strong recognition that even with the best will in the world things will go wrong; the crucial thing is to learn from what doesn't work – as well as what does – to keep getting better at spotting and managing risk.

Talking about risk in relation to people whom staff know, and encouraging them to work with the people themselves and others in their lives to find solutions based on what they know has worked for those people in the past, builds confidence in the staff team. Integrating risk identification and management in support planning makes the risk management process part of something that staff are confident about.

The aim of a revised approach to risk management is to enable managers and staff to identify what the risks are, to work out suitable control measures, and to transfer the information to the support plan. Integrating information about risk into the person-centred support plan enables staff to see that supporting someone safely is central to their job, and that risk management is not something separate.

There may be concerns that reducing the amount of risk assessment paperwork will mean that staff do not have access to all the information they need to maintain safety. However, limiting and prioritising the information in risk assessments means that staff are provided with manageable amounts of the information they need, and managers can test staff knowledge and competence more easily. Staff are clear about what they are expected to know and are provided with vital information to ensure safety, and managers are reassured that staff understand the risk and control information they need to support people safely.

Supporting people to take risks in order to develop and try new things presents a huge challenge to service providers because each of their aspirations has the potential to go wrong. There is rightly an expectation that, if it does, then society, relatives, service procurers, the courts and the media will scrutinise the organisation paid to support the person involved. The HSE *Principles of Sensible Risk Management* establish that the legislative framework is not a barrier to positive risk taking as long as organisations and individuals act responsibly.

There is evidence to show that providers, who have been subject to legal consequences in relation to support for people, fail to control risk on a basic level. A list of prosecutions, published by the HSE in relation to harm caused to people being supported, identifies that it's the fundamental events in their day-to-day lives where risks are not being adequately controlled.[119] In the five years to 2010, the list of prosecutions that have been brought against social care providers in the UK for causing harm to people they supported include one person who drowned in the bath, two who fell from hoists, one who burned a leg against a radiator, three who were harmed through a failure to use bed rails correctly, and one who died after drinking a poisonous substance that was being stored in a water jug. None of these cases reflects a wish by the person supported to take such risks. They represent the day-to-day activities that employers design and manage, and staff carry out. We are all fallible; and these cases make it clear where social care providers need to exercise effective control of risk.

A robust risk enablement system, designed to deliver safe support in relation to things that are important for people, and to clearly demonstrate that those risks are managed, is essential. Keeping a person safe, when using equipment or being supported to take medication is non-negotiable. All staff must be trained and supervised to ensure that they work within the system as designed, and the system itself must be subject to monitoring and audit to ensure it remains suitable and sufficient to deliver safety. Staff must receive clear information, instructions and guidance, appropriate and timely training and supportive supervision so that their knowledge and competence are tested and confirmed by managers. The system must deliver staff who are both competent and confident, and who have the skills, knowledge and experience to make the risk management decisions required of them at work.

The robust system can be used to address risk in relation to things that are important to people, and then to support them to take positive risks in order to fulfill their hopes, dreams and aspirations.

The person-centred approach extends to encompass the management of risk to staff. Identified risks include workplace stressors and the hazards associated with lone working, such as isolation and a greater risk to personal safety. Ownership is crucial. United Response strives to make sure that organisationally required risk assessments are written in consultation with the staff themselves so that the control methods make sense to the individuals who will work in line with them.

A person-centred risk approach alone, encompassing a positive vision of success, is not enough to guarantee that people will be supported to take positive risks. One must add recognition of the immense cultural shift that is required to acknowledge that people in receipt of services have the right and, importantly, must be supported, to take risks in their lives, in full recognition and expectation that they will suffer the same setbacks and heartaches that we all do.

In order to provide support and reassurance for staff when exercising their judgement and making reasonable decisions, it is crucial to:

- make explicit the encouragement to staff to explore what's important *to* the people they are paid to support, and to involve the people themselves and others in their lives in managed risk taking to make progress

- provide support both from the line management function, and from subject experts, so that decisions are scrutinised thoroughly

- make it clear in the risk management policy that staff engaged in reasonable risk taking are acting under their employer's instructions

- provide sincere, swift and wholehearted support for staff when positive risk taking results in injury or harm.

This last item on support for staff is not a carte blanche. Staff must know that decisions will be examined to ensure that lessons are learnt at the earliest opportunity and by everyone in the organisation. This means that if a near miss or an accident occurs it need never be repeated. However, an investigation does not seek to apportion blame. Scapegoating a staff member destroys the trust that the organisation must have with its staff; they are trusted to support some very vulnerable people, often alone, and for extended periods of time. An investigation seeks to find out how and why an incident occurred and to identify corrective actions to prevent recurrence. If staff teams need more training, better information or closer supervision, it will be put in place. There are very few people working in social care who would act in a way that would deliberately expose the people they support to harm, and so, while some actions or failure to act may seem incomprehensible at first, only by seeking out and understanding the immediate and underlying causes of an incident can corrective action be implemented.

Through this culture of accountability, but not of blame, staff know that the reasoning behind their decision, recorded in an assessment of risk, will be examined to reduce the risk of recurrence, but that sound judgement and reasonable decision making will not result in kneejerk punishment of the individual. Without that approach, staff will not feel supported to encourage the people they support to take the risks we do in life. Staff working in an atmosphere of fear or a blame culture, or who do not feel supported or competent, will never be emboldened to support the people they work for to take managed risks.

Appendix – risk assessment template

NOTE: Only assess risks which actually exist. Risk assessments should contain VITAL information to maintain people's safety.

Risks posed to the person supported from their environment
(Please list specific risks that exist)

Date of assessment: Prepared by:

Others involved in drawing up this assessment, including the person themselves, family, advocate and multi-disciplinary team:

Name	Date	Signature	Organisation (if appropriate)

- How does this assessment reflect what's important *to* the person being supported?
- How might the person be harmed?
- Is the risk adequately controlled? (List all the precautions that already exist. Do they reduce the risks as far as is reasonably practicable?)
- Further actions to control the risk
- Date when this assessment will be reviewed.....................................

Chapter 11

Measuring and Improving Quality

We must always change, renew, rejuvenate ourselves; otherwise we harden.

Johann Wolfgang von Goethe[120]

Introduction

There are almost as many definitions of quality as there are experts in it. *The Concise Oxford Dictionary* defines it as 'The degree of excellence of a thing'.

People who use services may not be able to 'define' quality in the same ways as business literature, but they know it when they see and experience it.

Crowther, Mumford and McFadzean remind us that values are worthless unless they are reflected in the behaviours of the people working in the service.[121] This is arguably the most important judgement about quality for human services. It is the actual experience of the relationship between the individuals receiving services and their support staff that matters – our values into practice on a day-to-day, hour-by-hour basis.

One of the characteristics of a person-centred organisation is the determination to get better and better, to continually learn and improve. This quest for continual improvement, and figuring out how to make sense of measuring quality, are the focus of this chapter. We will look at the relationships between quality and purpose, defining the quality you are looking for in a service, and then what's worth measuring and how you can do this. As we hope that the whole of the book is about improving the organisation to become more person-centred, we have focused more on measurement in this chapter.

What does measuring and improving quality mean in a person-centred organisation?

Thinking about how we define, measure and improve quality has to start with the purpose of the organisation, and its vision, mission and values. How successful we are depends on what we set out to do in the first place. If your purpose is to keep people safe, then you will be asking how you can check how safe people are, and you may conclude that the number of accidents or injuries could be helpful in knowing if you are successful. An organisation that sees its purpose as supporting people to live the life that they want will be thinking about how they know how people want to live, and how well their staff support people to achieve that.

Services that are genuinely striving to become person-centred will need to honestly assess whether each of their activities and outputs contributes to or detracts from their expressed purpose, and then to make any necessary changes to the way that they work.

Deming, one of the leading thinkers in quality, locates problems with quality at the feet of managers, suggesting that they are responsible for between 80 per cent and 94 per cent of quality problems.[122]

Therefore all members of staff will need to be clear in the light of the organisation's purpose what their core roles and responsibilities are, where they can use their judgement and creativity and what is not their job (for example, through using the Doughnut). Staff must have a clear vision of what success will look like, from the perspective of people using the service, their families and friends, and the wider community.

Involving everyone in deciding what quality means in the organisation

There are many ways of establishing what quality looks like – what you are aiming for in services. It is important that an understanding of what good quality looks like is co-produced with people using services, and staff and managers. Here are some examples, and how person-centred thinking can be used.

Individuals receiving services – at an individual level, quality means being supported in a way that reflects what is important to the people concerned, and in the way that they want to be supported. It will also mean working towards and achieving the goals or outcomes that the people have for their life. Person-centred thinking and planning are ways to discover and record what is important to the people now and in the future, and what good support means to them. Therefore a good one-page profile or person-centred plan representing an individual's personal definition of quality is essential. Improving quality for that person can start with simply regularly asking what is working and not working and changing what is not working.

Staff – it is important that staff are involved in defining what quality means for them in relation to how they are supported, and are able to contribute to what quality means overall. Here are a couple of examples involving one-to-ones and teams.

In a health and social care team, every staff member was asked what was working and not working about their one-to-ones, and what people would like to see in the future. This information was collected anonymously, and then a group of staff and managers developed a 'good practice guide' for one-to-ones. This explicitly said what to avoid (based on what was not working for people) and what to work towards (based on what was working and what people wanted in the future). Each manager was asked to review these with people in their next one-to-one. People were asked to use the good practice guide to share with their manager one thing that the manager was doing well, and one thing to work towards in one-to ones.

In a provider organisation team members are asked to think about what success means for their team, and what quality looks like for them in relation to the people they support, as a team, and as part of the organisation. Team members work with the individuals they support to define success or quality with them. These success statements are then part of their team plan, and they review them every four months using the 4 Plus 1 questions person-centred thinking tool.

Involving everyone in specifying what quality means in the organisation

Person-centred descriptions (for example, one-page profiles) represent what quality means to people from their perspective. It is important to involve everyone to establish what quality means for the organisation.

Working Together for Change is a way to define quality standards with everyone who uses the service's contribution. Part of the process is looking at what people say is working and not working in their lives. Staff, managers and people who use the service then identify the root causes of what is not working and decide on success statements for each area. These co-produced statements can then be used to establish a baseline of where we are now, and key performance indicators to work towards. Here are three examples of how organisations have defined what quality means to them, involving people supported and other stakeholders.

In the provider organisation, IAS, quality was defined based on statements of purpose. The process for creating the statements of purpose with individuals, families, staff and managers is described in Chapter 3. Once these were created and agreed by everyone, a quality group was established. This group included people who used services, family members, staff and managers. The group worked together to use the Doughnut to draft the staff core responsibilities, in each area of the statement of purpose, and where staff could use their creativity and judgement. They also defined what the 'bottom line' was, their promises, which they would always deliver, and how these should be measured.

In United Response, a group of people who used services and staff defined staff competencies together. They also introduced a process called 'quality checkers', involving a number of people supported in regular visits to other services to review the quality of support. They used the support of Skills for People, a Newcastle-based organisation that helps disabled people to speak up for themselves and have more control in their lives, to implement this. The quality checkers – all people supported by United Response – are trained and paid for their work as 'experts by experience'. The results have been extremely positive – providing a perspective and a richness of information that simply couldn't have been achieved via 'traditional' processes. One key outcome of one of these quality checks was to ask Skills for People to evaluate United Response's 'Getting it Right' quality assurance manual – to review whether it really did promote person-centred approaches to the way that staff provide support, and to make amendments appropriately to ensure that it did.

In a local authority, a group of care managers and people who used services worked together to define what best practice meant for support planning. They used the principles of appreciative enquiry [see p.266] and interviews based on storytelling to enable people to share the best of their experience of support planning. The group then used this to develop best practice statements.

Here are the person-centred practices that are useful in measuring and improving quality.

Person-centred practices	How each practice can help in measuring and improving quality
Important to and for	Information about what matters to the person and how they want to be supported is the person's personal definition of quality of life now. All efforts at measuring and improving quality have to start here.
Working and not working from different perspectives and person-centred reviews	Looking at what is important to and for the person and asking them what is working and not working is how to evaluate the quality of the service they are receiving, and then acting on that information to improve their service and therefore improve quality (in a person-centred review). For staff, you can evaluate the quality of the support that staff receive by asking what is working and not working about their support as described in their one-page profile. A team can review their work through using a team person-centred review.
Working Together for Change	This is a process of using the information from person-centred reviews to co-produce with people, families, staff (and external stakeholders) what quality means (through developing shared success statements that can be developed into performance indicators) and how the organisation is doing (evaluating quality through what people are saying is working and not working for them). It results in action plans to develop and improve quality.

How are you doing?

Looking at the organisation's purpose, and involving people in being clear about what good quality looks like are the first steps in thinking about quality and performance management.

The following table is a way to rate what you are doing at the moment in thinking about, measuring and improving the quality in your organisation. You can use this table to rate your own performance using a scale of 1–5, where 1 is very poor, 2 is poor, 3 is fair, 4 is good and 5 is excellent, to give a rough first assessment of your progress as an organisation.

Measure	Rating (1–5)
Our approach to quality is focused on learning how to improve what we do, and ensuring we are delivering on our commitments to people – providing person-centred support.	
Knowing what 'quality' means for individuals supported and how each person wants their support delivered (for example, a detailed person-centred description).	
We measure things that matter, in relation to our purpose.	
Everyone in the organisation has a shared understanding of what quality means and what the organisation's key performance indicators are.	
Performance measures and indicators are widely and regularly communicated.	
The implications of performance indicators and measures for action are discussed regularly and widely across the organisation.	
We have a clear, integrated way of measuring quality without duplication – including internal and external approaches.	
We have a balance of approaches – using numbers and metrics and also stories and examples.	
Information from measuring quality always leads to action – there is no measurement without action.	
We have a good balance of investment (time and money) in measurement and investment in action.	
There are ways that people we support help us learn about quality and give their views (including people who don't use speech).	
We evaluate our services in partnership with individuals and families, and share information from this and what we are going to do to become more person-centred.	

Improving performance

Once you know what you are working towards – what good quality or 'success' means for your organisation, the next question is how do you support people to move towards this?

Improving performance is covered throughout the book, for example:

- using team meetings as a way to discuss issues with staff and for them to support other team members in developing their competence (Chapter 9)

- using the personal development part of the performance management process (Chapter 8 for the Developing Excellence process used in United Response)

- creating learning opportunities (Chapter 8)

- managers coaching staff to develop performance (Chapter 9)

- Working Together for Change (Chapter 5)

- using Progress for Providers (Appendices 1 and 2)

- managing employee relations to enable people to develop (Chapter 8)

- managing change effectively (Chapter 12)

- developing effective business strategies and plans (Chapter 3).

What is important here is having an integrated, consistent way of working that combines some or all of these approaches and techniques. One place to start is with measurement, to establish a baseline of where you are now before you start, and then to continue to invest in change, closely tracking progress as you move forward.

Measuring and improving quality

When you have thought about what quality means in your organisation and how you can enable people to deliver this, you need to think about how you can know how well (or otherwise) you are doing. What you decide to measure is very important for two reasons. The first, of course, is to provide the information you need to check your progress and to continue to develop. As we said earlier in the chapter, there should be no measurement without action, and you need to focus on measuring what you have the capacity to do something about and improve. The second is that 'What gets measured gets done'.[123] What you measure sends significant information to people about what is important to the organisation, and therefore it is more likely that this will be what people focus on.

When thinking about what is worth measuring, another important question is how much time and effort you want, or can afford, to spend on measuring quality. There is an argument, as Crosby suggests, that effort and energy measuring whether something has happened is too late, and instead that effort and energy needs to go into prevention and getting it right.[124]

Prevention is the only system that can be used. (Crosby 1979)[125]

What are you measuring already?

Once purpose is clear and you know what you want to measure quality against, the next question is how. You can start by looking at what you already measure, and what other information you have about the quality of what you deliver and how you work.

This could include external audits, internal measures and other information about quality – for example, comments and complaints. Once again we recommend ensuring that this is drawn from multiple perspectives but, crucially, the perspective of the people using your service. It is important that your performance measures are clearly and obviously linked to purpose and what success means to the organisation. The effort and cost of collecting and analysing data must be justified by the value of the information you get. As stated earlier, there should not be any data collection without action.

External audits

Given that health and social care are already externally regulated, what else needs to happen to measure quality? Is external assessment sufficient, and should providers therefore just focus their resources on delivering quality rather than measuring it?

Some organisations do solely rely on external inspections. Others ensure that their quality strategy does not repeat what external inspectors assess, but add in their own; and, finally, other organisations decide what they want to focus on themselves, regardless of what the external inspections are looking for. External inspection is not just delivered by regulators – people who use services, and those who have expertise through their experience of using services themselves, can be commissioned to evaluate services. One example is quality checkers, described earlier in this chapter. The quality checkers process is now embedded in all four of United Response's divisions, giving the organisation, for the first time, the opportunity to formally and systematically invite people they support to conduct quality checks of the support provided.

Many organisations look to other types of external quality assessments such as the Canadian Council on Quality, EFQM or Baldrige.[126, 127, 128]

Internal measures

These refer to any information that you collect in addition to what you are required to measure for external audits. For example, earlier we talked about how the Quality group in IAS worked from the statement of purpose and used the Doughnut to develop internal measures for the organisation. In United Response the procedure is to observe and interview staff and people supported at a sample 20 per cent of support locations per year to provide quantitative information on a number of core measurements, including levels of assistance and contact from staff, community involvement, family contact and contact with friends, participation in daily life and choice and access to employment or regular day services.

Another example is a regular checks system, which requires that managers conduct four quarterly checks per year covering multiple aspects of risk management. Three of these are at the location(s) for which the manager is responsible, the fourth at a location for which they do not have operational responsibility. The manager checks that appropriate health and safety systems are working effectively.

Organisations can use best practice self-assessments such as Reach (on which the quality checkers process is based)[129] and the Progress for Providers tools you will find in Appendices 1 and 2.

Other information about quality

There are many other ways that you can learn about the quality of the service that you are providing. These include surveys, complaints and staff turnover.

Surveys

Outcome 1 of the UK Care Quality Commission's *Essential Standards of Quality and Safety* says that:

> People who use services can influence how the service is run as they are given opportunities to take part in decision making through general discussions with the provider, on an informal basis, as the person who uses services wishes – and *through periodic surveys or gathering of their views.*[130]

To comply with this, most organisations do annual surveys of people they support and their families. Staff satisfaction surveys are also a good source of additional information about quality in general and, in particular, issues such as treatment of people and the management of diversity.

We think that Working Together for Change is a more powerful and effective way of gathering information than surveys. This still fits the requirement of 'gathering of their views' but without the challenges inherent in surveys.

Complaints

It goes without saying why measuring things such as accidents and incidents, or failures of health and safety checks are important. Perhaps a less obvious one to the staff directly concerned is complaints – often seen as a bad thing, but in United Response, like many other positive thinking organisations, encouraged as providing more opportunities to get feedback from 'customers' and improve quality.

A complaints system gives you an ideal opportunity to identify what people are unhappy about, whether there are any trends that you need to react to organisationally, and how quickly and effectively you respond to people's concerns.

Staff turnover

The people you support will have a better quality of life if they are supported by people they know, and who know them, and where support staff are happy with the work that they do ('people's needs are best met by people whose needs are met').[131] Therefore, looking at your staff turnover is important to consider when you are thinking about quality. It is not just an issue of turnover per se, but asking, 'Are we keeping our great staff?' Levels and reasons for staff absence and the volume of use of temporary agency staff provide important information to explore in relation to quality.

Some of the 'normal' areas that you measure are critically related to your core purpose – for example: diversity of the staff population is critical to measure, not because there is some regulatory requirement, but because it is good business. If an organisation wants to profess to be person-centred, then it is impossible to be non-diverse. Diversity adds to the quality of staff, by bringing a broader range of skills, knowledge and experience, and therefore to the quality of the 'product'. The 'product' becomes more attractive to prospective purchasers because they can see it is related to their own diversity and what they perceive as high quality.

What else do you want to learn about and change?

Once you have looked at your purpose and what you want to learn, and then considered whether your existing quality measures give you that information, you will be able to see where the gaps in your measurement process are, and to decide what to do about them. It could be that taking a random sample around a particular issue – for example, identified through Working Together for Change – is more helpful than trying to develop a comprehensive set of measures that would be regularly and routinely applied.

> In older people's services, in a local authority in the North West, the senior managers in a local authority were concerned that their care management process was not very person-centred. They decided to get together managers and staff from the care management service with carers and providers to look at the issues together. They mapped out the care management process together on large pieces of paper across the room. Then they identified the areas that could be improved, and asked everyone to share what was working and not working from the perspectives of everyone in the room. This enabled them to see what they needed to keep going with, and what needed to change. Then they asked whether any of the person-centred thinking tools could help. As a result of this they discovered:
> - that they were duplicating reviews (they decided to introduce person-centred reviews instead, and to review thoroughly, in a person-centred way)
> - to introduce one-page profiles at the beginning of assessments
> - to focus on decision-making agreements within three weeks of people becoming supported by providers.
>
> Now they have decided to measure the number of one-page profiles and person-centred reviews that actually take place.

Earlier in the book (Chapter 3) we described how Positive Futures developed a 'one-page strategy' that clearly communicated to everyone in the organisation what success meant, how person-centred thinking tools and practices could be used to help achieve it, and what they were measuring to see how successful they were being. Success was measured by determining their key performance indicators.

> Key Performance Indicators are like the tips of an iceberg – the 10 per cent of things that can be seen and measured that provide evidence of the existence of the other 90 per cent. When groups of people get together to search for 'Key Performance Indicators' that measure progress toward a particular long term outcome, those that are most likely to be *useful* for people who use services, *feasible* to measure (without wasting valuable time and resources), and *accurate*.[132]

Some challenges to consider

There are some challenges to consider when thinking about measurement. Here are five to be mindful of.

1. Be careful what you count. Check that you are not setting up perverse incentives, or giving a different message from the one you intend. For example, there is a danger in counting the number of plans that have been written, because this gives a message that it is the paperwork that matters. This can be addressed, instead, by counting one-page profiles that have actions based on what is working and not working for people. Counting action plans of course does not mean that they have been achieved, or are being worked towards; however, if you count the number of actions that have been achieved, you set up a perverse incentive for staff to make sure that only 'easy to achieve' goals are set.

2. Be specific about what you are counting. For example, a good indicator for some services is the number of people who have a job. However, 'job' means different things to different people – some may consider voluntary work as a job, others (probably including those doing the work) will not. Therefore you will want to be precise and define your measure as perhaps 'the number of people who have work paid at or above the minimum wage, and who work for 16 hours or more a week'.

3. Don't reinvent what is already available. If you are looking at using measures in social care, for example, you might want to consider:

    • the measures used by IBSEN to assess the Individual Budget Pilot[133]

    • the measures used by Janet Robertson, Eric Emerson and colleagues to assess the impact of person-centred planning[134]

    • the approach to measuring personal outcomes developed by the Council on Quality and Leadership (their method uses structured interviews to gather information on 25 personal outcomes).[135]

4. Don't only rely solely on numbers. Numbers by themselves are insufficient for learning about what you are doing well and what needs to change. What they can do is alert you to where further conversations need to take place.
    Other ways of doing things could include the following.

    • Using storytelling – stories have an important role in understanding and explaining change and we talk about this in Chapter 12. It's worth spending time on a story to work out what you can learn from it and what it is telling you in some detail about the support you provide, so that you can use that learning and apply it elsewhere.

    • Appreciative enquiry – an approach that begins with the premise that change starts by finding out what is good, positive and working, and then doing more of it.[136]

- Some processes that combine measurement and action – for example, the Social Role Inventory (www.inclusion.com) combines measurement and a change process. In this approach, measures are co-produced as part of taking steps to develop organisational capacity.

5. Be cautious about surveys. Service user surveys (or equivalent) are required by regulators. However, surveys for people who use services are fraught with challenges – for example, how can you mitigate against the impact of people probably having fewer life experiences and lower expectations of services than the general population? How can you address the different ways that people communicate through a survey?

Sometimes we may need to gather information that is more subjective – for example, measures of quality of life might look at people's own impressions of how they are living, and the meaning that they attach to their lives.

Working Together for Change, using information from person-centred reviews, is a way to learn about quality from people who use the service, without taking people's time through surveys and focus groups. Providers are starting to use person-centred reviews as a way to hear everyone's perspective of what is working and not working (therefore fulfilling the regulators' expectations), and then Working Together for Change as a way to address together what is not working, and to celebrate and build on what is working. This combines reviewing quality and improving quality, in a co-produced way, in line with person-centred values.

Conclusion

Thinking about quality has to start with purpose. What are we trying to achieve, and then how well are we doing? A person-centred approach to measuring quality naturally involves a range of perspectives, starting with the people supported. What does quality mean to an individual? This is found in the information about what matters to the person, and how best to support them – this is each person's individual definition of their quality of life. Finding ways to fully involve everyone in measuring and developing quality, including people who don't use speech, can be achieved through person-centred reviews and using this information about what is working and not working in Working Together for Change. In a person-centred organisation you will hear about numbers (but only counting things that matter) and stories, in conversations about quality, and you will see action based on what is learnt to continually improve and develop.

Chapter 12

Managing Change

Change is the law of life and those who look only to the past or present are certain to miss the future.

John F. Kennedy[137]

Introduction

We devote a separate chapter here to managing change clearly because of its universal importance to the life of any organisation or the people it supports and serves. In health and social care, trying new things, enabling thoughtful risk taking and expanding the boundaries for people with their communities are the lifeblood of providing person-centred support. In the modern world, the speed of innovation and communication is such that all of us are constantly adapting to new environments, stimuli and ways of doing things. The advance of technology such as the smartphone alone demonstrates the global impact this change can have.

So understanding what constitutes change, knowing what is happening during change, and having the skills to manage the impact is vital knowledge for any manager and practitioner in every field. In person-centred terms, of course, this means being very adept at change management because it affects each individual, and having that knowledge and skill embedded across the organisation.

Earlier in the book, we give examples of cultural and business change, and supporting this with person-centred HRM approaches – for example, in relation to performance management. In this chapter, we share how person-centred practices can be used in making change happen, or in managing change activities and projects.

Here you will find some definitions of change, some of the typical issues that arise, a guide to what good change management looks like in a person-centred organisation, practical examples of the theory in practice, a guide to the key areas to address in change management, and some example exercises to help you in using the person-centred tools and techniques we recommend for this purpose. We pay particular attention to the role of storytelling in change on pp.286–289.

What does managing change mean in a person-centred organisation?

> There is nothing more difficult to take in hand, more perilous to conduct, or more uncertain in its success, than to take the lead in the introduction of a new order of things. (Machiavelli 1515)[138]

The Commander in Chief of change management points out that courage is required to begin the process of change. Leaders need the strength and wherewithal to carry through what has been started. Our definition of change management is the way in which an organisation improves itself and aligns to what is important to the people it supports by doing things differently and adapting to the context and environment it works in. This is a constant process, and may consist of change at a number of levels. Gerald Smale, in his book *Managing Change through Innovation*, identified a first and second order of change.[139] He defines them as follows:

- A first order change is a change *within* the rules of a given system; *within* the existing pattern of relationships between people even where tasks change significantly. First order change takes place without change in the existing role relationships between people.

- Second order change occurs when there *is a change in the nature of the relationship between people, a change in the rules, a change in the nature of the system*; when rules and the boundaries of a system of relationships change in an unprecedented way, when patterns of relationship are altered. The roles of each party in a relationship change.

Smale's definitions add much to the understanding of the complexities of change. We need to be clear that personalisation and introducing person-centred practices are second order changes, because they fundamentally change the power relationships within organisations and with people and professionals. It is easy to think that you are just introducing a new set of tools (a first order change) rather than fully appreciating the change in power and relationships this requires (a second order change).

Smull, Bourne and Sanderson suggest looking at three levels of change.[140] These are:

1. team level
2. organisation level
3. system level.

This is also shown diagrammatically in Figure 12.1.

The diagram illustrates how we expect team members and the team manager to use person-centred practices to change what they can within their sphere of influence, and address what is not working for the people supported. These are called Level 1 changes, and may include enabling people to choose who they want to support them, and when, and making these changes to the rota. When what is not working for people requires change that is beyond what they are directly responsible for ('what they can't change'), then this has to be shared with the people in the organisation who

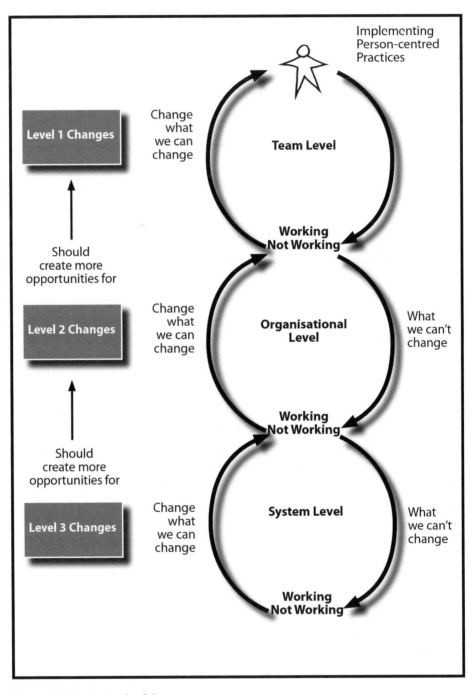

Figure 12.1 The three levels of change
Source: Smull, Bourne and Sanderson (2009)

can make the necessary changes. These are likely to be changes in policies, procedures and structures, and are called 'Level 2 changes'. An example might be if a team manager wants to change the rota structure completely – for example, to change from a standard rota system to a flexible, personalised rota, which requires change in policy and in the IT system in relation to the rota. If the changes required to deliver what is important to people are beyond what the organisation can change without changes to commissioning or regulation, for example, then these are 'Level 3' changes. This could include a situation in which people are in charge of their own budget through an individual service fund and agree a process of creating an individual budget allocation with the commissioner.

Models of change

We are not going to review all the models of change management, because there are so many. Instead, initially, we want to cover in summary one of the most popular approaches to planned change – Kotter's eight-step model.[141] Later in the text we will refer to other relevant sources of information we have considered. Kotter's model is perhaps typical of many of its kind, some more or less complicated in their approach. Many tend to take a top-down, leadership-driven approach, focusing less on the efforts required throughout an organisation to align people to a new way of working. Summarised in this way, the process seems over-simplified, which of course it is not.

In the following table we show how person-centred practices can help deliver each of the eight stages.

Kotter's eight stages of change	How person-centred practices can help
1. Establishing a sense of urgency	'Working/not working' and Working Together for Change identify the key areas of focus required by the people supported, staff, the organisation and other stakeholders.
2. Creating the guiding coalition	A relationship map can help to think about the membership of the guiding coalition. Using Positive and Productive Meetings will ensure that everyone is able to contribute, be listened to, and that decisions are made effectively. A decision-making agreement can be useful in clarifying the scope of the coalition's authority. The Doughnut can help to clarify the individual roles of each member, and the responsibilities of the group. If each member of the group has a one-page profile, this will help people to know how to support each other individually, and can be the basis of using 'matching' to get the best fit between roles and people. A one-page team plan can capture who the group are, what is important to them and the support they need from the organisation to be successful. A team contact chart would enable people to know the best ways to be in touch with each other in between meetings.

cont.

Kotter's eight stages of change	How person-centred practices can help
3. Developing a change vision	Purpose posters or success posters can be useful here to think about the vision from different perspectives. The Presence to Contribution tool can be used to enhance the description of the vision and explain more about how things will change.
4. Communicating the vision for buy-in	A one-page strategy can communicate how you will be working to achieve success and how this will be measured. Relationship mapping can help to ensure that all appropriate stakeholders are picked up. The Doughnut can clarify everyone's responsibilities in relation to communication. A history map could be helpful for people to see this change in the context of the history of the organisation.
5. Empowering broad-based action	Clarifying roles through the use of the Doughnut can help effectiveness here. The Matching tool can be useful in matching tasks to people.
6. Generating short-term wins	Focusing on the priorities highlighted by use of the 'Working/not working' tool and Working Together for Change will help to identify those areas where quick wins are possible. The 4 Plus 1 questions tool used regularly to review progress can inform further action and recognise and celebrate successes. Learning logs can be used to track learning and act on this.
7. Never letting up	The 4 Plus 1 questions tool is particularly helpful here in identifying what people are pleased about, and what still remains to be done to go further. A review of the original information generated through the use of the Presence to Contribution tool can also inform this process. A person-centred review of the guiding coalition can help people reflect on how they are working together and what's working and not working about the processes used to achieve change.
8. Incorporating changes into the culture	Using the Working Together for Change process to consolidate the views of multiple stakeholders, recognise successes and achievements, and transfer priorities into the normal business planning process to take them forward is valuable here.

How are you doing in the way that you manage change?

In many ways 'managing change' covers everything in this book. However, in order that you can assess how you are doing, we have picked out a number of key criteria as relevant to the key areas of person-centred change management. These are clear purpose, leadership and strategy; changing the culture; and learning from individuals and acting on what is working and not working for them. Here we explain why these are important in managing change:

Clear purpose, leadership and strategy – it is essential that the meaning of any change is understood, aligned to the vision, mission and values of the organisation, and that the leaders are seen to align themselves with the change. It is also even more important that the change is in the direction desired by the people supported.

Changing the culture – this is an important area to consider, because changes to culture are far more difficult to achieve than staying with what you have got, or aligning closely to what has gone before and to the needs and desires of the people supported.

Learning from individuals and acting on what is working and not working – this is a key principle of the person-centred approach and important to change management, because without this input from the many and various stakeholders the change you plan may not go in the direction required by people who use your services.

The following table gives some examples of excellence in using a person-centred approach to change management – for individuals and the organisation. You can use this table to carry out a quick rating of your own performance using a scale of 1–5, where 1 is very poor, 2 is poor, 3 is fair, 4 is good and 5 is excellent, to give a rough first assessment of your progress as an organisation.

Criteria	Measure	Rating (1–5)
Changes for individuals		
Working towards the outcomes that the person wants for the future	We know what each individual wants for their future – their dreams, hopes and aspirations.	
	We know what is working and not working for people now. We have a process to identify and act on outcomes for each person (based on what the person wants in the future and what is working and not working for them now).	
	We have action plans with identified ownership to change what is not working. There are specific, measurable and achievable actions to deliver each individual's outcomes. These are reviewed through team meetings, one-to-ones and in person-centred reviews.	
Changes at a team level		
Staff feel that their opinions influence change	Team members feel confident in suggesting new ideas or changes to each other and their manager.	
	We have a process for making sure we hear from staff about what needs to change in the organisation.	
	Staff know what the vision for change is, and what it means for them, and what progress has been made.	
Changes at an organisational level		
Identifying changes required together	People who use services, their families and other stakeholders contribute their views about what is working and not working for them. We have a way to gather and organise this information and use it to inform our strategy.	

cont.

Criteria	Measure	Rating (1–5)
Changes at an organisational level		
Leadership and strategy	Our change strategy is based on a good understanding of where we are now, and on what is working and not working for people, the current context and the aspirations of the people we support and other stakeholders. The senior team actively supports the strategy and we are all held accountable for delivering on it.	
	Our strategy is delivering results – it is helping us to deliver more personalised services.	
Communicating change	We inform, engage and feed back to people about the changes we plan to make or have made in a way that makes sense for them.	

Now that you know how you are doing, we want to share an example of what this can look like in practice and then suggest ways that you can develop further in taking a person-centred approach to change management.

Managing change in United Response

The challenge for United Response was how to go from the very successful pilot in the North West division to scaling up and using person-centred thinking tools and practices to become national practice and part of the culture and DNA of the charity.

Bob Tindall, Managing Director of United Response, explains the significance of this escalation of the change, and the impact of this on how the organisation's mission and values were communicated and embedded.

In the spring of 2007, there was further investment in the original pilot change process by extending it to all of the organisation. This required Trustee approval for financial investment in the programme.

Such a scaling up of the person-centred thinking tools and practices had never been attempted before on the size of this programme. The major success achieved through the implementation of the programme, however, suggested that organisational culture change could be scaled up effectively in a large organisation. In order to achieve change on a larger scale – and in addition to thinking about the resource implications – thought needed to be given to the translation of the concepts into an overall context that would be recognisable across the organisation.

It was important that this became 'the way we do things around here' – and not be seen as the latest fad, or flavour of the month. And so, we consciously badged the rollout of the programme as 'Developing the Way We Work'; borrowing from the successful practice in creating the original Way We Work poster and merging external good practice with internal good practice to create a blend that would feel coherent to internal staff in particular. It made it clear that we were – at a conscious and visible level – adapting the original Way We Work process by incorporating the positive and essential new learning from the original pilot programme.

There was top-down sponsorship, but not a one size fits all approach or direction; however, it was important that we shared the learning from the pilot programme and it was recognised that the infrastructure that had supported the pilot – the hallmarks – had had a significant impact on it success. These were:

- A leadership team – an extended version of the divisional management team which included managers and staff from varying levels, and was charged with steering the overall direction of the programme, and ensuring that we listened to people we support and families.

- Coaches and coaches' teams – most of whom were managers, and who provided the one-to-one support for people in applying the skills and knowledge they had acquired, and shared knowledge and learning across the division.

- Trainers and trainers' teams – who delivered training in the person thinking tools, techniques and thinking, and shared knowledge and learning across the organisation. In the pilot we brought HSA in to deliver this, and now we wanted to work with HSA to build our own capacity of accredited trainers in person-centred thinking to deliver training across the charity.

There were some issues concerning change management at this time. The divisions that had not been incorporated with the programme in its pilot stage were beginning to warm up to the implications of its introduction. There were concerns about a perceived lack of information and a lack of preparation. An event was organised in response to this. It was a joint learning event where people from the North West division enthusiastically presented to the people from the rest of the organisation their experiences around implementing the changes. This event was successful and marked the formal hand-over of the programme from myself to all the divisional directors.

The extended programme began to be rolled out across the organisation in April 2007 and has now had a significant positive effect on work across all divisions.

A point was reached, however, at which this rather long and transitional title of 'Developing the Way We Work' felt no longer appropriate. Investment in person-centred thinking training, and a redrafting of training on person-centred active support training in order to give it equal prominence alongside person-centred thinking training, had brought us to the point at which we had a broader understanding of how to provide person-centred support. This was illustrated in the updated 'Way We Work' poster that included person-centred practices and person-centred active support. We decided simply to declare that the transitional process was over by reverting to the use of the Way We Work title.

By this point it was clear, given all of the learning and positivity generated by the pilot and the extended Developing the Way We Work programmes, that thinking had moved on so far that there was no danger of colleagues confusing the 2003 Way We Work process with the use of the same title in its updated context. Essentially, colleagues understood the reversion to the Way We Work title as what it was – a confirmation that all of the extra learning of the last few years was both here to stay and fully compatible with all we had been doing prior to it.

The impact of the change

Implementing the change programme as a pilot, followed by a national rollout has, beyond doubt, been very beneficial for the people supported and has boosted staff morale and creativity. A recent (2010) evaluation study of 20 per cent of the services showed that the percentage of staff who indicated that they were likely to leave in the next 12 months had dropped by two-thirds since 2005.[142] In addition, turnover has continued to fall, accompanied by a significant decrease in the costs of temporary agency staff. The ratio of management costs to staff has also continued to reduce, as skill and knowledge – and the confidence to use them – has been spread out to staff across the organisation, supported by the leadership teams and coaches.

Here are some of the key elements of the change in United Response:

- An analysis of the 'as is' situation, for example:
  - The organisation focuses on the people we support and strives hard to deliver what it is that they want.
  - The organisation is welcoming and supportive and collectively proud, despite being highly dispersed.
  - The emphasis on getting systems right can detract from what was originally set out to achieve.
  - There is a strong health and safety and risk management focus in the organisation.
  - Good training is a feature of the organisation.
  - There is a very busy, hardworking culture (this is probably expressed to emphasise both positive and negative).
  - Perceptions and aspirations of senior managers differ from those on the ground – reality on the ground is stressful.
  - The selection of a pilot area with a keen champion and strong sponsorship, and external expert support.
  - Strong leadership, and providing training and support to give people the skills to deliver the changes.
- Alignment with a vision, mission and values that express where United Response wants to be, for example:
  - Person-centred practices that recognise people's rights and enhance the possibility of a valued social role.

- An understanding that what is important to people, and how best to support them, is best delivered by someone who has what is important to them recognised and is supported in the way that makes sense to them – so extending person-centred practices to the management of staff is important too.

- A reinforcement of gains made through person-centred active support by the development of tools and teamwork that supported judgement and initiative on the part of staff.

- A definition of the areas that had to change, to fully implement person-centred practices, which included the following:

  - attitudes and beliefs

  - skills and competencies

  - work practices and behaviours

  - processes that produce systems of shared understanding, such as:
    - financial management
    - people management
    - decision making
    - planning
    - recruitment and selection
    - training
    - quality management approach
    - consultation
    - communication
    - support practices
    - identification of the roles of all staff in culture change.

What is lasting?

Beyond initial impressions, however, it is what sticks that matters. This is where the programme of learning and development in the use of the person-centred thinking tools and practices has been particularly effective. In summary, the key elements of the programme have been as follows.

- A defined set of person-centred thinking tools for all staff to use.

- Mandatory training for all staff in person-centred thinking.

- A supporting infrastructure of leadership teams whose role is to guide the development of the process and training, and ensure it makes a difference in people's lives.

- Trainers and coaches with extra training in person-centred practices who are deployed close to the staff on the ground to give regular support and guidance to those using the tools.

- Modelling of values, attitudes and beliefs – centred on person-centred thinking – at the highest levels of the organisation.

Developing your practice in managing change in a person-centred way

Our preference is for the type of learning-led change that you have seen in the story of United Response. Here, a concentration on instilling the knowledge and tools across the whole workforce *pulled* change through the organisation. The change began with a top-down impetus, but its momentum is maintained by staff across the breadth and depth of the organisation.

Using the learning from this experience in United Response and drawing from Kotter's model and other authors on the subject of change management, we have developed our own thinking on what is appropriate for a person-centred organisation. The work of Daryl Conner is very relevant in this respect, and in particular when he discusses the nature and process of change; the roles involved; and resistance, culture and levels of commitment.[143] We have also been informed in this thinking by Plant,[144] Beckhard and Harris,[145] and the many areas of change management pulled together by Cameron and Green.[146]

So now we summarise in simple language what seems to work as a structure and process for change in this kind of person-centred way, using the tools and practices you are by now familiar with. This covers all the key areas of change management that typically you would expect to find in a change management project or action plan. Clearly the emphasis that you place on each element will vary according to the scale and nature of the change you are undertaking. We would recommend, however, that you give each of these elements some consideration in developing your actions for any change, no matter how small it may be. Even what we think may be the most minor of changes can cause reactions that we did not expect!

You will find as you read on that the elements do have impacts on and consequences for each other. So, for example, if it is important to you that you involve people in the change, then the way to decide to do it would clearly not be by hiring an external project manager to impose it on your workforce or other stakeholders. Alternatively, if you need to bring a change about quickly because of a legal or regulatory problem, then deciding how to bring about the change is easier – you must do it – but you may want to spend more time on being clear with people what the change is and why it is necessary, to avoid stronger resistance to it than you can afford to have.

Being clear what the change is and why you are doing it

Many changes fail because people are not clear about what is supposed to happen, or, in the end, something different happened from what was expected. Writing down a detailed description of what will change and, equally important, what will not change is vital. A tool that can help you with this is Presence to Contribution, for example. This defines where you are going and what it might look like, sound like and feel like when you get there.

This reflects Kotter's model in terms of creating a vision and establishing a sense of urgency to bring the change about – because it is clear to all concerned where you are going, and why it is important.[147] This appeals directly to people's desire to make a change, if they are attracted by a strong vision for the future (making lives better for people supported, for example) or if they see that something needs to be put right because it is not working for them or the people supported and other stakeholders.

> If you always do what you've always done, you'll always get what you've always got. (Anonymous)

This quote from an unknown helper points out that a key requirement of a change project is to demonstrate the need for the results or outcomes to be different. If not, then indeed why change the way of doing it? We might add to this that there must be something that demonstrates the value of being somewhere else, and also that we need to think differently, so that the future may not actually be just like the past.

Exercise 1 in the Appendix provides tools to help with this part of the process.

Getting and keeping permission to do it

Again, many changes fail because the key people who need to authorise and promote them either don't know what is happening, or something different happens from what they think they authorised, or expected. So stakeholder analysis is important here, to identify those who need to be on board early to give permission to go ahead. By 'stakeholder' we mean anyone on whom the change will have an impact, including those who authorised it to happen, internal and external groups, and individuals. Next, a stakeholder management plan is critical to manage the communication and expectations of those key stakeholders in particular. The tools that can help here are as follows.

- Relationship map – to identify the key stakeholders.
- 'Working and not working' – using this for each group of stakeholders will help to gain support for changing the aspects that are not working. It can also be a review tool during the course of the project.
- 'Important to and for' – knowing where to focus the project aims for stakeholders.
- 4 plus 1 questions – regularly reviewing where the project is up to and how well it is meeting its aims.

Exercise 2 in the Appendix explains more about using the tools for this part of the process.

Deciding how to do it

Intuitively, a person-centred organisation would want to bring about change in a way that engaged and involved as many of its staff and other stakeholders as possible. It would seek to manage the expectations and resistance of those stakeholders in detail, and consult with them on the design of the change project or activity to take advantage of their detailed knowledge of the work that is to be done, and especially the outcomes that need to be achieved.

In the alternative situation, a person-centred organisation would also know when to take a more directive approach to change. This is because the analysis of what is important for the health of the organisation and its stakeholders is done regularly and widely communicated.

Many articles on change management would seem to suggest that a change project has one style of approach – perhaps we might call it 'engaging' on the one hand, or 'directive' on the other. Clearly this is not the case, and most projects or activities lend themselves to different approaches for separate parts of the undertaking, or for different stakeholders. Being clear about what style to adopt for each of these parts, *and communicating that to the affected stakeholders* will help the progress and effectiveness of the change. The tools that will help with this are as follows.

- 'Working and not working' – and the level of criticality of what is not working.

- 'Important to and for' – and the level of urgency for something that is important to be done better or to be in compliance.

- 4 Plus 1 questions – what has been tried already and the level of success it had.

Exercise 3 in the Appendix explains more about using the tools for this part of the process.

Knowing how it affects people

In conventional approaches to change projects, understanding the impact of change is a common technique used to aid the smooth progress of the project. In larger projects it is often run as an ongoing activity, so, as the design of the project fluctuates or it goes through different implementation stages, the impact can be tracked and responded to.

The impact of change analysis can take many forms, and there are a number of tools used for it. The starting point is always some form of stakeholder analysis, clearly because you need to know who you might be affected before you can assess the impact of change on them. Often also, the initial stakeholder analysis and any ongoing impact of change analysis are combined to produce an additional stakeholder management document, which may take the form of a simple communications plan, or a more complex engagement strategy and detailed action plan, depending upon the complexity and numbers of stakeholders and impacts. Stakeholders can be identified individually or in groups, again depending upon the complexity and their numbers.

A common approach also is to categorise impacts in some way. For example, impact may be assessed as to how it affects stakeholders in terms of culture, structure, jobs and tasks, learning and development, communications, policies and procedures, systems and data, or facilities and equipment.

This matches very well with the person-centred approach, and, although the tools might differ, the basic principles of identifying who is affected and paying attention to the impact upon them (provided there is a positive reasonable response), chimes well with our preferences.

Exercise 4 in the Appendix offers some more advice on using the tools for this part of the process.

Managing reactions to change

It is a truism of change management that whatever the change there will be a reaction, whether the change is positive or negative, and more often than not, that reaction will take the form of some type of resistance, be it overt or covert, active or passive. So the best advice we can give is to accept that reality, and perhaps not sit back and enjoy it but plan for it and deal with it.

Reactions to change – again it is a reality that everyone will travel through some sort of reactions from disbelief to acceptance or points in between. Primarily it is the speed of their transition and their level of discomfort, and therefore their need for support that differs from person to person. Simply acknowledging this, and assuming positive intent, is very much a person-centred way of working.

Change readiness – plotting out the characteristics of change readiness and being able to recognise when someone has got there, or how far they need to travel, is therefore a worthwhile activity. Coupling this with a set of active and accessible responses to support people towards readiness is good practice, and compatible with taking a person-centred approach to understanding that different people with different abilities will move at different paces, and the level of support will not be the same.

Resistance management – a stream of activity for this will often appear in project plans. Resistance is perhaps a strong word to use, but it does take many forms, naturally, because its root is in the many different ways in which we all look at the world about us. In this sense, it is entirely consistent with a person-centred approach to have a very detailed understanding of how people think or feel about a change we are suggesting to them, to respect the frame of reference that they have, and to respond to their concerns in a positive yet robust way. Robust because, if a change has been properly designed to deliver better outcomes for the people supported, the customers who keep us in business, then it must achieve those outcomes. That does not mean, however, that listening to the resistance cannot lead to a better way of doing something, and it often does.

Exercise 5 in the Appendix explains more about using the tools for this collection and analysis of information.

Talking and listening

Many of the popular approaches to change management talk about communications strategies and plans to underpin the change efforts. These are often broken into phases, and many talk about there being some kind of first phase of unfreezing or unblocking, a second phase of making the changes or a transition, and the third being 'refreezing', or perhaps in Kotter's terms incorporating the changes into the culture in the new situation.[148]

As we said earlier, it would seem common sense that, as people will naturally go through a series of reactions to any change, then a communication strategy should try to mirror the transition that individuals make, so this kind of phasing or sectioning of the communications strategy and plans is useful.

In a person-centred organisation, the emphasis is of course on understanding as many as possible of the people on whom the change has an impact, how they react, what is important to and for them as the change occurs, and what is working and not working for them as the change is implemented. Added to this should be a section of the communication plans that follows up after the change has been built into the normal culture or operations, and regularly checks that it is still working. Here the 4 Plus 1 questions can help in carrying out a review. Thus, for example, a change that was made to the absence management process in United Response at the beginning of 2008 is still reviewed quarterly with staff representatives several years later, and adjustments are made because of those reviews. The learning here, of course, is to keep repeating the message, and give yourself more opportunities to listen to the feedback of those who know about how the change can continue to improve.

Try Exercise 6 in the Appendix for more about using the tools for this part of the process.

Making sure it fits

Peter Drucker said, in our view wisely, 'Company cultures are like country cultures. Never try to change one. Try instead, to work with what you've got.'[149]

Again, a number of the conventional approaches to change management would recommend trying to achieve alignment with the existing culture in as many facets of a change as possible in order to optimise success. Many do still, however, talk about 'changing the culture'.

Perhaps Drucker goes too far, because there certainly are examples of organisations where the culture has changed. The key for us is that the change that is sought is seen as congruent (note that congruent does not mean 'the same as') with the current culture by stakeholders in a number of aspects as follows:

- *What they see as 'important to' and 'important for' people* – this can help you figure out how the change might align with the culture. It can tease out those aspects that you need to know about and be congruent with.

- *What is working and not working for people from different perspectives* – the tool can help you assess where the current ways of working do not align with the culture. If you know what is not working, then designing your change to make it work will undoubtedly attract believers. On the other hand, if there is a strong belief that something is working, then you may mess with it at your peril if you have not put hard work into convincing stakeholders that it can still work, but in a better way with better outcomes for all.

The information from these tools and analysis of the outputs can then be built into communications, stakeholder management, and resistance management strategies and plans.

Selecting and training the leaders of change

Successful change projects require an infrastructure of their own to make them work. This means that an organisation has to be prepared to put in a range of resources to support the change. In terms of Kotter's model, this will probably fall into the areas of 'Creating the guiding coalition' and 'Empowering broad-based action', and was very effective in the United Response example. Our recommendations are that this should look something like this:

- A committed project leader/main change agent (such as the leader of the pilot project in the United Response example) who has the organisational gravitas and knowledge to command respect for the change. This project leader must also have the sponsorship of the person(s) authorising the project. Regular discussion of what is 'important to' and 'important for' each party should take place, and either a review of what is working and not working or one using the 4 Plus 1 questions.

- A leadership team that takes on the accountability for the progression of the change project and providing the resources to do that. In the United Response example, this took the form of a multi-discipline/multi-layer group, operating at a divisional level. This was essentially the project management group. In due course, this leadership team evolved into a wider group, engaging with clients and their families, and involving them in the overall operation of the division, so keeping the momentum of the new culture going. Of course, the size of the leadership team required will vary according to the size of the project, as will the requirement for a full-time project manager or managers. These are clearly all questions of scale and the need for dedicated resources.

- The leadership team is supported by a change leader/advocate/agent or a number of these. In the United Response example, this took the form of individual 'coaches' who were also formed into teams, with usually two teams supporting a division. These coaches (most of whom were managers) are extensively trained in person-centred thinking and tools, and additionally in coaching skills. The coaches' teams meet regularly to swap ideas and carry out knowledge management of good practice and positive outcomes.

- The coaches provide support to all other staff in the organisation at a local level. It was mandatory in United Response for all staff in addition to have two days of training in person-centred thinking and tools. Coaches collect and share knowledge and good practice from the local staff, and ensure that the project aims are being met at ground level.

- Annual learning and reflection days that are organised at an appropriate divisional/area level, and culminate in the same exercise at national level.

Making sure people know what good looks like

All the leaders and coaches working on a change project communicate the aims and progress on the project through how they behave. This also applies to the leadership team of the whole organisation.

It is not sufficient to promote the aims of the project simply through 'talking the talk' and regularly saying the right things. People very quickly spot if actions do not match words, so key players must also be seen to be acting differently and showing people what the new way of working looks like by doing it themselves. Last but not least, the practice of catching people doing something right is very useful here. Spotting the new way of working and publicly recognising good behaviour will reinforce the changes.

Person-centred thinking tools that can help here include the following.

- 4 Plus 1 questions – for identifying what we are pleased about, what remains a concern and what we are going to do about it.

- Praise and Trouble – clearly identifying what will be positively recognised and what will attract the opposite. If people are very clear about the negative consequences of continuing to work in the old ways, as well as the positive consequences of changing, it tends to promote the aims of a project.

Have a look at Exercise 7 in the Appendix, which covers more about using the tools for this part of the process.

Involving people in the change

Clearly a person-centred approach favours the involvement of as many stakeholders as possible as frequently as possible. There are multiple opportunities for engagement, in the design of new ways of working, in assessing the impact of change, in understanding communications needs, in project decision making, and so on. The person-centred tools that can help here are as follows.

- One-page profiles and 'Important to and for' – to understand what is important to people, how they like to work, and what we need to know to be able to work effectively with them.

- 4 Plus 1 questions or 'Working and not working' – to review progress on the project and decide corrective action as appropriate.

One aspect not to underestimate here is the quality of learning and development that individuals require to be able to accommodate change and be able to work in new ways. So spending time with people in understanding these needs is time well spent, and will pay dividends in terms of project outcomes and longevity. Many projects fail because the project leaders have skimped on the quality of and time spent on training. In a learning-led approach to change, this is critical.

Exercise 8 in the Appendix may help you with some ideas about using the tools for this.

Reviewing the 'customer experience' of the organisation

Another way of identifying, reviewing and monitoring changes made or required in the organisation is to review the experiences of people supported or their representatives (customers) as they interface, or try to interface with the organisation. You can look at this from the customer perspective, preferably getting their direct feedback by using the approach that is often called the 'customer journey'. This approach was used, for example, by United Response in reviewing the overall processes to support the move towards personalisation and individual budgets, and in deciding what changes might be needed to ways of working, systems, and so on.

Where you might use it

The approach can be used for process description or analysis, and therefore for subsequent purposes such as waste elimination and process optimisation, as well as for communication or marketing.

Benefits and drawbacks

The benefits of this approach are as follows.

- The ease of use by the customer or other stakeholders or interested parties.

- Having a process description that allows the organisation to look at what it does from a customer or stakeholder perspective, the premise being that looking at a business operation in this way will make the business more successful.

- Having a marketing tool that enables staff to explain how it all works to a prospective client very quickly.

- It highlights waste in the process.

- It is very effective for training.

- It is a challenge to any proposed change to ensure that the customer is still foremost.

There may be some drawbacks as follows.

- You need to be reasonably certain that you have had input from a range of stakeholders, and that their needs are being met.

- It has to be kept up to date.

- There are always some people for which a diagrammatic approach like this doesn't work.

What it is

See the example in Figure 12.2. The clue is in the title – the customer journey is essentially a roadmap of how a customer travels through an organisation, covering the full life cycle of the potential relationship from initial attraction of potential clients to the termination of the relationship and assisting a client to move on elsewhere.

The customer or potential customer can, of course, make use of as much of that life cycle as they wish for what is important to and for them, or what is working and not working for them, or to review the relationship (for which we would of course use a tool such as 4 Plus 1 questions).

How to use it

As in the example in Figure 12.2, the basic graphic is a roadmap. On this are written the stops along the way, where potential or actual customers wish to interface with the organisation, and a short description of how they do this.

The roadmap can work better when it is coupled with a 'total systems' approach that looks at the systems and processes that support the customer interface in a holistic way, ensuring that customers can bridge from one interface to another, and that data and information are used effectively and minimally to support those bridges.

Thus a customer, or the organisation, can review or interrogate the entire relationship without multiple or complex transactions with numerous and varying systems and processes.

The aim is to make it easy for customers to find their way into an organisation's complexity and to obtain the information, support or service they require quickly and in an understandable form. Thus the customer journey roadmap is best created with the input of stakeholders and not by an organisation in isolation.

Telling stories that illustrate the change we are looking for

A particular aspect of person-centred organisations weaves its way through all the areas covered in this book, and that is the use of stories to build and strengthen the organisation. In the areas of knowledge management and outcome measurement alone, the value of stories is immense. In terms of outcome measurement, it is one of the most valid ways in which true progress can be measured. In terms of encouraging and reinforcing change, storytelling is an invaluable tool, and so we include it for special attention in this chapter.

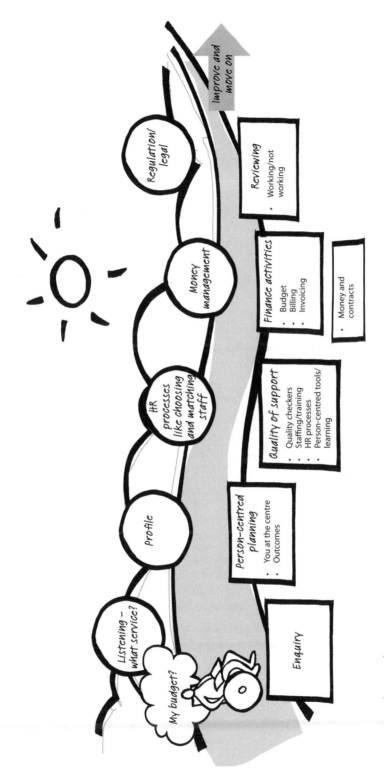

Figure 12.2 The United Response customer journey

Storytelling has received much more attention in recent years as its importance in areas such as team creation and building, resourcing, management development and culture has been more recognised. This has not been exclusive to the social care sector, but also occurs in other public and private sector organisations. Stories can be used in many ways to inform and motivate an organisation, and are a powerful indicator of the health of an organisation's culture. Stories must be true, of course. They also give the opportunity to give recognition and praise for the achievements of those who may not often get the limelight. The table that follows says more about how stories can add value in each subject considered in this book.

This table covers the other chapters in the book and indicates where you might consider active collection and sharing of stories. The importance of actively looking for stories was highlighted by the experience of United Response during a learning and reflection day. Stories are invited at these events to share good practice. The organisation had stressed to colleagues that they would be supported in taking risks that had been properly thought through, and were done with the intent of affording people supported the opportunity to try something new or have a more fulfilling life. It became apparent that there were no stories being told about situations where risks had been taken, and all had not gone well, but the colleagues concerned were supported by their managers. Senior management made special efforts to find these stories, in order to check that the stated culture was being carried out in reality, and colleagues were not risk-averse unnecessarily.

Chapter subject	Look for stories that
Vision, mission, values and strategy	Show how the vision, mission and strategy are being reinforced by leaders of the organisation, are demonstrated consistently through the depth and breadth of the staff teams, or show the direction for people to follow.
Organisation design	Point out how the people we support can easily get high-quality response and service from the organisation structure and processes, or show how hierarchy and position are less important than working effectively to contribute your best.
Working together	Show how engaging wider groups of or individual stakeholders led to more positive and productive outcomes for people we support, or relate how the wider community rallied to achieve an aim.
Creating a person-centred culture	Demonstrate the power of the culture and how focused it is on meeting the needs, aspirations and desires of the people we support.
Quality	Give a meaningful measure of the outcomes that the organisation is focused on, or that demonstrate what is really valued in the organisation.

Human resources	Support the process of performance management and show how people are developed and encouraged to acquire new skills and knowledge that add value to themselves and the people we support.
Managing change	Show how change really did turn out well in the end, how doing something differently is encouraged and supported, that it is OK to be wary of change, and how resistance or concerns are dealt with calmly and even-handedly.
Person-centred teamworking	That strengthen the belief that people working as a team can generate much more than they can as individuals.
Leadership	Show people how behaving in the right way is valued, recognised and rewarded in the organisation.
Enabling risk	Give examples of where taking a measured risk paid off, or where something did go wrong, but it was still OK, and the staff were supported in taking the risk.

More recently in United Response, the use of storytelling has been advanced into video, using simple and cheap video capture to record and distribute 'one-minute stories' of people achieving things and trying out new ideas, or demonstrating good practice. This has proved to be an extremely effective way of knowledge and good practice sharing.

Summary of tools and techniques

The following table summarises some of the typical issues arising in change and the potential tools and techniques (both conventional and person-centred) that can be used to help analyse, understand and deal with these.

The exercises in the Appendix to this chapter give more detail of how the person-centred tools can be used to meet specific needs. The person-centred thinking tools can be used on their own or in combination with the more conventional tools.

What do we want to do?	What would be a conventional way of addressing this?	What person-centred tools can I use for this?	Exercise number
Being clear what the change is and why you are doing it	Project mandate and planning documents Vision statement New standard operating procedures From/To chart	Presence to Contribution Doughnut Success from different perspectives	1

cont.

What do we want to do?	What would be a conventional way of addressing this?	What person-centred tools can I use for this?	Exercise number
Getting and keeping permission to run a change project	Project mandate and planning documents Budgets Project review meetings	Working/not working Important to/for 4 Plus1 questions	2
Deciding what style to adopt in running the change project	A compliance or engagement approach	Working/not working Important to/for 4 Plus 1 questions	3
Understanding how the change will affect the organisation	Impact of change analysis Stakeholder analysis	Success from different perspectives 4 Plus 1 questions Working/not working from different perspectives	4
Managing reactions to change	Management instruction Compliance Focus groups Surveys	Working/not working Important to/for 4 Plus 1 questions	5
Communicating change	Communications strategy and plan Project newsletter Monthly reports	Working/not working Important to/for From/To	6
Managing culture	Communicating what the new culture will be Identifying the parts of the old culture that will still align after the change	See Chapter 6 for more detail	N/A
Making sure people know what good looks like	Project rollout Performance measures	4 Plus 1 questions Praise and Trouble	7
Engaging people in the change	Focus groups Project sub-groups Individual questionnaires 'Walk the Wall' reviews and feedback	One-page profiles Working/not working 4 Plus 1 questions	8

Conclusion

As we said at the beginning of the chapter, managing change is a thread that runs through all the subject matter of this book, and indeed through life and work generally, so it deserves the application of special attention and skill. We hope that we have also shown that person-centred practices can contribute to ensuring that we are changing what people want to change (based on what is working and not working) and in ways that bring together everyone's contributions.

We need to see changes with people supported that are moving in the direction that they want their lives to go. Teams are responsible for delivering the changes that are within their sphere of influence, and ensuring that senior managers and others in the organisation know what else needs to change. At the beginning of the book we quoted Think Local, Act Personal in saying that personalisation requires significant changes for organisations. The three levels of change are important in sharing that change is expected at all levels of the organisation and, like quality, is everyone's responsibility.

Exercises

Exercise 1: Being clear what the change is and why you are doing it

Purpose: To be able to define in detail what will happen when the change project has done its work. This needs to include what will be different and what will remain the same.

Audience: All stakeholders in the change project.

Typical uses:

- To seek or maintain authorisation for a change project.
- To communicate the need for change to stakeholders.
- To maintain focus on the project with stakeholders.
- A context for project decision making.

How to do it:

Presence to Contribution – this can describe the range of activities that the organisation might undertake, and what it is planned to move away from and towards in terms of greater benefits or better results.

From/To – use this with a list of characteristics of the change to describe how life will be different.

The Doughnut – this can be used to clarify how new roles and responsibilities for an organisation, team or individual will be.

Success from different perspectives – use this to define exactly what you want to change and what this will look like. This could be generated through Working Together for Change.

Exercise 2: Getting and keeping permission to run a change project

Purpose: To ensure that a change project has authorisation and support or sponsorship in place from its outset through to completion.

Audience: All stakeholders who are in a position to authorise or sponsor the progression of a change project.

Typical uses:

- To gain project authorisation from a leadership team.
- To gain budget approval.
- To get resources to progress a project further.
- To satisfy external stakeholders' interest or concerns.

How to do it:

'Working/not working' – list these aspects of the current situation to demonstrate what is not good enough now, and why there needs to be change.

'Important to/for' – use this to demonstrate to authorising stakeholders and leaders how your proposed change matches what the organisation has set itself out to achieve, or should be achieving.

4 Plus 1 questions – this tool can be used to carry out a review with stakeholders or project authorisers of the current state of the organisation and what is not performing as well as it should, and to agree what steps need to be taken to address shortfalls.

Exercise 3: Deciding what style to adopt in running the change project

Purpose: To be clear about the way in which a change project will be put across to its stakeholders and the way in which it will be managed.

Audience: Project leadership team.

Typical uses:

- To decide the givens in a change, and the parameters for flexibility.
- To clarify the way in which decisions will be made.
- To clarify how resistance will be dealt with.
- To decide on levels of involvement.

How to do it:

'Working/not working' – use this to highlight the priority areas that are not working, and how severely they are affecting the organisation.

'Important to/for' – match what is working and not working with what the organisation's priorities for action and results are ('important to' the organisation) in order to derive a sense of urgency or compliance requirements.

4 Plus 1 questions – using this tool you can establish with groups of stakeholders or individuals where their main concerns are, what is currently OK, and therefore again derive the level of need for direction and compliance versus the scope for building on what is working and engaging with stakeholders.

Exercise 4: Understanding how the change will affect the organisation

Purpose: To ensure that the project leadership and change agents have an understanding of the impact of the change on stakeholders and can plan to manage that impact.

Audience: All stakeholders in a change project.

Typical uses:

- To assess the impact of change on individuals and groups of stakeholders.
- To manage the impact of change and amend the project design and implementation accordingly.
- To encourage involvement of stakeholders.

How to do it:

Success from different perspectives – this gives people the opportunity to talk about the desired change from their perspective and the impact this could have on them.

4 Plus 1 questions (future focus) – use this tool with individuals or groups of stakeholders and involved parties to discuss the proposed changes in detail, looking at what each of the questions could mean to them in the future, and gather from them their feedback on how they will be affected, and the level of feeling about that impact. This tool will also allow you to collect data on what such stakeholders think should be done about anything they are concerned about.

'Working/not working' from different perspectives (future focus) – ask people to imagine what could work and not work from their perspective about the future change, and therefore what their hopes and fears could be.

Exercise 5: Managing reactions to change

Purpose: Ensuring that the project leadership and change agents understand the levels and forms of reactions to the change, and can manage them effectively.

Audience: All stakeholders in a change project.

Typical uses:

- Engaging stakeholders in the design and implementation process.
- Consulting with staff representatives.
- Discussing issues with individuals or teams.
- Reinforcing the purpose of the change in communications.

How to do it:

'Working/not working' – asking these questions will allow stakeholders to voice what they feel about the change, and your interpretation of the detailed comments will tell you where they are in the reaction curve towards acceptance.

'Important to/for' – using this tool will enable you to probe into the detail of how people feel they are affected by the change, and where it is causing them to feel uncertain about what is important. Analysing the data collected will point to the critical areas where resistance to the change is likely.

4 Plus 1 questions – use this approach to carry out detailed reviews of progress with individuals and groups of stakeholders. The advantage of this tool is that, as well as surfacing potential resistance, it leads respondents towards finding actions to respond to any concerns.

Exercise 6: Communicating change

Purpose: Ensuring that stakeholders receive and understand the key messages about the change.

Audience: Project team/management team members concerned with communications.

Typical use: To form the content for communications and engagement strategy and plans.

How to do it:

'Working/not working' – this tool helps identify the areas that will change either because they are working but can be improved, or because they are not working, for communication to stakeholders, and justification of the proposed changes.

'Important to/for' – keying into what the organisation (and even better, the stakeholders) see as important can be used to reinforce the need for change.

Exercise 7: Making sure people know what good looks like

Purpose: To encourage people to maintain the momentum and quality of the change project or process.

Audience: Project/leadership/management team members. All stakeholders in the change project.

Typical use: To review the change and decide actions to progress further and to ensure it is sustained and improved.

How to do it:

4 Plus 1 questions – use this to carry out regular reviews of the change to identify what progress has been made, and where positive reinforcement of the good is called for, and where different tactics might be needed to overcome resistance and motivate people further.

Praise and Trouble – in discussion with individuals and groups of stakeholders, this tool will help gather information about whether people perceive there has been a change, and what managers are currently recognising as good or bad (through an analysis of the feedback they are giving people). You can then analyse and judge whether this is line with the change expectations or not.

Exercise 8: Engaging people in the change

Purpose: To ensure that organisation and project leaders understand where stakeholders are in relation to the change, and to gain their input into the improvement of the project implementation and change outcomes.

Audience: All stakeholders in the change project.

Typical uses:

- Developing the design of new ways of working or systems.
- Assessing resistance.

- Assessing the impact of change.

- Assessing readiness for change.

- Assessing project progress.

- Assessing a go/no go decision.

How to do it:

One-page profiles – having as many of these as possible helps people to work together more effectively. In a change environment this is important where colleagues need to get up to speed with working together in a project team. Alternatively, it can be used for teams to review how they are working together with new ways of working or systems.

'Working/not working' – this tool gathers detailed information from a range of perspectives about the current reality, and can be used at intervals to review the progress of change with stakeholders.

4 Plus 1 questions – this can also be used as a detailed review tool, to get information from stakeholders on how they feel about a change, and steps that can address any concerns.

Chapter 13

Conclusion

People will forget what you said. People will forget what you did. But, people will not forget how you made them feel.

Maya Angelou[150]

How many times have you asked someone to describe something and they have replied, 'Well, I can't put it into words, but I know what it feels like?' Being in a person-centred organisation is a bit like that. Nevertheless, we hope that we have described enough of it for you to be able to know what it feels like, looks like and sounds like to be part of a person-centred organisation. The essence of person-centredness is in those interpersonal moments that we experience, in our relationships with each other, whether that is being supported by someone or in our interaction within the organisation.

A friend is one that knows you as you are, understands where you have been, accepts what you have become, and still, gently allows you to grow. (Anonymous)

It is that understanding and acceptance of people, as well as enabling growth, that you will see and feel in a person-centred organisation.

In this conclusion, we try to pull together into a final summary for you what makes a person-centred organisation and the contribution of person-centred practices.

Here are some of the characteristics of a person-centred organisation that we have explored throughout the book:

1. There is a complete focus on people supported and services are designed around individuals. Support reflects both what is important to the people now and what they want in the future, and it is delivered exactly how the people want and need it.

2. The people direct their own service and therefore decision making is as close to those receiving the service as possible. This means that teams are empowered to make decisions, with as little bureaucracy as possible.

3. Staff are encouraged to 'bring the whole person to work' and use their talents and interests to deliver the best service to people. They are thoughtfully matched to get the best fit with people they support and roles within the organisation.

4. Leaders and managers work with staff in a person-centred way – ensuring that all teams have a shared purpose and know what is important to each other and how to support each other; what their core responsibilities are; and where they can use their judgement and be creative.

5. The organisation embraces and encourages thoughtful risk taking, creativity, innovation and continuous learning. There is a culture of trust, empowerment and accountability.

6. You can see the values of the organisation in the lives of the leaders throughout the organisation.

7. There is a clear and inspiring vision and mission, and everyone in the organisation can talk about what that is, and what it means to them in their role.

8. Community matters – people supported by the organisation and the organisation itself are part of and contribute to communities.

9. People supported have a direct impact on organisational development and business planning. Business development and organisational change are driven by what is working and not working for people receiving the services.

10. You see the thoughtful use of person-centred thinking tools and practices at all levels of the organisation, to achieve its purpose. People can tell you both how they use them, why they use them and the difference they make in people's lives and in the way the organisation runs.

In the following table, we return to the organisation assessment criteria offered in Chapter 4, and summarise the key areas we have covered, and how person-centred practices are used.

Performance criteria	A summary of how this can be achieved through person-centred practices
Vision, mission and strategy	The vision, mission and values are expressed in a powerful visual way to all colleagues, and reinforced through repetition in multiple forms of business communication, and in learning and development and the one-to-one and annual review process. These priorities are expressed in terms of what is important to and for the organisation to be successful. The business strategy and planning process, and the performance management process use person-centred practices (success from different perspectives, 'Working/not working' from different perspectives; the Doughnut; 4 Plus 1 questions and Working Together for Change) to assess performance in relation to the vision, mission and values of the organisation.

cont.

Performance criteria	A summary of how this can be achieved through person-centred practices
HR processes	Colleagues are selected using the matching process to ensure that they bring the appropriate skills and gifts to their particular role. They participate in defining their role using the Doughnut, and undertake to work together to deliver what matters to the person, in the way the person wants to be supported, ensuring that the person has maximum choice and control in their life. Progress for the person supported is made through reflection and action, through person-centred thinking tools such as 'Working and not working' and 4 Plus 1 questions. One-page profiles are a way to know what matters to each person and how they need to be supported in their role. Regular communication of what is going well and not so well is also done using the 'Working/not working' tool or the 4 Plus 1 questions, emphasising what is important in the role. This is done prior to any resort to formal employee relations processes.
Financial processes	Financial reporting and analysis identifies where there are threats to the delivery of what is important to and for the stakeholders of the organisation. Focusing resources effectively to enhance what is working and to correct what is not working is enabled by the management information available. Assisting and collaborating with people we support and other stakeholders when there are financial difficulties is an accepted way of working.
Technology	Colleagues are trained in the 'technology' of the use of the person-centred thinking tools. They are supported by modern IT systems to which they have access according to what information is important to and for them, the people they support and other stakeholders in order to be successful. There are numerous opportunities for knowledge and good practice sharing both within the organisation and with external experts and professional bodies. Assistive technology is used where appropriate to enable people to be supported in ways that make sense to them.
Performance measurement and improvement	Colleagues use the full range of person-centred thinking tools to encourage and acquire multiple perspectives on the performance of both individuals and the organisation as a whole. This information is fed into the business improvement strategy through the learning and reflection and Working Together for Change process. Team meetings and other staff forums review performance using the 'Working/not working' and 4 Plus 1 questions tools. Performance is measured on a core set of indicators that are agreed as important to and for the organisation, and may be communicated through a one-page strategy.

Compliance	Standards are set using the Doughnut tool to define individual role requirements and thinking about organisational requirements related to the vision, mission and values, and to external compliance needs. Standards and practices challenge the rules and regulations to explain why something cannot be done and to enable it to happen, if it is important to the person.
	The compliance reporting process offers person-centred information to support compliance. This is gained from feedback from people supported using 'Working/not working' in a person-centred review. It demonstrates that working practices are meeting regulatory and legal requirements by delivering what is important to and important for people supported.
Reward and recognition	The person-centred review evidences staff contribution to what is important to and for the person supported. Managers are alert to contributions from individuals and teams that are in support of the vision, mission and values; reward and recognise this immediately; and create opportunities for those colleagues to share their good practice with others.
Risk enablement	There is a focus on enabling rather than preventing. There is a published statement of support for risk taking where colleagues have acted reasonably to try something new. The risk assessment process uses the person-centred thinking tools to identify what matters to the person in relation to the risk as well as what is important for the person and the organisation or others in taking the action. The process focuses on real risks, and does not produce 'good paper' for the sake of it.
Performance management	There is a common performance management process using the same language of person-centred thinking. Performance management focuses on the core purpose of the organisation, and also encourages creativity and innovation in individual and team roles within defined parameters. The performance management process includes a mandatory personal development discussion. One-to-ones and annual reviews use the person-centred thinking tools to assess competencies and how individual gifts and contributions are being used to support people well, and to learn whether staff have the support they need to do their best work. The areas for creativity and innovation for each individual and team are identified via the Doughnut tool. Contributions are strongly linked to the central vision and mission statements of the organisation.
Decision making	Decision making is made as close to people supported as possible, and clarified through decision-making agreements. Decision making leading to business strategy and planning is informed by the input from many perspectives using Working Together for Change and person-centred thinking tools such as 'Working/not working' and 4 Plus 1 questions with many different stakeholders.

cont.

Performance criteria	A summary of how this can be achieved through person-centred practices
Learning and development	Colleagues are given full education, support and coaching in the use of person-centred thinking tools, in addition to the practice and technical training for their job. Staff one-to-ones and annual reviews use person-centred thinking tools to create personal development plans and individual portfolios of learning. Learning logs are used to encourage the recording and sharing of learning. Multiple channels of learning and development are offered to suit individual learning and communication styles.
Communications	The vision, mission and values are focused for all colleagues in a visible way, such as the Way We Work posters or one-page strategies. This is reinforced through learning and reflection days using the Working Together for Change process, which gathers input to business planning. Storytelling is a key component of communications. There are regular forums for communicating business performance and good practice to colleagues. Visual performance indicators are used to communicate performance regularly to all colleagues.
Organisation structure	Hierarchy alone is not highly valued. Structures are determined by what is important to and for the people supported, learned from when things are working and changed when something is not working. Contributing knowledge and leadership is a key measure of status and position in the organisation. The structure facilitates the creation of subject matter expertise and the sharing of knowledge and resources.
Leadership and management style	Managers use the 'Working/not working' and the 4 Plus 1 questions tools to explore problems and issues with individuals and teams, and to propose solutions in the workplace. Requests for additional support and resources are communicated to others using the information from this analysis and an explanation of what is important to and for the organisation and the team to fix or improve. Managers obtain feedback from multiple perspectives from other stakeholders about what is working and not working for the individual colleague, and use the 4 Plus 1 questions tool to assess and discuss this feedback with the colleague and agree any improvement actions. Managers are skilled in coaching staff to use person-centred practices. Person-centred thinking and tools are modelled by managers throughout the organisation.
Business continuity	The Working Together for Change process ensures forward plans are directly linked to the people supported. Stakeholders are fully engaged in the business, and will provide support when times are tough. The quality versus cost equation is used effectively in obtaining business, by demonstrating that the service or 'product' is directly meeting the aspirations, needs and desires of the people supported.

What next?

The following organisation design and development diagram (Figure 13.1) is our one-page summary of how you can decide what to do next. It starts at the top of the page with your mission and vision for the organisation. We share many processes for helping you decide where you are now (and where you want to be), and in the middle are some of the common organisational challenges that resonate with your organisation. We could not cover every one, but have summarised common challenges. The arrows then point to the person-centred practices that could be helpful in addressing those issues.

This analysis will lead you to your organisation development plan, or at least targets, and you can then allocate these to resources through a change management plan as required.

We hope that the range and combination of tools and techniques we have offered you will give you plenty of options to take your organisation forward to become truly person-centred.

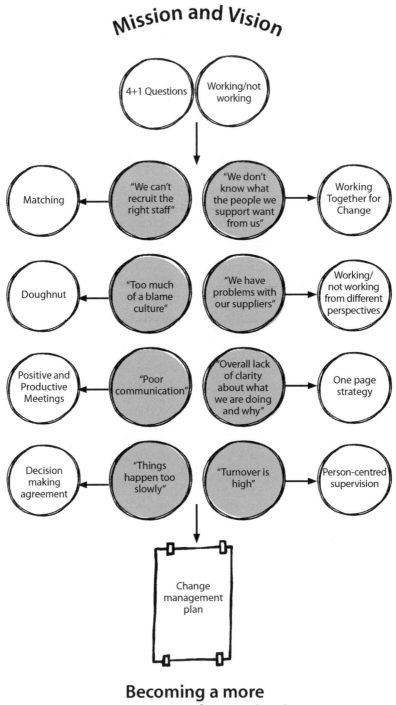

Figure 13.1 Getting started

Appendix 1

Progress for Providers

1 Leadership and strategy
Strategy

Tick one box ✓

1	We have not considered the impact of the personalisation agenda and don't know if this will impact on our organisation.
2	We think that personalisation will have an impact on our organisation although we are not sure what this will be nor how we need to respond. We are not sure that all of our senior managers are convinced of the need to develop a strategic response.
3	We have identified some of the areas of our business that we think will be affected by the personalisation agenda. We have also started to engage with local commissioners and other stakeholders, including people who use our services, in order to work in partnership on these changes.
4	Following discussions with all stakeholders, we have developed a strategic plan for delivering the changes we think we need to make. This includes the impact on all staff, including finance and back office functions. The senior team (and trustees if relevant) have signed up to this and are supporting it.
5	We have a clear vision and strategy for delivering personalised support and for remodelling our business to ensure we have a sustainable model for the future. Our strategy is based on a good understanding of where we are now, and on the aspirations of the people we support and other stakeholders. We have considered the resource implications of these changes and planned accordingly. The senior team actively supports the strategy and we are all held accountable for delivering on it. Person-centred approaches inform all activities, including our back office functions and finance.

2 Creating a person-centred culture
Changing the culture

1	We don't think that we need to think about changing the culture of our organisation.
2	We think that personalisation will have an impact on our culture and the way we operate but are not sure if this goes beyond some changes to the way we organise our finances and who we contract with.

3	We have started to think about what personalisation and what being person-centred will mean for our culture and the way we operate, both in terms of the delivery of support and our systems. We have had some discussions with managers and support workers and think we know how to proceed. We have not yet included our back office staff.	
4	We understand that personalisation will have a significant impact on our culture, systems and processes. We have a strategic plan to implement this change and are working with all staff across the organisation to help them understand what this means (including back office staff). We have lots of opportunities for discussion within a range of staff about what this means for them.	
5	We have worked with our staff, the people we support and other stakeholders to identify the culture change that needs to occur throughout the organisation and ensure that our leaders are modelling the change we want to see, and actively support our managers to do the same (through training, coaching and problem solving). We have looked at all the ways that we communicate in the organisation and have made sure that we are giving the same key messages.	

A person-centred approach to risk

1	We try to ensure that staff and people avoid taking risks. This is a major focus of our work and all potential risks relating to the people we support is recorded in detail and authorisation is needed before we support people to try certain activities.	
2	We realise that we need to adopt a new approach to risk to ensure that people have a chance to do the things they want. We are not sure how to put this into practice.	
3	We have decided to review our approach to risk, in relation to the people we support, and want to develop an approach that takes account of individual circumstances and aspirations.	
4	We have developed a new approach which is based on the premise that people should have the chance to do the things they want and that we should support them to do this.	
5	We developed our approach to risk in conjunction with the people we support, their families and other stakeholders and believe we have an approach to risk that is based on listening to what is important to people. This approach is embedded across the organisation and all staff are clear about their responsibilities in this respect. Positive risk taking is rewarded and we accept that this will not always be successful. We have a no blame culture and learn from successes and mistakes as an organisation.	

3 Community focus

1	We focus very closely on certain support tasks such as keeping people healthy and safe and think that this is our primary responsibility.	
2	We are aware of the need to promote community connections and citizenship but are not sure where to start and how to go about this.	
3	We have begun to think about promoting community connections and citizenship and understand why this is important for both the organisation and the people we support.	
4	We are actively looking at how we promote community connections and citizenship and recognise that this needs to be a clear priority for our work. We have some examples of supporting people to make community connections and we are learning from this. We are beginning to support our staff to work in this way and are learning from others.	
5	We have a clear commitment and focus on community and understand the importance of working alongside the entire community to effectively support people to become citizens. We undertake specific community development activities as an outcome of people's support plans and aspirations. We also engage with a range of community resources on a corporate basis and have a demonstrable local commitment.	

4 Support planning and review

Person-centred planning and support plans   Tick one box ✓

1	We provide support to groups of people, according to the specification provided by the local authority or primary care trust.	
2	We realise that we need to provide support to people as individuals but are not sure how to move from the current arrangement.	
3	We are beginning to make efforts to translate the care plan into a more person-centred document. We are introducing person-centred thinking to some of our staff.	
4	We are committed to person-centred support planning and ensure that all the staff in the organisation are trained and coached to use person-centred thinking, tools and approaches. Individuals have up-to-date person-centred support plans that are acted upon by staff. We use person-centred thinking tools and reviews to record what we are learning and to continue to develop and update the support plan.	
5	We use person-centred thinking extensively and ensure that everyone we support has a costed person-centred support plan that is outcome focused. Plans have clearly identified outcomes, linked to the funding available. We use person-centred approaches across the organisation, including non-operational functions, and person-centredness is embedded in all that we do.	

Outcome Focussed Reviews

1	Our reviews are focused on services and contracts. We discuss services with the local authority or primary care trust.	
2	We realise that we need to focus on outcomes when reviewing services but are not sure how to do this or what needs to change.	
3	We have begun to identify outcomes with people and have tried to do this with some people we support. We have begun to train staff in person-centred reviews that focus on outcomes.	
4	We ensure that all the people we support have person-centred reviews that are outcome focused and that the person and those close to them are at the centre of this process. People review how they are spending their money.	
5	We use information from person-centred reviews to help us evaluate how well we are meeting people's outcomes and what we need to change in the way we work and support people. We involve stakeholders in this process.	

5 Finance

Costing services

1	We cost our services as locations/building/groups and the service is delivered through aggregate contracts with funders not individuals.	
2	Even though the majority of the services we deliver are funded through aggregate contracts, we realise that we need to understand what it costs to provide support to individuals. We are not sure how to do this.	
3	We cost our service on an hourly rate that includes what it costs to run the service (e.g. management charges) as well as the direct cost of support. We can explain how we have calculated our hourly rate and have begun to develop individual costs for people we support.	

Tick one box ✓

4	We know what it costs to deliver each individual's support package, and we provide people we support with information about how much their support costs. If someone is interested in buying a service from us, we can provide detailed individual costings based on their support plan.	
5	We provide detailed costs for each individual we support and for people who may want to buy our service or products. We are clear with people that they can use their money flexibly, and not just to buy hours of support. People can buy as much or as little of our service as they want.	

Contracts

1	We have contracts with the local authority or primary care trust, a mixture of block and spot, which are generally focused on hours delivered and/or tasks.	
2	We think we might need to adopt other contractual models but are not sure where to start.	
3	We have contracts with local authorities and some with people who control their funding and are beginning to explore what this means for the way we do things. We are trying to make our contract documents easy to understand and read and want to talk with our commissioners and other stakeholders about creating individual service funds for other people we support.	
4	We offer an individual contract to all of our new customers, based on their support plan and their personal budget. We are actively working with our commissioners and other stakeholders to move people we already support from a block contract to individual service funds. We are looking at 'virtual budgets' within our block contracts to give people more flexibility.	
5	All of the people we support, regardless of whether they control the funding or not, have an individual contract with us based on their person-centred support plan. The contracts we use are easy to read and understand. We have individual contracts with a range of individuals, trust circles and family members.	

Invoicing

1	Our invoicing processes are designed to meet the needs of contracts with funding authorities. We struggle with deviations in billing.	
2	We realise that we need to look at how we can adapt our invoicing system so that we can invoice individuals but are not sure how to start.	
3	We can produce a mixture of invoices, including those required for block contracts and for individual services and have cost centres for each of our services. We are developing systems for individual invoicing.	
4	Although we currently have a mix of block contracts and personal budgets, our invoicing system can produce individual invoices. We have cost centres for each individual with a personal budget and self-funders.	
5	We invoice personal budgets holders and have systems that can be flexible, taking into account the different ways that people want to spend their personal budget. We can offer people different ways to pay us, through invoicing, direct debits and through systems such as Shop4Support. We have developed a range of accessible invoices.	

Accounting

1	We track the money we spend on a service-by-service/cost centre basis.	
2	We realise we need to account for support individually but cannot do this within our existing systems and processes.	

Tick one box ✓

3	We have begun to work on monitoring staff time and what we are spending on people's individual support. We are beginning to understand what changes we need to make to our accounting system.
4	We can show links between what people are spending their money on and the outcomes identified in their support plan. We are working on how we can make our financial information on how people are spending their personal budget easy to understand.
5	Our monitoring and accounting systems mean that we provide information for each individual about how they are spending their budget, how this relates to what is in their support plan, and whether they are under or over budget. We provide this in ways that people find easy to understand and use, and have worked with people and families to achieve this.

6 Human resources
Selecting and recruiting staff

1	Managers and paid staff select and recruit staff for our organisation based on formal job descriptions that we have developed.
2	We think we need to find a way of involving people in recruitment and selection but are not sure where to start
3	We are exploring ways to involve the people we support and their families in selecting staff and developing job descriptions. Some people have been involved to date.
4	We have trained some people who we support and families to be on interview panels with us and worked with them to improve our job descriptions, adverts, etc. They help us recruit staff to the organisation.
5	We work closely with individuals and their families in all aspects of the selection and recruitment process. People are involved as much or as little as they want to be, with some people/families leading all aspects of the process with appropriate support. Each job advert and person specification is based on the person, including their interests, and interview questions are mostly taken from the individual's person-centred support plan. Adverts are placed locally in a range of ways (post office, local radio, etc) and we actively recruit local staff. Staff are always recruited to an individual not to a pool of staff employed by the organisation.

Supporting, supervising and appraising staff

1	Staff support, supervision and appraisal is based on the manager's feedback only.
2	We supervise staff through meetings. We think we need to take people's views into account but are not sure how to do this.
3	Managers have frequent, regular supervision sessions with each staff member and conduct annual appraisals. We have made efforts to give people and families a voice and role in this and plan to do more.
4	Managers use people's person-centred support plans when supervising and appraising support workers, to check the progress being made in delivering the support people need and want. Support workers are clear about their core responsibilities and where they can use their creativity and judgement. People who use services are given the opportunity to get involved in this in a way that makes sense for them.

Tick one box ✓

5 We use person-centred support plans as the foundation of how we support and supervise support workers. Before supervision and appraisal, we ask the person (their family or trust circle) about how the support worker is doing and ensure that supervision and appraisals focus on how we can deliver the best service to the people we support. Supervision sessions also recognise what is important to and for staff, and are opportunities to consider what is working and not working and to think and problem solve together. We have a way of feeding back to people and families in a positive way. Listening to individuals and families forms part of our performance management system.

Workforce development

1 We have some training days in our organisation and these are based on statutory requirements such as lifting and handling and food hygiene. We meet minimum legal and regulatory requirements.

2 We have begun to think about how we might talk to staff about the changing culture of the organisation, their role in this and what new skills we might need to develop to meet new demands.

3 We have begun to think about the impact of becoming more person-centred and have started a programme of training that helps support staff and their managers to understand what they can do to make sure people have more choice and control in their lives. This has included practical tools such as person-centred thinking tools, and helping staff to understand what individual service funds are and the wider context for the organisation.

4 We understand that personalisation means that we need to review all aspects of the service we provide. We are working with senior managers across the organisation (including back office, non operational functions) to help them think about what personalisation means to them and their role and what new skills and knowledge they may need. We are developing an in-depth training programme as part of our workforce plan.

5 We have developed a detailed workforce strategy and training programme based on input, ideas and involvement of staff, individuals and their families. This includes what will need to change about the way we train, support and deploy our staff, and the way we organise and govern ourselves if we are to be a truly person-centred organisation.

Policies and procedures

1 We have policies and procedures on how we work. We meet minimum legal and regulatory requirements and don't take into account personalisation.

2 We recognise that our policies and procedures will need to change to reflect personalisation and being person-centred but have not started to make changes.

3 We have begun to review our policies and procedures to make sure that they are person-centred and reflect personalisation. We are working on ways of making sure people have a voice in this process.

4 We are working with staff, people we support and other stakeholders to identify where our policies and procedures need to change to ensure that they actively promote people having more choice and control in their lives. We are trying to streamline them so that we have as few as possible.

5 We have changed our policies and procedures to ensure that they are person-centred and actively promote enabling people to have choice and control in their lives. We worked with people who use services, families and staff to develop these, and they are presented in a way that is easy to read and understand. There are as few of them as possible.

7   Marketing
Customer focus

Tick one box ✓

1	We see our customers as the local authority or primary care trust.
2	We say that our customers are the people who use our services and their families, but the ways that we provide our services do not always match this. We know that the local authority or primary care trust are also our customers.
3	We have started to rethink how we work with people and their families, and understand what their 'customer journey' is, and how we need to change.
4	We have started to make changes to our service to reflect the journey that we want people to have with us. We are working on how people find out about us, how we tell them what we can offer, how we learn about people in a person-centred way and design and deliver individual costed services. We have also thought about the customer service we provide to the local authority or primary care trust.
5	We put people at the centre of what we do. We recognise that we have a variety of customers and partners and work with each of them in an individual, person-centred way. We don't always get it right but we learn from our mistakes, and make sure we reflect and learn from this.

Communication and promotion

1	We are focused on selling our services to the local authority or primary care trust.
2	We know that we need to think about how we communicate with people who may want to buy our services themselves (individuals or their family) or who want information on our services (for example care managers, brokers, user led organisations, peer advocates or others) but are not yet sure where to make changes.
3	We have begun to think about how we might market ourselves to people better, and what we need to change about our information. We have made some effort to communicate directly with people and families, and other people who may be interested in our services (care managers, brokers, user led organisations, peer advocates or others).
4	We have begun to develop information for different people and we are aware of the need to do this in a way that is meaningful, accessible and meets people's needs. We are also considering new marketing methods such as Shop4Support.
5	We have a clear strategy/approach to communicating with and marketing ourselves to individuals, families and circles, and everyone who may be interested in our services. We use a range of accessible and user friendly approaches, which we have developed in consultation with people and families. We actively seek feedback from people about how we are doing and have developed processes to make sure this happens and is acted upon.

8   Reviewing and improving our service (quality)
Mission and standards

1	We focus on achieving our regulator's standards.
2	Our organisation has a mission and standards, but they do not very clearly connect with each other. We do not measure whether we are achieving our standards and are not sure how to measure this.
3	We have a mission, vision, values and standards. We measure progress on some of our standards and are thinking about how these things connect and want to do more work on this.

4	Our mission, vision and values are connected and reflect our commitment to personalisation/person-centredness. We have a set of standards that we regularly measure against. We set actions based on this to improve the way we deliver person-centred services.	
5	Our mission, vision and values were developed with people we support, families and staff. They reflect the ideas behind personalisation in everyday language and we use them in our training and our meetings, and everyone knows them. We evaluate our services in partnership with individuals and families, and share information from this and what we are going to do to become more person-centred. Our approach to governance includes listening to and involving people and families.	

Improving people's lives and achieving their outcomes

1	Staff are busy keeping people healthy and safe.	
2	We try to help people change things if they want to and to have a fulfilling life, but we do not use a process for doing this nor do we understand how to adapt our approach.	
3	Most people have some sort of review of the support they receive. We have thought about outcomes and are beginning to work with people to identify what they want to change about their lives.	
4	Everyone has a person-centred support plan and a review that focuses on what is and is not working for them, and what they want for the future. We focus on supporting people to achieve their outcomes and make sure we can demonstrate this.	
5	We use person-centred support plans and reviews to enable people to think about their lives and what they want to change. We work together to make these changes happen. We support people to move towards their aspirations and contribute to their communities. Managers see themselves as responsible for making sure great planning takes place, that actions happen, and people are supported the way they want to be.	

Learning from individuals to inform strategic change

1	We do not have a way to systematically and strategically review our business/organisation.	
2	We undertake a strategic review of our organisation and involve employees in this review and decision making about what we will do the next year. We realise we need to try to involve the people we support, families and other stakeholders in this process.	
3	We have begun to consult with and directly involve people who use our services, families and other stakeholders when we review the service we provide. We then use this information to influence strategic decisions.	
4	We have established a range of mechanisms to enable people to comment on the performance and strategic direction of the organisation. We make sure that we use feedback from people's experiences to inform our future plans.	
5	We have a way to ensure that everyone's experiences count when we review our progress. People who use services, their families and other stakeholders contribute their view about what is working and not working for them through person-centred (or outcome focused) reviews. We aggregate information from these reviews together with people and their families. This information sets the direction of the organisation and provides important information for our business and strategic planning. We feedback to people about the changes we have made in a way that makes sense for them.	

Appendix 2

Progress for Providers for Managers

1 Person-centred thinking tools and approaches
Knowledge, skills and understanding

Tick one box ✓

1	No one in my team has any understanding or experience of using person-centred thinking tools or approaches.
2	I know that we need to develop our skills, knowledge and understanding of person-centred thinking tools but have not developed any plans to do this and I am not sure how to begin.
3	I have a plan to develop our understanding of person-centred thinking and some of the team have begun to use person-centred thinking tools and approaches. We have started to look at some of the information available on person-centred thinking (for example, Michael Smull's podcasts on YouTube).
4	I am using person-centred thinking tools and approaches myself, and all the team know and are successfully using several of the tools. I have a one-page profile and so do each of the team, and we are using this in our work together.
5	We all have our own one-page profile and we use this to inform our practice, and we are all confident and competent in using person-centred thinking tools. Everyone can describe at least five person-centred thinking tools (why and how you can use them and the benefits to the person) and talk about their experience of using them and the outcomes doing so achieved. As a manager I demonstrate enabling people supported to have as much choice and control as possible in their lives; working in a consistently person-centred way and proactively and competently using person-centred thinking tools in all areas of my work.

Supporting team members individually

1	No one in the team has a personal development plan and we are not using any process to reflect on how we work and how to develop our skills.
2	I recognise that all staff need ongoing support and opportunities for development to build their skills and knowledge and a way for their progress to be monitored. I am not sure how to go about this.
3	I have started to talk to each team member about how they are doing in using person-centred thinking tools and approaches in their work. This is on an adhoc basis.
4	I talk to each team member on a regular planned basis about how they are developing their skills in using person-centred thinking and approaches and how I can support them in this. I have a record of the progress that team members are making (for example, using the person-centred thinking rating scale).

5	Each staff member has a regularly reviewed individual development plan that includes how they are developing their competence in using the person-centred thinking tools and approaches. This includes celebrating successes and problem solving difficulties. I ensure that each team member reflects on their own practice and is accountable for this. We use a range of ways to ensure each team member has individual support in using person-centred thinking tools and approaches (for example, peer support, mentoring and person-centred thinking, as a standing agenda item for supervision). There is a mechanism for recording and sharing best practice across the organisation.	

Support and development as a team

1	We don't meet as a team and when we do meet, we solely focus on processes and procedures.	
2	I recognise that it is important that we meet and reflect about the team's ongoing development but we are struggling to prioritise this or find the resources to allow this to happen.	
3	I make sure that we set aside time during team meetings to reflect on practice and sometimes this includes how we are using person-centred thinking tools and approaches.	
4	I use person-centred thinking tools and approaches in our team meetings. I also have other ways that we work together to develop our understanding of person-centred thinking tools and approaches, and to reflect on successes and challenges together.	
5	We have a strong culture of reflective practice around our experience of using person-centred thinking tools and approaches. In the team we have a variety of ways (for example, standing agenda item in team meetings, sharing best practices and problem solving, practice groups, person-centred thinking tool of the month) to support team members to develop their skills in using person-centred thinking and approaches. The information is gathered and collected to inform organisational training and development planning.	

2 Using person-centred thinking tools and approaches to support individuals to have choice and control in their lives

Seeing the person as an individual and appreciating gifts and qualities

1	We have information about the person's support needs - this is usually provided by the person who commissioned the service. This information is focused on their needs. Staff struggle to describe the person in a positive way and feel uncomfortable doing this.	
2	We recognise the importance of seeing the person as a whole person, including their gifts and qualities, but we don't record this.	
3	We have a commitment to see the person as a whole person and to develop ways of gathering a range of information in our care plans about the person, including recognising their gifts and attributes.	
4	We collect person-centred information about each person we support. This includes recording the person's gifts and skills (for example, in a one-page profile). We don't just record this information, we try to use it; for example, in conversations with the person.	
5	We know and have a record of each individual's gifts and qualities and we have found a variety of ways to communicate this to them and people important to them (for example, appreciation books, one-page profiles). We actively use this information to support people to develop relationships and become contributing citizens. People are described positively, and individually, as a matter of course, and we encourage others to do the same.	

Understanding the person's history

Tick one box ✓

1	All we know about the person comes from the care plan, commissioners or our recent experience of supporting them. If we know anything about their history it is more likely to be in the context of negative experiences or behaviour.
2	We understand the value of knowing the person's history and background in a balanced way, so we can support them better, but do not have any way to do this at the moment.
3	We have a commitment to finding out about the person's history and have started to work with a few people to talk about their history and record this.
4	We have recorded histories for some of the people we support. We have different ways to share this information, and are working towards having recorded histories for everyone we support.
5	We know and have a record of each individual's personal history. This is recorded in a way that works for the person, for example on a history map, life story book, timeline, scrapbook, memory box or DVD. We always use this information as the foundation of current and future approaches to support.

What matters to the person now

1	We know and focus on how to keep people healthy and safe, but do not know or record what is important to each person as an individual.
2	We know we need to recognise what's important to people and support people to have what is important to them, and to record this. We are looking at how we can do this.
3	We have started to use some person-centred thinking tools to gather information about what is important to each individual we support (for example, good day and bad day, relationship maps and learning about people's routines). This information is starting to change how we support people.
4	We have information about what matters to most of the people we support and this is recorded (for example, in a one-page profile). Team members use this to support people.
5	We know what is important to each individual we support. This is clearly recorded and includes specific, detailed information including relationships, routines and interests. Everybody we support has a one-page profile. Staff intentionally work to make sure what is important to the person is happening in their day-to-day life and identify where there are obstacles to achieving this (including where it is our organisation's own procedures and practices that cause these obstacles).

Working towards the outcomes that the person wants for the future

1	We provide support based on the care plan and commissioning; we are unsure what people want for the future.
2	We realise that in order to support people effectively we should understand their aspirations for the future. However, we are not sure how to do this, or whether it is really our role.
3	We are trying different person-centred approaches to enable people to think about their future and we have recorded goals for some people, and we are working on our role in achieving these goals.
4	We have made good progress in ensuring that everyone we support has an opportunity to think about their future by using person-centred thinking and planning. This is recorded for most people, and there are clear outcomes that we are working towards.

5	We know what each individual wants for their future – their dreams, hopes and aspirations. We have gathered this information from the person and those who know and care about them (using person-centred thinking, planning or person-centred reviews). There are specific, measurable and achievable outcomes that move in the direction of these future aspirations and we are working with the person to achieve these. We are clear about our role in this, and review progress with the person. The information is used to develop a strategic plan and to hold the organisation to account. All the people we support have outcome-focused reviews.	

How the person wants to be supported

1	We have established policies and procedures for how we support people and we support everyone in the same way.	
2	We know that to support people effectively we need to find out how they would like to be supported. We are unsure how to do this and record the information. Currently our approach is not flexible enough to allow this to happen. We are task orientated rather than people orientated but we want to change this.	
3	We acknowledge the importance of finding out from people what good support looks like for them individually, and we have begun to explore with people what this looks like and have developed a plan to gather this information for everyone, using person-centred thinking tools and approaches.	
4	Everyone in the team is clear about what good support looks like for each person they support. We have started to record this (for example, in one-page profiles). Staff understand what this means for their practice on a day-to-day basis and are using this information to inform how they support people.	
5	We know and act on how the person wants to be supported. This is clearly recorded, is detailed, specific to the person and staff use this to deliver individual support. The information includes the support people want in their routines, in their relationships and interests, and how to help people be healthy and safe. We review team members' performance on their ability to provide support in the way that someone wants.	

How the person communicates

1	We support people following our policies and procedures; we do not specifically record how people communicate.	
2	We realise that we need to understand more about how people communicate and what they are trying to tell us.	
3	We have started to introduce communication charts as a first step. Staff are now beginning to understand that all behaviour is communication and are developing their skills in observing recording and communicating with people.	
4	We use communication charts with the majority of the people we support; increasingly staff understand their own role in effective listening and communication.	
5	We know and respond to how the person communicates (particularly if they don't use words to communicate). This is clearly recorded, for example, on communication charts, or communication passports, and staff know what the person means when they behave in certain ways and how staff should respond. All staff consistently use this on a day-to-day basis and update regularly.	

How the person makes decisions

Tick one box ✓

1	The people we support are not involved in significant decisions about their life.
2	We realise that people should be involved and included in any decisions about their life; we also recognise that this could help people feel more in control. We do not know how to do this yet. We use best interest meetings.
3	We have started to develop decision-making agreements with people and have tried out different approaches to help people to make decisions. We are using best interest meetings and engaging families to assist in the process.
4	The use of decision-making agreements is common, and we have many examples of people making decisions about what is important to them. We are struggling to ensure that this is for all people with capacity or communication issues. Staff are engaged and support people to record their decisions.
5	Staff know the decisions that are important to the person, how to support the person with these decisions and how the final decision is made. This is recorded, for example, in a decision-making agreement. We make sure people get representation if they need it. We have supported some people to make decisions that we didn't agree with and manage the tension in this.

Acting on what is working and not working

1	We do not know what is working or not working for the people we support.
2	We want to learn what people think is working and not working in their lives. We are not sure how to do this and are fearful we will not be able to respond and make the changes they want.
3	We have started routinely to ask people what is working and not working from their perspective about their life and the service they receive (for example as part of a person-centred review).
4	Staff are confident in supporting people to tell us what is working and not working. This happens for everyone at least once a year. There is an action plan developed from this. We have created a system that will gather this information from people so that we can plan strategically what needs to happen in the service.
5	We have a process for asking and recording what is working and not working from the person's perspective. We have actions (with a date and a named person responsible) to change what is not working. The action plan is regularly reviewed and this information is shared to inform change in the organisation.

Supporting people in their friendships and relationships

1	The only people in the person's life are paid staff. We don't see it as our responsibility to support people with relationships.
2	We realise that people might want to meet and make more friends but we are fearful that this could expose people to harm and risk and we are not prepared to accept the responsibility for this. We are not sure how we would begin to find out who is important in the person's life.
3	We have started to work out how we can support people to build and maintain relationships. We are still worried about the risk and how to manage this. We have started to understand what's in the local community and we are developing relationship maps. Staff are putting a greater focus on people's interests and friendships.

4	We have tried a number of approaches to support people with their friendships and relationships. We know who is already important in the person's life (for example, by using a relationship map) and people are now having opportunities to meet new people (who are not paid to be with them). We are gathering the learning and sharing good practice.	
5	We support people to meet new people and make new relationships and friendships in their community (outside of staff and any other people who live with the person). We know who is important to the person and support them to maintain these relationships. This is recorded, for example, on a relationship circle or inclusion web. We have a strategic approach to friendships and relationships. Staff see this as a main purpose in their role.	

Being part of their community

1	It is not our job to connect people in the community.	
2	We think it would be good if people we support were out and about in the community more but we can't see how we can do this within our current resources.	
3	We are committed to exploring ways of people being part of their communities, and we have started thinking about how to do this with a few people we support (for example, using community maps, recording gifts and Presence to Contribution).	
4	We support some people to go out and be part of their community and we use person-centred thinking tools in the way that we approach this.	
5	We know the places in the community that are important to the person, and other places they may like to be part of. This is recorded, for example, on a community map. We have a specific, measurable plan to enable the person to be fully part of their community, and making a contribution (for example, through using Presence to Contribution). This is regularly reviewed and there is evidence that people are becoming part of their community.	

3 Using person-centred thinking tools and approaches to create a person-centred culture within teams
Clear purpose

1	We have an organisational mission statement created by the senior manager/management team/owner. This complies with requirements. We have not considered how this should be reflected in the way we work.	
2	We think it would be helpful for the team to think about our purpose as a team but we are not sure how to go about this.	
3	We have begun to talk with staff about what our purpose is and to think about how we can record this.	
4	We are clear about our team's purpose and how this fits with the organisation's mission statement. We have developed this together as a team and with people using the service.	
5	The organisation's mission statement informs the team's purpose. Everyone understands the connection between the mission and their individual purpose and role. The team knows what their team purpose is; what we are trying to achieve together and all team members know their purpose in relation to the people they support, their team and the rest of the organisation. This is recorded, for example, in a purpose poster or team purpose statement. The team's purpose informs the work of the team, and there is evidence of this in practice.	

An agreed way of working that reflects values

Tick one box ✓

1	We don't really think about values; we just get on with the job.
2	We realise that we need to explore our values and beliefs as a team and how this can inform our practice.
3	We have started to think together about our team values and how we work together. We know what is working and what needs to change.
4	We have agreed our values and team principles and developed an action plan that addresses what needs to change, in partnership with people we support.
5	The team has a shared set of beliefs or values that underpin their work, and agreed ways of working that reflect these. These reflect working in a person-centred way and include working in ways that ensure people have maximum choice and control in their lives, as part of their local community. The team principles and ways of working are clearly documented (for example, ground rules, team charter, person-centred team plan, team procedure file, etc.). The team regularly evaluates how they are doing against these agreed ways of working (for example, by using what is working and not working from different perspectives).

People know what is important to each other and how to support each other

1	My team do not know each other very well.
2	I have started to work on ways that I can help the team know more about each other; what matters to them as people and how they can support each other at work (for example, starting with one-page profiles for everyone).
3	I am learning what is important to my team and how best to support them. We are all aware of how to support each other and what is important to each other and we are working at putting this into practice.
4	My team and I have all documented how best to support each other and what is important to each of us. We know how we make decisions as a team, and the best ways to communicate together.
5	As a team we know and act on what 'good support' means to each person. This information is recorded, for example, in a person-centred team plan. We regularly reflect on what is working and not working for them as a team, and what they can do about this. We have a culture where we appreciate each others' gifts and strengths and use these in our work wherever we can.

Staff know what is expected of them

1	I think that each team member has a general sense of what is expected of them.
2	All staff have a generic job description and work to organisational policies and procedures.
3	I know that staff need to be clearer about what their important or core responsibilities are and where they can try out ideas and use their own judgement. We have started to have discussions in the team about this.
4	Some staff are clear about what is expected of them and where they can make decisions themselves. There are still some grey areas that we need to explore more. We are using person-centred thinking tools (for example, the Doughnut) in clarifying expectations and decision making.

Tick one box ✓

| 5 | As a team we know and act on what 'good support' means to each person. This information is recorded, for example, in a person-centred team plan. Staff know what is expected of them – they are clear about their core responsibilities and where they can try new ideas in their day-to-day work. Staff are clear about their role in people's lives and know what they must do in their work around the people they support, and any team, admin or finance responsibilities. Staff know how to use person-centred thinking to deliver their core responsibilities. Staff know where they can use their own judgement and try new ideas or approaches and record what they are learning about what works and does not work when they use their own judgement. Roles and responsibilities are clearly recorded (for example, in a Doughnut) and this is reflected in job descriptions. | |

Staff feel that their opinions matter

1	I make all decisions; I don't involve my team. I chair team meetings and set the agenda. I set the agenda for supervision and appraisal.	
2	I recognise the need to find a way to listen to my staff team, value their opinions and engage them in decision making. I am trying to improve how I do this.	
3	My team have some involvement in setting team meeting agendas. I still make most of the decisions.	
4	I regularly meet with my team and discuss issues that they raise (in team meetings and other day-to-day opportunities). They contribute to team meeting agendas and make suggestions for supervision discussions. Some staff make suggestions for new ideas or changes. We are starting to use person-centred thinking tools to listen to each other.	
5	Staff feel that their opinions are listened to. Team members are asked for their opinions and consulted on issues that affect them. Team members feel confident in suggesting new ideas or changes to me. We regularly use person-centred thinking tools in the team to listen to each others' views and experience (for example, 4 Plus 1 questions).	

Rotas - staff are thoughtfully matched to people and rotas are personalised to people who are supported

1	I write staff rotas based upon staff availability. The rota meets the requirements of the service. There is a system for staff and people who use the service to make requests.	
2	I have identified the preferences of people who are supported and the staff (for example, using the Matching tool and one-page profile). I write the rotas and take these preferences into consideration where possible.	
3	Sometimes people who are supported are matched to people with similar interests but service need still takes priority.	
4	My team and I know what people's preferences are, how they like to be supported and what is important to them. These preferences are acknowledged in the way that the rota is developed, so that we get a good match between the person and the staff who support them. The rota times are based around how people want to be supported.	
5	Decisions about who works with whom are based on who the person supported wants to support them. Where the team leader makes this decision, it is based on which staff get on the best with different individuals, taking into account what people and individual staff members have in common (for example, a shared love of country music) as well as personality characteristics (for example, gregarious people and quieter people), necessary skills and experience. Rotas are developed around people using the service based on the support they want and the activities they want to do, and who they want to support them.	

Recruitment and selection

Tick one box ✓

1	Staff are recruited to the team based on formal job descriptions that have been developed by the organisation.
2	I know I should involve the people who receive a service in recruitment but I am not sure how to go about this.
3	I have started to look at 'good practice' examples of ways to involve people in recruiting their support staff. We have started to explore how we can develop job descriptions that reflect what is important to people we support.
4	We have worked with people and identified ways for them and their families to be involved in recruitment and selection of their staff. This happens some of the time. We have developed personalised job descriptions and adverts based on what is important to the person and how they want to be supported. We use the Matching tool in our recruitment processes.
5	Our recruitment and selection process demonstrates a person-centred approach. We recruit people who can deliver our purpose by selecting people for their values and beliefs, and characteristics, not just their experience and knowledge. Job descriptions are individualised to the people who are supported wherever possible, using information from matching staff. It is common practice for people to be involved in recruiting their own staff, in a way that works for them.

Enabling risk

1	I encourage my team to make sure people are safe and do not take risks. We adhere to all required legislation.
2	I am aware that I need to encourage my team to become less risk averse. I am not sure how to do this.
3	I am working with the team to help them take a responsive and person-centred approach to risk. We are starting to use this in some situations.
4	We use a person-centred approach to risk most of the time. We involve the people, family and others in thinking this through. I ensure everything is documented and adheres to the relevant legislation.
5	We ensure that risks are thought through in a person-centred way that reflects what is important to the person and decisions are clearly recorded. The person and their family are centrally involved in the way that we do this.

Training and development

1	All training is based on statutory requirements. I make sure that we meet minimum legal and statutory requirements.
2	I recognise that I need to find a way for training and development opportunities to reflect the needs of the service we provide to people and motivate the staff.
3	I have started to think about how I can introduce learning and development opportunities to staff that will reflect the needs of people who receive a service and also engage and develop the team member. I have begun to look at what is working and what is not working for individuals and also researching what is available.
4	We have identified all training needs, learning and development opportunities and have a plan in place. Training and development opportunities reflect the needs and wishes of people who receive a service and have been agreed with team members. Person-centred thinking and approaches are central to our approaches to training. We are compliant with all legal and statutory requirements.

| 5 | We provide development and training opportunities to all staff that focus on increasing choice and control for people we support and delivering an individual, person-centred service. Within a few months of starting with the organisation, new staff have induction training that includes using person centred thinking and approaches to deliver our purpose. Our training enables staff to be up to date with best practice in delivering choice and control, and using person centred thinking to enable people to live the lives they want. We know that the first-line managers are key to delivering a person-centred service, and we have specific training and support to enable them to use a person-centred approach in all aspects of their role, and to be able to coach their staff in using person-centred thinking skills. | |

Supervision

1	I set the agenda and make the arrangements for staff supervision. I meet the minimum requirement.	
2	I am aware that staff support and supervision practice needs to be reviewed. I am not sure how I can change the current arrangements.	
3	I have started to think about involving people who receive a service in staff supervision. I have talked to people and staff about how we might go about this. Most members of staff have supervision meetings.	
4	All staff are supervised, and people who staff support usually contribute through sharing their views with me before the supervision session. Supervision results in actions and the meetings are documented. I have started to use person-centred thinking tools in supervision sessions.	
5	Each team member has regular, planned, individual supervision. Supervision includes giving staff individual feedback on what they do well, as well as what they can improve on (for example, coaching staff to develop their skills in working in a person-centred way). There is a clear link between training and supervision and what people do when they are at work (for example, when people attend training, managers expect to see a difference in their work, and this is discussed in their individual supervision). The views of people supported are very important in the supervision process, and people are asked their views before supervision.	

Appraisal and individual development plans

1	Most of my staff have an appraisal. I set the agenda and assign objectives.	
2	I have recognised that people who receive a service and their families should be given the opportunity to feed back on the support they receive from staff. I am not sure how I should go about this. Staff have an appraisal but do not really contribute to the agenda or any development plan.	
3	I have a plan in place to ensure that each member of staff receives an annual appraisal. Where possible, I try to seek the views of people who receive a service and their families.	
4	We have a variety of ways for people who receive a service and their families to contribute their views to staff appraisals. All staff are asked to reflect on what they have tried, what they have learnt, what they are pleased about and if they have any concerns. We then agree what actions need to be taken from all the information gathered.	
5	Team members get positive feedback about their work and have annual appraisals and individual development plans. Annual appraisals include feedback from people supported about what is working and not working about the support they receive and results in an individual development plan with clear goals that build on strengths, focus on working in a person-centred way, and further developing skills.	

Meetings

Tick one box ✓

1	We have occasional team meetings but not everyone attends or contributes.	
2	There are frequent team meetings. I set the agenda and chair the meeting. There is little structure to the meeting and they are not as well attended as they could be.	
3	I schedule regular team meetings. The meeting tends to be an information-giving forum and does not often include problem solving or celebrating successes.	
4	We have regular structured team meetings which are documented. Actions are agreed, recorded and followed up on. They are well attended and most people contribute.	
5	Our team has regular, productive team meetings that are opportunities to hear everyone's views, and everyone contributes. Team meetings include sharing what is going well and problem solving difficulties (for example, practising using person-centred thinking tools to solve problems).	

Endnotes

1. Sanderson, H. and Lepkowsky, M.B. (2012) *Person-Centred Teams*. Stockport: HSA Press, p.3.
2. Think Local Act Personal. Available at www.thinklocalactpersonal.org.uk/Browse/ThinkLocal ActPersonal, accessed on 21 January 2012.
3. Sanderson, H. and Lepkowsky, M.B. (2012) *Person-Centred Teams*. Stockport: HSA Press.
4. Sanderson, H. and Lewis, J. (2011) *A Practical Guide to Delivering Personalisation: Person-Centred Practice in Health and Social Care*. London: Jessica Kingsley Publishers.
5. Williams, R. and Sanderson, H. (2003) *What Are We Learning about Person-Centred Organisations?* Available at www.helensandersonassociates.co.uk/media/16516/what%20are%20 we%20 learning%20about%20person%20centred%20organisations.pdf, accessed on 13 March, 2012.
6. Ibid.
7. Ashman, B., Ockenden, J., Beadle Brown, J. and Mansell, J. (2010) *Person Centred Active Support – A Handbook*. Brighton: Pavilion Publishing.
8. Department of Health (DoH) (2010) *Personalisation through Person-Centred Planning*. London: DoH.
9. Department of Health (DoH) (2001) *Valuing People: A New Strategy for Learning Disability for the 21st Century*. White Paper. London: DoH.
10. Department of Health (DoH) (2007) *Putting People First*. London: DoH.
11. Robertson, J., Emerson, E., Hatton, C., Elliott, J. *et al.* (2005) *The Impact of Person Centred Planning*. Lancaster: Institute for Health Research, Lancaster University.
12. Smull, M., Bourne, M.L. and Sanderson, H. (2009) *Becoming a Person Centred System*. Available at www.elpnet.net/documents/BecomingaPersonCenteredSystem-ABriefOverview.pdf, accessed on 13 March 2012, p.3.
13. Sanderson, H. and Lewis, J. (2011) *A Practical Guide to Delivering Personalisation: Person-Centred Practice in Health and Social Care*. London: Jessica Kingsley Publishers.
14. Smull, M. and Sanderson, H. (2005) *Essential Lifestyle Planning for Everyone*. Stockport: HSA Press.
15. Handy, C. (1994) *The Age of Paradox*. Boston, MA: Harvard Business School Press.
16. Mount, B. (1987) *Personal Futures Planning: Finding Directions for Change*. Doctoral dissertation, University of Georgia.
17. O'Brien, J. (1987) 'A Guide to Lifestyle Planning'. In B. Wilcox and G.T. Bellamy (eds) *The Activities Catalog: An Alternative Curriculum for Youth and Adults with Severe Disabilities*. Baltimore, MD: Brookes Publishing.
18. Duffy, S. (2004) *Keys to Citizenship: A Guide to Getting Good Support Services for People with Learning Difficulties*. Birkenhead: Paradigm Consultancy and Development Agency.
19. Scown, S. and Sanderson, H. (2011) *Making it Personal for Everyone – From Block Contracts towards Individual Service Funds*. Stockport: HSA Press.
20. Ibid.
21. Smull, M. and Sanderson, H. (2005) *Essential Lifestyle Planning for Everyone*. Stockport: HSA Press.
22. Myers, I.B. with Myers, P.B. (1995) *Gifts Differing*. Palo Alto, CA: Davies-Black.
23. Handy, C. (1994) *The Age of Paradox*. Boston, MA: Harvard Business School Press, p.70.
24. Smull, M. and Sanderson, H. (2005) *Essential Lifestyle Planning for Everyone*. Stockport: HSA Press.

25. Ibid.

26. Timebanking UK. Available at www.timebanking.org, accessed on 14 March 2012.

27. Mary Lou Bourne, personal communication.

28. Memo dated 25 March 2004 from Owen Cooper of IAS Services to the heads of service regarding historical analysis.

29. Wertheimer, A. (2007) *Person Centred Transition Reviews: A National Programme for Developing Person Centred Approaches to Transition Planning for Young People with Special Educational Needs.* London: Valuing People Support Team.

30. Sanderson, H. and Lewis, J. (2011) *A Practical Guide to Delivering Personalisation: Person-Centred Practice in Health and Social Care.* London: Jessica Kingsley Publishers.

31. Scown, S. and Sanderson, H. (2011) *Making it Personal for Everyone – From Block Contracts towards Individual Service Funds.* Stockport: HSA Press.

32. Michael Smull, personal communication.

33. Department of Health (DoH) (2009) *Working Together for Change: Using Person-Centred Information for Commissioning.* London: DoH.

34. Quinn, R.E. (1991) *Beyond Rational Management: Mastering the Paradoxes and Competing Demands of High Performance.* Oxford: Jossey-Bass.

35. Mohandas Gandhi (n.d.) Available at www.gandhiserve.org/cwmg/VOL074.PDF, accessed on 13 March 2012.

36. Covey, S.R. (2004) *The 7 Habits of Highly Effective People.* London: Free Press, p.3.

37. Collins, J. (2001) *Good to Great.* London: Random House Business Books.

38. Options. Available at www.options-empowers.org, accessed on 13 March 2012.

39. Williams, R. and Sanderson, H. (2009) *What Are We Learning about Person Centred Organisations?* Stockport: HSA Press.

40. Ibid, p.16.

41. Friedman's approach is called 'Results-Based Accountability' (RBA), also known in the UK and Australia as 'Outcomes-Based Accountability' (OBA).

42. Friedman, M. (2005) *Trying Hard is Not Good Enough.* Bloomington, IN: Trafford Publishing.

43. Collins, J. (2001) *Good to Great.* London: Random House Business Books, p.74.

44. Ibid.

45. David Hanna, The RBL Group. Available at http://dave-hanna.net/, accessed on 28 November 2011.

46. John Hespe, personal communication.

47. Nadler, D.A., Tushman, M.L. and Nadler, M.B. (1997) *Competing by Design: The Power of Organizational Architecture.* Oxford: Oxford University Press.

48. David Hanna, The RBL Group. Available at http://dave-hanna.net/, accessed on 28 November 2011.

49. Galbraith, J.R. (1995) *The Galbraith 'STAR' Model of Organisation Design. Designing Organizations: An Executive Briefing on Strategy, Structure, and Process.* San Francisco, CA: Jossey-Bass. Cited in *Designing Dynamic Organisations, A Hands-On Guide for Leaders,* Kindle edition, Location 327 of 4582. The Galbraith 'STAR' model was first developed by Jay Galbraith in the 1960s, and a more complete discussion of it can be found in Galbraith, J.R. (2002) *Designing Organizations,* revised edition. San Francisco, CA: Jossey-Bass. It has been considered in detail again in Galbraith, J., Downey, D. and Kates, A. (2002) *Designing Dynamic Organizations: A Hands-on Guide for Leaders at All Levels.* New York: Amacom.

50. Nadler, D.A., Tushman, M.L. and Nadler, M.B. (1997) *Competing by Design: The Power of Organizational Architecture.* Oxford: Oxford University Press.

51. McKinsey 7S Model, cited in Wickham, P.A. (2000) *The Financial Times Corporate Strategy Casebook.* Harlow: Pearson Education.

52. Scown, S. and Sanderson, H. (2011) *Making it Personal for Everyone – From Block Contracts towards Individual Service Funds.* Stockport: HSA Press.

53. Henry Ford. (n.d.) Available at www.brainyquote.com/quotes/quotes/h/henryford121997.html, accessed on 30 January 2012.

54. Originally published as Arnstein, S. R. (1969) 'A ladder of citizen participation.' *JAIP 35*, 4, 216–224.

55. Taylor, M. (2011) *Co-Production, What's That?* Matthew Taylor's blog. Available at www. matthewtaylorsblog.com/public-policy/co production-what%E2%80%99s-that, accessed on 13 March 2012.

56. North Yorkshire Council, Engagement promise. Available at www.northyorks.gov.uk/index. aspx?articleid=2926, accessed on 13 March 2012.

57. Scown, S. and Sanderson, H. (2011) *Making it Personal for Everyone – From Block Contracts towards Individual Service Funds.* Stockport: HSA Press.

58. Ibid.

59. Bailey, G., Sanderson, H., Sweeney, C. and Heaney, B. (2009) *Person Centred Reviews in Adult Services.* Stockport: HSA Press.

60. Bennett, S., Sanderson, S. and Stockton, S. (2012) *Working Together for Change.* Available at www. groundswellpartnership.co.uk, accessed on 14 March 2012.

61. Department of Health (DoH) (2009) *Working Together for Change: Using Person-Centred Information for Commissioning.* London: DoH.

62. Kline, N. (1998) *Time to Think: Listening to Ignite the Human Mind.* London: Cassell Illustrated.

63. Circle of support. Available at www.circles-uk.org.uk, accessed on 14 March 2012.

64. Collins, J. (2001) *Good to Great.* London: Random House Business Books.

65. What Makes Us Tick (2011). Available at http://whatmakestick.wordpress.com, accessed on 14 March 2012.

66. Plas, J.M. (1996) *Person Centred Leadership: An American Approach to Participatory Management.* Thousand Oaks, CA: Sage Publications, p.21.

67. Bower, M. (1966) *The Will to Manage: Corporate Success through Programmed Management.* New York: McGraw-Hill.

68. Hofstede, G. and Hofstede, G.J. (2005) *Cultures and Organisations: Software of the Mind.* Columbus, OH: McGraw-Hill, p.402.

69. Bower, M. (1966) *The Will to Manage: Corporate Success through Programmed Management.* New York: McGraw-Hill.

70. Hofstede, G. and Hofstede, G.J. (2005) *Cultures and Organisations: Software of the Mind.* Columbus, OH: McGraw-Hill.

71. Schein, E.H. (2010) *Organisational Culture and Leadership*, 4th edition. Oxford: Jossey-Bass.

72. Michael Smull, personal communication.

73. Helen Sanderson Associates (2006) *Person Centred Thinking Minibook.* Stockport: HSA Press.

74. Scown, S. and Sanderson, H. (2011) *Making it Personal for Everyone – From Block Contracts towards Individual Service Funds.* Stockport: HSA Press.

75. Stephen Covey. (n.d.) Available at www.brainyquote.com/quotes/authors/s/stephen_covey.html, accessed on 30 January 2012.

76. Kouzes, J.M. and Posner, B.Z. (2008) *The Leadership Challenge*, 4th edition. San Francisco, CA: Jossey-Bass.

77. Plas, J.M. and Lewis, S.E. (2001) *Person Centred Leadership for Nonprofit Organisations: Management that Works in High Pressure Systems.* Thousand Oaks, CA: Sage Publications, p.42.

78. Covey, S.R. (1992) *Principle Centred Leadership.* London: Simon and Schuster.

79. Handy, C. (1995) 'Trust and the virtual organisation: how do you manage people whom you cannot see?' *Harvard Business Review*, May–June, 40–54.

80. Covey, S.R., Merrill, R.A. and Merrill, R.R. (1994) *First Things First.* London: Simon and Schuster, p.203.

81. Handy, C. (1995) 'Trust and the virtual organisation: how do you manage people whom you cannot see?' *Harvard Business Review*, May–June, 40–54.

82. VARK. Available at www.vark-learn.com, accessed on 14 March 2012.

83. Blanchard, K. and Johnson, S. (1983) *The One Minute Manager.* London: Harper Collins Publishers.

84. http://www.gandhiserve.org/cwmg/cwmg.html, vol. 51, p.302.

85. Schultze, H. (1994) Available at http://www.12manage.com/quotes_hr.html, accessed 13 June 2012.

86. Armstrong, M. (2006) *A Handbook of Human Resource Management Practice*. London: Kogan Page.

87. Enrico, R. (1995) Availablt at http://www.leadershipnow.com/relationshipsquotes.html, accessed on 13 June 2012.

88. Kirkpatrick, D.L. and Kirkpatrick, J.D. (2009) *Evaluating Training Programmes: The Four Levels*. Oxford: Jossey Bass.

89. Cited in Daft, R.L. (2010*) The Executive and The Elephant: A Leaders Guide for Building Inner Excellence*. Oxford: Jossey Bass.

90. Plas, J.M. (1996) *Person Centred Leadership: An American Approach to Participatory Management*. Thousand Oaks, CA: Sage Publications, p.79.

91. Buckingham, M. and Coffman, C. (2001) *First, Break All The Rules*. New York: Simon and Schuster.

92. Ibid, p.28.

93. Drexler, A., Sibbet, D. and Forrester, R. (1994) *The Team Performance Model*. San Francisco, CA: Grove Consultants International.

94. Sanderson, H.L. (2000) *Critical Issues in the Implementation of Essential Lifestyle Planning within a Complex Organisation: An Action Research Investigation within a Learning Disability Service*. Manchester: Manchester Metropolitan University.

95. Covey, S.R. (2004) *The 7 Habits of Highly Effective People*. London: Free Press.

96. Belbin Associates *Belbin Team Roles*. Available at www.belbin.com, accessed on 16 May 2012.

97. Ashman, B. and Beadle-Brown, J. (2006) *The Valued Life Report – A Valued Life: Developing Person-Centred Approaches so People Can be More Included*. London: United Response and Tizard Centre at University of Kent.

98. Blenko, M.W., Mankins, M.C. and Rogers, P. (2010) *Decide and Deliver: Five Steps to Breakthrough Performance in Your Organisation*. Boston, MA: Harvard Business School Publishing.

99. Lepkowsky, M.B. (2009) *Person Centred Thinking Coaching Cards: A Series of Cards for People Who Help Others in Their Mastery of Person Centred Practices*. Stockport: HSA Press in partnership with Tri-Counties Regional Centre, card 2.

100. Landsberg, M. (2003) *The Tao of Coaching*, 2nd edition. London: Profile Books.

101. Blanchard, K.H., Zigarmi, P. and Zigarmi, D. (1996) *Leadership and the One Minute Manager: Increasing Effectiveness through Situational Leadership*. London: Collins.

102. Center for Leadership Studies. Available at www.situational.com, accessed on 16 May 2012.

103. John O'Brien, personal communication.

104. Office of Public Sector Information (1974) *The Health and Safety at Work etc Act*. London: HM Stationery Office.

105. Health and Safety Executive (1999) *The Management of Health and Safety at Work Regulations*. London: HM Stationery Office.

106. Ministry of Justice (2008) *Mental Capacity Act Deprivation of Liberty Safeguards Code of Practice*, p. 15.

107. Smull, M. and Sanderson, H. (2005) *Essential Lifestyle Planning for Everyone*. Stockport: HSA Press.

108. Health and Safety Executive (2006) *Principles of Sensible Risk Management*. Available at www.hse.gov.uk/risk/principlespoints.htm, accessed on 16 May 2012.

109. Department of Health (DoH) (2001) *Valuing People: A New Strategy for Learning Disability for the 21st Century*. White Paper. London: DoH.

110. Maslow, A.H. (1943) 'A theory of human motivation.' *Psychological Review 50*, 4, 370–396.

111. Robens, Lord (Chairman) (1972) *Safety and Health at Work*, Cmnd 5035. London: HM Stationery Office.

112. Confederation of British Industry (CBI) (1991) *Developing a Safety Culture*. London: CBI.

113. Heinrich, H.W. (1959) *Industrial Accident Prevention: A Scientific Approach*, 4th edition. New York: McGraw-Hill.

114. Health and Safety Executive (1999) *The Management of Health and Safety at Work Regulations*. London: HM Stationery Office.

115. Commission for Social Care Inspection (2008) *Experts by Experience: The Benefit of Experience: Involving People Who Use Service in Inspections.* London: Commission for Social Care Inspection, p.42.

116. Care Quality Commission (2010) *Guidance about Compliance: Essential Standards of Quality and Safety.* London: Care Quality Commission, p.42.

117. Health and Safety Executive (2006) *Principles of Sensible Risk Management.* Available at www.hse.gov.uk/risk/principlespoints.htm, accessed on 16 May 2012.

118. Health and Safety Executive (1999) *The Management of Health and Safety at Work Regulations.* London: HM Stationery Office.

119. Health and Safety Executive (2009) *Prosecutions and Notices Register.* Available at www.hse.gov.uk/prosecutions, acccessed on 16 May 2012.

120. Johann Wolfgang von Goethe, German dramatist, novelist, poet, and scientist (1749–1832). Available at www.quotationspage.com/quote/38926.html, accessed on 13 March 2012.

121. Crowther, C., Mumford, B. and McFadzean, G. (2011) *Great Interactions: It Ain't What You Do… It's the Way that You Do It.* Milton Keynes: MacIntyre.

122. Deming, W.E. (1986) *Out of the Crisis.* Cambridge, MA: MIT Press.

123. Osborne, D. and Gaebler, T. (1992) *Reinventing Government.* Lexington, MA: Addison-Wesley.

124. Crosby, P.B. (1979) *Quality is Free: The Art of Making Quality Certain.* New York: McGraw-Hill.

125. Ibid.

126. Canadian Council on Quality and Leadership (CQL). Available at www.c-q-l.org, accessed on 14 March 2012.

127. EFQM Excellence Model. Available at www.efqm.org, accessed on 14 March 2012.

128. Baldrige Performance Excellent Programme. Available at www.baldrige.com, accessed on 13 March 2012.

129. Paradigm. Available at www.paradigm-uk.org, accessed on 13 March 2012.

130. UK Care Quality Commission (2010) *Guidance About Compliance – Essential Standards of Quality and Safety*, p.47.

131. Isabel Ros Lopez, personal communication.

132. Neill, M. and Bailey, G. (2008) *Quality In Services Striving for Person Centredness.* Unpublished paper.

133. Individual Budgets Evaluation Network (2008) *Evaluation of the Individual Budgets Pilot Programme Final Report.* Available at www.dh.gov.uk/prod_consum_dh/groups/dh_digitalassets/@dh/@en/documents/digitalasset/dh_089506.pdf, accessed on 13 March 2012.

134. Robertson, J., Emerson, E., Hatton, C., Elliott, J. *et al.* (2005) *The Impact of Person Centred Planning.* Lancaster: Institute for Health Research, Lancaster University.

135. The Council on Quality and Leadership (CQL). Available at www.c-q-l.org, accessed on 13 March 2012.

136. Barrett, F.J. and Fry, R.E. (2010) *Appreciative Inquiry: A Positive Approach to Building Cooperative Capacity.* Lima, OH: CSS Publishing Company, p.5.

137. Address in the Assembly Hall at the Paulskirche, Frankfurt, 25 June 1963.

138. Machiavelli, N. (1515) *The Prince.*

139. Smale, G.G. (1998) *Managing Change through Innovation.* London: HM. Stationery Office, p.130.

140. Smull, M., Bourne, M.L. and Sanderson, H. (2009) *Becoming a Person Centred System.* Available at www.elpnet.net/documents/BecomingaPersonCenteredSystem-ABriefOverview.pdf, accessed on 13 March 2012.

141. Kotter, J.P. (1996) *Leading Change.* Boston: MA: Harvard Business School Press. A summary is available at www.kotterinternational.com/kotterprinciples/changesteps, accessed on 30 January 2012.

142. United Response (2010) *Annual Survey of Services*, not published externally.

143. Conner, D.R. (2006) *Managing at the Speed of Change: How Resilient Managers Succeed and Prosper Where Others Fail.* London: Random House.

144. Plant, R. (1987) *Managing Change and Making it Stick.* London: Collins.

145. Beckhard, R. and Harris, R.T. (1987) *Organisational Transitions, Managing Complex Change*, 2nd edition. Boston, MA: Addison-Wesley.

146. Cameron, E. and Green, M. (2004) *Making Sense of Change Management: A Complete Guide to the Models, Tools and Techniques of Organisational Change.* London: Kogan Page.

147. Kotter, J.P. (1996) *Leading Change.* Boston: MA: Harvard Business School Press. A summary is available at www.kotterinternational.com/kotterprinciples/changesteps, accessed on 30 January 2012.

148. Ibid.

149. Cited in Harper, T. (2010) *Leading from The Lion's Den: Leadership Principles from Every Book of The Bible.* Nashville, TN: B&H Publishing Group, p.47.

150. Maya Angelou. (n.d.) Available at www.brainyquote.com/quotes/quotes/m/mayaangelo392897.html, accessed on 30 January 2012.

About the Authors and Contributors

The authors

Helen Sanderson has led the development of person-centred thinking and planning in the UK over the last 15 years. Helen was the Department of Health's expert advisor on person-centred approaches to the Valuing People Support and Putting People First Teams. She co-authored the first Department of Health guidance on person-centred planning, and the 2010 guidance 'Personalisation through person-centred planning'. She has worked in health and social care for over 25 years.

Helen is the primary author of *People, Plans and Possibilities: Exploring Person-Centred Planning* (1997), the first book on person-centred planning in the UK, emerging from three years' research. Her PhD is on person-centred planning and organisational change and she has written over 15 books on person-centred thinking, planning, community and personalisation. She has worked extensively with organisations to enable them to become more person-centred.

Helen leads HSA, an award-winning international development agency passionate about how person-centred thinking and planning can create person-centred change and contribute to changing people's lives, organisations and communities. She is Vice-Chair of the International Learning Community for Person-Centered Practices and has provided consultancy in Europe, Japan, Australia and America.

Helen lives in Heaton Moor, with Andy and her three daughters, Ellie, Laura and Kate, together with a dog, cats and hens. She is a black belt in karate, but is now trying to spend more time doing yoga, and learning mindfulness.

Stephen Stirk is an experienced Human Resources and Organisation Development Director, with knowledge of the public, private and not-for-profit sectors. He has worked in all aspects of human resources and organisation development, with experience at national and international level. He is a specialist in organisation development, having spent a number of years in these roles in the pharmaceutical industry. Stephen has also worked in the FMCG field and has specialist knowledge and qualifications in logistics operations. In more recent years, he has focused on social care, with time spent in leading learning and development for the government regulator, and in leading a number of functions in one of the largest UK providers of support for people with learning disabilities and mental health issues. Stephen is married with three children, one of whom is disabled, hence his particular interest in furthering the aims of organisations that wish to become person-centred and improve the way they do business, especially for those people who may be disadvantaged in some way. He and his family live in County Durham.

Other main contributors

Shonagh Methven CMIOSH is Director of Learning, Quality and Risk Management at United Response. Shonagh has worked in the field of health and safety risk management for 20 years, spending six years providing advice and training to Londoners through the London Hazards Centre. She has published on developing a person-centred approach to risk, notably in the Tizard Learning Disability Review, to drive an increase in choice and control for people in receipt of social care services. Shonagh is an HSA-accredited trainer in the use of person-centred thinking and tools, and a powerful advocate of the rights of vulnerable people.

John Hespe is a specialist in organisation design and role transition coaching. A member of the Organisation Design Associates consortium, John's time is divided between consultancy and coaching work on a commercial basis, working with a number of charities as a pro bono advisor and ongoing research into people and performance at work in conjunction with Leeds Metropolitan University's School of Business and Law where recent research interests include the development of internal coaching capability, narrative and identity development at work, significant events in development coaching, the role of mentoring in accessing tacit knowledge in organisations and role transition coaching.

Other providers of material for the book

Su Sayer OBE co-founded the disability charity, United Response, in 1973. It is now in the top 100 charities with a turnover of over £64 million and 3000 staff. Awarded an OBE in 2000 for services to disabled people, she has won several prestigious charity awards, including one for Outstanding Achievement and another for Lifetime Achievement. On receiving the latter award, she was described as 'a true innovator' and 'a pioneer who championed care in the community long before government interest'. She has served on the boards of several government bodies and a range of charities including Save the Children and NCVO, and was Chair of ACEVO for three years. Currently she is Vice-Chair of the Prostate Cancer Charity, a member of the Students' Union Evaluation Initiative Validation Panel and an Honorary Senior Visiting Fellow in the Faculty of Management, Cass Business School, City University.

Bob Tindall is Managing Director of United Response. Bob has 36 years of experience of working with people with learning disabilities and their families, and also with people with mental health difficulties. He has been Managing Director of United Response since 1997, having previously worked at a senior level in local government. He is the former Chair and a current board member of the Association for Supported Living. Bob introduced and steered through United Response the work on the development of a person-centred culture.

Diane Lightfoot is Director of Communications and Fundraising for United Response.

Nick Rogers is North West Divisional Director for United Response.

Index